100
years

PAUL KELLY

100 years

THE AUSTRALIAN STORY

ALLEN & UNWIN

First published in 2001

Allen & Unwin
83 Alexander St
Crows Nest NSW 2065
Australia

Phone: (61 2) 8425 0100
Fax: (61 2) 9906 2218
Email: frontdesk@allen-unwin.com.au
Web: http://www.allenandunwin.com

National Library of Australia
Cataloguing-in-Publication entry:

Kelly, Paul, 1947–.
   100 years: the Australian story.

   Includes index.
   ISBN 1 86508 531 6.

   1. National characteristics, Australian. 2. Australia—
   Forecasting. 3. Australia—History—20th century. 4.
   Australia—Politics and government. I. Title.

994.04

Designed by Nada Backovic
Set in 11/13 pt Bembo by Midland Typesetters, Maryborough
Printed by Griffin Press, South Australia

10 9 8 7 6 5 4 3 2 1

Contents

In memory of my mother, Sybil Kelly

100 Preface years

This book originated with the ABC television series '100 years—the Australian story'. The series was conceived in a collaboration between the Walkley Award-winning ABC producer, Sue Spencer and myself. The idea was for a documentary that coincided with the centenary of Australia's Federation. Our series is not about Federation as a movement or event. It attempts, rather, to capture Australia over its 100 years of nationhood. The focus is our political character, our leadership and, above all, the transformation in Australia during the century.

This involved a major undertaking to find primary and secondary sources. I am heavily indebted to both Sue Spencer and the series historical researcher, Kate Evans, for their extensive research efforts. I have drawn upon their work to reinforce my own research and interpretations for this book. Of course, they have no responsibility for the final product. The television series also had the support of an invaluable team at the ABC including Deborah Masters and Paul Cantwell. It is the television series that led to the book.

I am grateful to the ABC for accepting the treatment that Sue Spencer and I submitted and for commissioning our series for broadcast in 2001. I am also grateful to the National Council for the Centenary of Federation, in particular Tony Eggleton and Rodney Cavalier, for the Council's decision to provide substantial funding for the series. Without this support there would have been no television series. It was provided, ultimately, as an act of faith, as editorial independence for every aspect of the television series rested with Sue Spencer and myself.

In preparing the series I was privileged to have the advice of one of Australia's leading historians, Professor Geoffrey Bolton, who served as a consultant. Once again, he has no responsibility for this book.

The decision to write the book was taken in 2000 after talks with Matthew Kelly from ABC Books and my own publisher, Patrick Gallagher from Allen & Unwin. The book is highly selective and makes no pretence to be a broad account of the past century. It falls into two sections—essays and interviews. Each essay deals with a different concept and each mirrors the five themes around which the television series is based. The interviews are edited versions of those I conducted for the television series. These are with four former prime ministers—Gough Whitlam, Malcolm Fraser, Bob Hawke, Paul Keating along with the current prime minister, John Howard and Leader of the Opposition, Kim Beazley. These interviews are not 'news and current affairs' but were designed to encourage the leaders to reflect upon our history and their own times.

I thank Kate Evans for her invaluable help in gathering photographs and illustrations. My final thanks goes to my editor at Allen & Unwin, Rebecca Kaiser, for her support, diligence and skill in making this book a reality.

Introduction

Australian history has been a series of experiments. The original was the most inauspicious, a gaol for human refuse. However, from the foundation amid the hunger and hopelessness, there was a spark of higher aspiration—to invest the colony with a deeper meaning. The tension in the Australian character has been between the 'survivor' mindset and the aspirational impulse. There have been opposing ways of interpreting Australia: a land of despair or hope; a nation of indifference or achievement; as a museum to a bizarre historical accident—Europeans stranded on the wrong side of the earth—or as a civilisation with the will to renew itself.

Federation in 1901 was an epic experiment in nationhood. Australia in 2001 is a multiple experiment in democracy, multiculturalism and globalisation. There have been many Australian experiments—the creation of an Australia–Britain nationhood in the South, the European venture as a shipwreck at the bottom of East Asia, the utopian endeavour to humanise capitalism, the encounter between European civilisation and Aboriginal society and the exploitation of empire in the quest for national survival. Such a list is merely an introduction to the great and small among Australian endeavours.

This book is about these five experiments. In the prelude to the 2001 centenary they have been on our minds. The debates over the republic, multiculturalism, economic egalitarianism, reconciliation between Aboriginal and non-Aboriginal Australians and Australia's place in the world have shaped the politics of the 1990s.

These new dramas are corollaries of old stories. Each originates as a distinctive element of the national character. In 2001, only a blinkered pessimist could see Australian history as dull or provincial. It is now, more than ever, about the great ideas occupying the world: the nature of independence and sovereignty, the quest for unity in cultural diversity, the partnership of economic justice and wealth creation, the search for reconciliation between indigenous and non-indigenous peoples and the fate of middle powers in the contest for survival and influence.

This book has three unifying themes. First, that Federation and the pre-World War I nation-building era was a far greater and visionary endeavour than is recognised. Second, that the latter half of Australia's first century saw a re-invention of the nation's political compact and the construction of a new national vision. And third, that Australia's past and future can be reconciled. Its founding vision and its re-invention are different but they are not at war.

This book, to use Geoffrey Blainey's spectrum, is neither a three cheers nor a black armband view of our history. Our history needs to be liberated from the triumphalist and the black armband stereotypes. They conceal and they confuse. The real Australian genius has been the skill to adapt. It is a complex story and it remains a work in progress.

There are many interpretations of Federation but ultimately it was about creating on this continent something better and greater for its people. It was ambitious and it raised a question that has been put throughout our history: what is Australia's purpose? The initial answer was to create a society based on Old World tradition yet fired by New World equality and optimism.

The Australian re-invention of the twentieth century began to answer this question in a new way. This was the decision to replace our sense of being British with a self-confident Australian identity; to define our society by cultural diversity, not cultural uniformity; to make our economy internationally competitive, not isolated from the global community; to recognise belatedly the injustice done to the indigenous people and embark upon reconciliation; and to relate to the world as Australians rather than an outpost of imperial power.

These changes are profound. They are a trauma for those who live by the old ideologies and stand for the old interests. These changes are also under assault from either the left or right depending upon the issue; the critics use history as their weapon. Their claims are elaborate but can be simplified—they are that Australia is betraying its past. The argument of this book is that there is no betrayal.

Australia has been re-invented not by denying its past but by learning from its mistakes, moral and temporal, and responding to new situations. This means recognising success but confronting failure. Our history is evolutionary, not revolutionary. Our political character is guided by pragmatic self-interest, a skill for adaptation and a sense of conscience. Beneath the tide of change there is a river of continuity. The changes are vast—in our numbers, our faces and our policies—yet there is a continuity about the Australian character, outlook and civic democracy. Each generation sorts out what works best for itself and for Australia. That is the skill of a vigorous country alert to its past but more interested in its future. The need for such skill has rarely been so urgent. These essays argue, finally, that the unresolved experiments in which Australia is now engaged pose challenges as great as any in our history.

Child of the Empire

Australia in 1901 was young, brash and experimental in a nineteenth century fashion. In Australia democracy sprang from the soil and the street, the absence of an aristocracy, and a working class that aspired to live well and enjoy itself. Democracy took root in Australia as firmly as in any nation on earth. Its companion was a racist nationalism central to the Australian aspiration: to create a cohesive and egalitarian society more successful than the hierarchy and privilege of Europe's old world.

Australians brought a humdrum pragmatism and an aggressive self-interest to their nation building. As a people they were more interested in results than in ideas. Yet their core beliefs were implanted by their British heritage and the French Revolution. So Australians embraced the rights of man, the rule of law, the Christian faith, a fair wage and, as they surveyed their surrounds, a place in the sun.

The Commonwealth of Australia, enshrined at Sydney's Centennial Park on 1 January 1901, was a unique event in world history: never before had such small communities divided by such distances voluntarily decided to form a new nation. The timing and geography exuded a symbolism— a nation for a continent and a new nation for a new century. Australia's birth saw a perfect harmony between the cycle of man and the design of time. The first continent upon which the sunlight of the twentieth century fell was Australia—a full twelve hours before it dawned on London, home of a great empire and a dying Queen.

At Federation 60 per cent of the people were native born. Most worked by hand and more than half lived outside the capital cities. The stereo-typical man was a meat eater with bad teeth, good lungs and self-reliant outlook. Married women were typically having three or four children. Most houses were connected with water but few had electricity. Most Australians had better living conditions than the British.

Australia was a new world society that drew strength from its old world heritage. Australians were steeped in the British tradition of parliamentary

The crowd at the entrance to Australian Commonwealth celebrations in Sydney's Centennial Park, 1901. 'One People' spans the arch joining New South Wales and Victoria.

gradualism. They borrowed, improvised and adapted. They took the Westminster system from Britain and the federal system from the United States. They united by choice, not by coercion. This decision was compelled neither by war nor revolution but rested upon an act of political will, driven by common interest and shared heritage. Australians debated, wrote and then endorsed by popular referendum their own Constitution. Their leaders were nineteenth century politicians preoccupied with the practical questions of governance, stability, income and employment—the issues that won votes. These politicians, liberals, conservatives and radicals, managed to sink their differences, ultimately, in a sea of compromise for a greater goal. The colonies of New South Wales, Victoria, Queensland, South Australia, Tasmania and, belatedly, Western Australia each surrendered powers to a new Commonwealth Government as they, in turn, became States. Would another generation or, for that matter, today's generation, have been able to accomplish so much?

The feat of those Australians who made the nation has rarely been appreciated. Australians take the past for granted and move forward. The post-Federation assumption that Australia was an inevitability has undermined a full recognition of the leaders who secured the nation—the NSW premier, old Henry Parkes, autocratic and vainglorious, instigator of the Federation Movement; a young Tasmanian lawyer, Andrew Inglis Clark, who planted American federalism at the heart of the Constitution; Queensland politician and lawyer, Samuel Griffith, grandmaster of the 1891 Constitutional Convention and the first Chief Justice; South Australian premier and pistol duel veteran, Charles Cameron Kingston, a burly broker of the compact; the fat and witty cartoonist's gift, NSW premier George Reid, who won for his State a more democratic Commonwealth; Reid's rival, the Victorian Liberal and visionary, Alfred Deakin, a roving mind and a tortured soul; and the final pilot of the cause, Edmund Barton, whose leonine head, ready thirst and political guile made him Australia's first prime minister.

Deakin said the Federation appeared 'to have been secured by a series of miracles'. Griffith marvelled at the unique constitutional path Australia had negotiated. Federation was a political event, launched and sustained by politicians. It was the conclusion reached by a British civilisation of less than four million people stranded upon a vast empty land in the South Pacific. Australians followed the logic of their situation: they chose unity, above all, to help them defend their claim to the continent and to help them establish an economic union as the best basis for their prosperity.

The Australian idea lay in a synthesis of indigenous nationalism and Empire loyalty. Nationhood was a prize claimed by Australia; yet it was a gift bestowed by Britain. This meant that an imperialist could be a nationalist and a nationalist could champion the Empire. Federation was able to encompass these two emotions and hold them together. This was its genesis and its genius.

Australia's first two prime ministers, Edmund Barton and Alfred Deakin, were nationalists and imperialists. This was not just by predeliction; it defined the nation's character. Deakin wrote that to many Australians 'the Mother Country is nearer in thought than their relations next door'. Deakin called himself an 'independent Australian Briton'. It is a term that is now extinct. World War I prime minister, Billy Hughes, said: 'A man may be a very loyal and devoted adherent to and worshipper of the Empire, and may still be a very loyal and patriotic Australian.' People would not say this today. The fusion of nationalism and Empire—

Australia's defining instinct 100 years ago—is neither alive nor necessary in 2001.

Republicanism, which had enjoyed a flourish in the 1880s, had faded by 1901. Republicanism was tantamount to isolationism, and isolationism was no option for Australia. For a young nation at its birth the protection of the world's greatest Empire was a prize to be valued, not repudiated. Some Australian nationalists and champions of the Irish working class wanted to break from Britain. But this was an emotional fantasy. For Australia, all the arguments based in practical self-interest dictated a deep Empire bond and the common man knew this.

It is this 1901 synthesis between Australian nationalism and Empire loyalty that determined much of the nation's future. In the Australian story the longevity of the British connection would be remarkable; even more remarkable has been its adaptation and evolution in the face of new circumstances. The foundation idea of Australian Britons was real and powerful. This duality was a source of strength: Australia was both a new nation and part of a mighty Empire. This was reflected in the path to Federation: the people endorsed their Constitution but it came into existence only as an act of the British Parliament. Australians never fought Britain for nationhood; they were encouraged to nationhood by London. Britain had long since absorbed the lesson of the American Revolution.

In early 1900 a delegation of Australian leaders travelled to London— Barton, Deakin, Kingston and others, with each colony represented. They carried the new Constitution and they expected the Westminster Parliament to endorse it in full. They had an audience with Queen Victoria who, according to Deakin, had 'limbs and senses failing her' and was 'reminded in a loud voice of who they were'. They negotiated at Whitehall with that consummate politician who ran the Empire, the Secretary of State for the Colonies, Joseph Chamberlain. But Chamberlain insisted upon a change to the Constitution: that the Privy Council, based in London, be the final judicial authority for Australia beyond the High Court. Chamberlain largely prevailed in a negotiated compromise.

On 5 July 1900 the British Parliament passed the *Commonwealth of Australia Constitution Act* to take effect from the following January. The Queen gave Royal Assent on 9 July. She offered Barton one of the copies of the Act, along with the pen, inkstand and the table she had used. The delegation returned triumphant. Australia became a self-governing nation within the Empire, not an independent country as that term is known today. The concession over the Privy Council symbolised the nature of this compact. The British Act referred to an 'indissoluble Federal Commonwealth under the Crown of the United Kingdom of Great Britain

Enjoying a banquet at Sydney's Commonwealth celebrations.

and Ireland'. The British monarch was Head of State. The Crown could disallow bills passed by the Australian Parliament. Executive power was exercisable by the Crown's representative, the Governor-General, and such powers were sufficient to uphold British interests in Australia. The Governor-General, of course, was a Briton appointed by Britain and owing his allegiance to British ministers, not Australian ministers. The ultimate judicial authority was the Privy Council. There was no suggestion that Australia would conduct its own foreign policy; it was part of an Empire and the Empire's policy was run from London. The decisions about war or peace would be made in Britain, not in Australia. Australia did not have its own flag, currency or navy. It had no diplomatic service. The entire idea of nationhood was crafted for integration with the Empire. The former Chief Justice, Sir Garfield Barwick, later remarked that the 'Constitution was not devised for the immediate independence of a nation' but it meant 'that the people of Australia were moving towards nationhood'. As W J Hudson and M P Sharp have argued, independence as it is understood now was not on the agenda in 1901.

This was mirrored in the celebrations at Sydney and Melbourne for the

The Duke and Duchess of Cornwall pass under the 'Edward VII' arch in Melbourne, May 1901.

creation of the Commonwealth and the opening of the Commonwealth Parliament. They were a mixture of Australian informality and Imperial pageantry. Australia was born in January 1901 as an open air democracy. It came into existence not in a grand building but in a people's park beneath the summer sky. The procession from Sydney's Domain to Centennial Park was inclusive, from politician to battler, from banker to shearer. Soldiers from around the Empire came to honour an Imperial event. At Centennial Park there were 100 000 people including, in a special enclosure, 7000 official guests and 300 press. The first Governor-General, John Adrian Louis Hope, 7th Earl of Hopetoun and a product of Eton and Sandhurst, took the oath in a distinctly non–Australian accent. Barton's first ministry was sworn in. Prayers were offered. Hopetoun, still recovering from typhoid fever, was unable to make the banquet at Sydney's Town Hall. The celebrations extended for ten days, featuring light displays, concerts and harbour events.

Five months later the Duke of York, the future King George V, together with the Duchess, arrived at the temporary federal capital, Melbourne. Queen Victoria had just died. Dark colours were compulsory. The Commonwealth Parliament was opened on 9 May in the Exhibition Building. The vestibule ceiling was draped by a Union Jack 21 feet long. The Duke read a message from his father, the new King, Edward VII. Rule Britannia was sung. The *Argus* newspaper boasted that Australians were just as attached to the Crown as the British were. Australian artist

Tom Roberts painted the official portrait. The ultra-nationalistic journal, *The Bulletin*, sneered with contempt that this great event warranted 'no tawdy trappings, no small accidental prince'. The more radical *Tocsin* slammed the Government House crowd as 'troglodyte shire councillors in crawling droves, the sad catspaws of ambitious title-hunting women'. But the crowds told another story, a story the nationalists and the radicals resented: the people liked their heritage and their monarchy. This sentiment had the force of numbers. More than half a century later the story would be replayed with the same effect.

This fusion of nationalism and Empire, now long gone, is often denied. For many of today's Australians it offends their 'grown-up' self-image; it contradicts their anti-British nationalism; and it demands too much of their impoverished political imagination. The result is a psychological barrier between the past and the present, between 1901 and 2001. This denial of the past, now the result of apathetic conceit, was founded originally in ideology.

In his book *A New Britannia*, Humphrey McQueen identified the tradition of historians who had seen Australia as a radical nationalist country. McQueen wrote: 'Their tale is a sad one. A tale of decline, of a once radical people corrupted by their own victories. In essence, they picture radicalism, and with it socialism, as chances gone forever.' McQueen nominated Russell Ward's evocative *The Australian Legend* as 'the most influential account of radical nationalism'. This tradition offered a powerful interpretation of our history. It was an endeavour to find in Australia a more lofty purpose in ideals of nationalism, mateship and democracy. The conclusion, however, was inescapable: Australia had betrayed the radical nationalism of its class politics, its Irish spirit and its bush mythology.

There is, of course, another explanation of what happened which has attracted some currency. It is that these historians misread the story, exaggerated our radical nationalism, and misjudged the true balance in Australia between radicalism and conservatism, between nationalism and the British tradition.

The most popular radical nationalist was Henry Lawson. In 'A Song of the Republic' Lawson asked Australians to make a choice:

Sons of the south, make choice between
(Sons of the South choose true)
The Land of Morn and the Land of E'en,
The Old Dead Tree and the Young Tree Green.
The land that belongs to lord and Queen,
And the land that belongs to you.

Australians gave Lawson a resounding answer. They refused to choose. They insisted upon both the Old Dead Tree and the Young Green Tree. They said that Lawson's was a phoney choice. The people wanted to be British and to be Australian. They wanted lord, Empire, Imperial security, British investment, the Crown and Imperial honours—but they also wanted their mates, their land, their new democracy, their 'fair go', equality of opportunity and their Australian nationalism. The people were smarter than Lawson. In 1901 they voted to have both worlds. It was reflected in their Constitution, a document for Australian Britons.

The prophet most disappointed proved to be Manning Clark. When the great historian published the final volume of *A History Of Australia* he took his subtitle from Lawson: 'The Old Dead Tree and The Young Green Tree'. In his last pages Clark demonised Sir Robert Menzies as the old dead tree and eulogised John Curtin as the young green tree. Yet the Australian people had a different view from Clark's. They believed, once again, that it was a false diagnosis. The people elected Curtin and then they elected Menzies. They took both according to the situation. This was the Australian penchant: to purchase off the shelf what worked best according to their needs, not the prescription of the poets.

In 1901 when the Duke of York left Australia at the end of his long tour he wrote home to his minister, Joseph Chamberlain: 'I am convinced that there exists a strong feeling of loyalty to the Crown and deep attachment to the Mother country in Australia which I expect you can hardly credit.' Britain was well pleased with Federation. It patronised Australia.

The 1901–14 era saw a vigorous and constructive Australian nationalism bent to the task of nation-building. This was an age of optimism; it was morning for both the liberals and the radical nationalists. The main laws and institutions of the nation were established—the High Court, White Australia, female suffrage, a strong trade union movement, protectionism as a national policy, the Conciliation and Arbitration Court, the Harvester judgment and the enshrinement of the fair wage, an Australian navy, an army along with a system of universal military training, Duntroon military college, the selection of Canberra as the national capital site, the establishment of the Commonwealth Bank and the Commonwealth's own note issue, and the Labor versus Liberal party system. This progress was driven, in particular, by Alfred Deakin's vision and the Labor governments of Andrew Fisher. But the stream of creation was derailed in 1914 by trouble in the Balkans and a cataclysm.

The Great War was the cathartic event for Australia since European settlement. It revealed the depth of the Australia–Britain bond; it delivered what Federation had lacked—Australia's spiritual birth through bloodshed; and it split Australia over the issue of loyalty. The naive self-confidence of the prewar period was destroyed as tragedy touched the families of too many Australians.

Federation had created a constitutional and political entity—yet it left a spiritual void. The success of Federation as a peaceful and practical endeavour was also its flaw. Australia was a nation but its nationalism was untested. It was a nation in search of vindication. The Great War was not just a military event; it was about Australia's essence and its identity. This debate began with bravado and ended in tears and glory.

Australia was plunged into the European conflict by our ties of kinship, loyalty, faith and Empire. Australia's response to the war was spontaneous and strategic. There was a popular instinct for involvement and a recognition among leaders that Australia's security was bound to the fate of the Empire. The revisionist view which gained currency decades later—that the Great War was not Australia's business or interest—had scant sway at the time. This is a patronising and insulting view of the Great War generation. It implies that they were fools rushing to their own doom for no good reason. Such notions are more revealing of the outlook of subsequent generations than they are of the World War I generation.

Governor-General Sir Ronald Munro-Ferguson, a soldier and veteran from the House of Commons, was impressed: 'You can hardly believe what solidarity of national life there is between Britain and Australia.' Five days before war broke out, the Liberal Prime Minister, Joseph Cook, declared: 'Whatever happens, Australia is part of the Empire right to the full. When the Empire is at war, so Australia is at war.' The same day, ALP leader Andrew Fischer declared that Australia would fight for Britain 'to our last man and last shilling'. Britain did not consult Australia before her declaration of war on 5 August 1914. By law and sentiment Australia was bound by Britain's decision. Communications between Britain and Australia went through Munro-Ferguson. The Governor-General put the PM under pressure. He cabled Cook: 'What seems now . . . to be urgent is the Government's line of action, so that I may report to the Home Government what support it may expect from Australia. I notice that Canada has already acted.' Munro-Ferguson sought a cabinet meeting and lobbied ministers. But Australia did not require pressure from the Governor-General. It was anxious to respond; it knew its forces would operate under Imperial command.

The Australian soldiers wore a wide-brimmed felt hat, looped up at the

A patriotic football event during World War I. 'John Bull' England is centre wearing a Union Jack waistcoat.

left side, with a badge of the rising sun. They were named the Australian Imperial Force and known by the initials AIF. Before their landing at Gallipoli one of the British commanders, General Ian Hamilton, reported to London that they were 'as wild as hawks but splendid men'. The troops, raw and untested, sensed that their landing at Gallipoli at dawn on 25 April 1915 was the great test for Australia.

Colonel John Monash anticipated 'great events which will stir the whole world . . . to the eternal glory of Australia . . . it is astonishing how light-hearted everybody is, whistling, singing and cracking jokes'. The landing, designed to strike against the Ottoman Empire, Germany's ally, was a disaster and the eight month campaign was a failure. A total of 7594 Australians died at Gallipoli with an overall casualty rate of one in two. Gallipoli was a military failure but a psychological victory.

The courage and fortitude of the Anzacs were seized as a vindication of Australia. This was the national rite of passage. It was Australia's entry into nationalism by blood. It was the event which allowed the writers, painters and politicians to create the legends by which Australians would interpret themselves. Gallipoli became a mighty legend because it was founded in a reality. War correspondent Charles Bean nominated as the central force that drove the Australian troops 'their idea of Australian manhood'. Bill Gammage found in the diaries of the Anzacs a 'tragic nobility' where 'the spirit of an age moves through their pages'. On the first Anzac anniversary a crowd of 100 000 gathered in Sydney's Domain. In London 2000 Anzac troops marched from the Strand to Westminster Abbey. In his speech Prime Minister William Morris Hughes, 'the little Digger', was rapturous: 'Soldiers, your deeds have won you a place in the Temple of the Immortals.' Australia, born of convict origin, had proved itself to the world. Even more, it had purged many of its own doubts about the quality of its nationhood. Such sacrifices had to be justified by elevation into a national shrine. If any event touched the Australian soul it was Gallipoli. This became the nation's true sacred site; paradoxically, far from Australia itself. The location was determined by Imperial strategy and arose directly from our fused identity between nation and Empire.

Ken Inglis in his book *Sacred Places* quotes his age-mate, Peter Shrubb, a child of the culture of the Great War, writing that 'Anzac Day was the only day of the year that had any kind of holiness in it'. After the war Bean dedicated his life to two monuments—the official war history and the Australian War Memorial. His history was written with one aim, to show the Australian soldier passing the supreme test and to offer this as a metaphor for Australia's elevation to genuine nationhood. The Australian War Memorial in Canberra has become a fusion of monument and cathedral. It is a place of national worship with unrivalled pulling power.

By the year 2000 thousands of young Australians were making this Anzac Day pilgrimage, searching amid the stony beaches, the headstones and the rugged heights for answers to the great mysteries. Bean has been vindicated in his assertion that 'Gallipoli never dies'. Before the war was over the Anzacs on the Western Front testified in combat to the power of the Anzac story. The legend was a reality; and the reality reinforced the legend. Gallipoli provided the spiritual focus for the nation that Federation could never generate.

The Anzac story has revealed a capacity for renewal and self-reflection that transcends generations. Neither a glorification of war nor the monopoly of generations who lived it, Anzac has become a spiritual force for inspiration and unity. It is interpreted and reinterpreted by each generation in turn. It is why 25 April and not 26 January is the true national day.

However, the Great War left another legacy—a division between loyalty to Australia and loyalty to Britain. It undermined the national identity authorised by Federation and it left a permanent fracture. The AIF was a volunteer army, unlike the legions of Europe. Britain and New

Zealand had introduced conscription and in August 1916 Hughes insisted it was Australia's turn.

A leader of the Waterside Workers Federation and member of the first Commonwealth Parliament, Hughes was a born war leader. He said that war was like a strike—one man had to take charge. Hughes was a passionate nationalist and imperialist. He believed that the magnitude of Australia's war contribution would determine its ability to leverage the support of the Empire, postwar, to manage the threat from Japan. But within the Labor movement there was a strong current of resistance to his plans. Labor's political success had been linked to a growing union movement and an assertive machine, many of whose leaders wanted a war for socialism, not a war for Europe. Hughes found that a majority of union leaders and the caucus opposed his conscription plan. His decision to seek a referendum was the product of politics, not the Constitution. Hughes was appealing to the people to overrule the anti-conscription stance of his own party so he could introduce conscription by statute.

There were two referendums, in October 1916 and December 1917. Hughes lost them both, the 'no' vote being 51.6 per cent the first time and above 53 per cent the second. In the process Australia was divided by class and religion. Hughes, facing expulsion from the party after the first referendum, walked out of the caucus with his backers, created a minority ministry, won the May 1917 election and formed a new non-Labor Nationalist Government. The word 'tenacious' is a pale imitation of his indomitable spirit.

The second referendum was dominated by the struggle between Hughes and the tall charismatic Catholic archbishop of Melbourne, Daniel Mannix, who had arrived from Ireland, aged 49, in 1913. Mannix argued that Australia 'has done her full share' and that 'boys of twenty will be driven to the trenches if conscription is passed . . . what right have we to sign the death sentences of our fellow citizens?'

Mannix did not oppose the war; nor did he oppose the Empire. He put the issue in elemental terms and he gave expression to that great tension implicit in Australia. Mannix said: 'Many Australians are prepared, apparently, to place Australia below the Empire in their affections. These imperialists are ready to sacrifice Australia. They are not ashamed to put the Empire first and Australia second. Now whether it comes from the pulpit, from the bench or from the bar, it is a very silly thing, as well as an unpatriotic thing, to say that Australians should put the Empire before their country . . . and it will not be accepted by the people of Australia.'

This struggle between Hughes and Mannix fractured forever the comfortable synthesis of nationalism and Empire loyalty. This battle was not

Billy Hughes with hands aloft at a conscription rally.

just over conscription. It was, as B A Santamaria argued, 'essentially a question as to what Australia ought to be'. Hughes carried a pistol as he campaigned. In his appeal for the AIF vote Hughes accused Mannix of preaching 'sedition in and out of season' and of encouraging an 'insatiable hatred of Britain'. There were calls for Mannix to be deported. But from the time of Britain's execution of the leaders of the Easter Rising in Ireland, Catholic opinion hardened against Britain and Hughes.

It was an assertion of Irish faith in Australian nationalism. The Irish were fighting not primarily for Ireland but for Australia. Patrick O'Farrell wrote: 'The dominant forces in Australian society sought to exclude or demean Catholics of Irish origin. Conscription seemed to be, in microcosm, the enslaving program of the ascendancy party.' Irish Australians were asserting their legitimate claim on Australia's destiny.

It was a complex and multifaceted split: Catholic against Protestant, the Irish tradition against the British, working class against the middle class, Australia first against Empire first.

Australia finished the war a relieved but diminished nation. Jeffrey Grey's summary is that Australia enlisted 416 000 men out of a population of about four million. Over half of the eligible white males enlisted and 80 per cent of these served overseas, mostly on the Western Front. Nearly

A dispatch rider at Gallipoli avoids being shot at.

20 per cent were killed and a further 45 per cent were wounded. A total of 58 961 died. In relation to population Australia's casualty rate was the highest apart from New Zealand's. The scale of the Australian effort is staggering and nearly a century later almost defies comprehension. War memorials appeared in every town and the 'Last Post' would echo down the century.

Australia had been a pro-war and anti-conscription country—a unique mixture. It now understood better its own vulnerability and the price of Empire. Hughes had been a divisive leader but Labor had failed the nation during the war. Australian politics now became alarmingly polarised. A shattered and diminished Labor Party cherished its conscription victories, embraced isolationism, turned to a more radical socialism and lost its prewar electoral strength. The non-Labor side became more conservative, imperialist, unimaginative and anti-union. Hughes stayed prime minister into the postwar years, a Labor man heading a conservative party, symbolic of Australia's convulsion. But Hughes's vision of an Australia that gained strength through the Empire still prevailed with the people. The conservatives would control the interwar years. Class conflict deepened and the prewar synthesis between nationalists and imperialists would only partly recover from its Great War fracture.

After the war the Empire was redefined in a series of Imperial Conferences during the 1920s and 1930s. In a remarkable move Britain decided to give equality to its Empire members and the Empire became a Commonwealth. The process was driven by South Africa, Canada and the Irish Free State, all of which possessed internal divisions and anti-British communities that far transcended those of Australia. It meant that Australia had the opportunity to assume the constitutional independence denied at Federation. But the conservative prime minister, Stanley Melbourne Bruce, was scarcely interested.

Bruce, who became prime minister in 1923, was the most British of all our leaders. Educated in England, he served with a British regiment in the Great War, winning the Military Cross. Bruce was casual, imperturbable and wealthy. Politics discovered him, not vice versa. He was recruited by business to lead the non-Labor side and for a while fulfilled its expectations. He was the most streamlined Australian leader in the imperialist–nationalist tradition and later became an influential High Commissioner to London. Historian Stuart Macintyre wrote that 'he assimilated so successfully into the English upper class that his capacity and resolution as a representative of Australian interests were seriously underestimated'.

Although a personality opposite, Bruce had similar views to Hughes's: Australia could not survive alone; Australia could not defend itself; the task of Australia's leaders was to make the Empire work for them. Bruce grasped the reality of Australia's position in the 1920s. Australia depended upon the Imperial preference system for trade; its national development and public infrastructure were financed by capital raisings from London; its modest population expansion depended upon British immigration. Bruce's policy was 'Men, Money and Markets', and in each sense Britain was the lynchpin. He had no taste for schemes designed to weaken the ties between the dominions and London.

The Colonial Secretary, Leo Amery, now occupied in Whitehall the vast room in which Joseph Chamberlain had once sat, with its walnut map case and picture of George Washington, a reminder of what happened when the Empire was maladministered. But Amery was planning to be generous at the glittering 1926 Imperial Conference. Amery knew that the 'purely British dominions' of Australia and New Zealand were relaxed about constitutional dependency. But the 'mixed grills' of South Africa, Canada and the Irish Free State wanted a fundamental change.

South Africa's prime minister, J M Hertzog, who governed a country where the Dutch outnumbered the English, led the charge: he wanted equality within the Commonwealth. Bruce had a different message. He said: 'The King is the visible symbol of our unity, the centre of all our loyalties and the link which binds us together.' Bruce saw the trend; he would not oppose it but nor would he embrace it. The key decisions were taken in a committee chaired by one of Britain's statesmen, Lord Balfour, and the final document was known as the Balfour Declaration. It represented the constitutional modernisation of the old Empire but it was sufficiently ambiguous to allow different leaders their own interpretations.

The document referred to 'self-governing communities of Great Britain and the Dominions'. They were 'autonomous communities within the British Empire, equal in status, in no way subordinate one to another in any aspect of their domestic or external affairs, though united by a common allegiance to the Crown'. The word independence was not used but its meaning was implied.

It was a constitutional revolution. The Governor-General would henceforth represent the King, not the British Government. He would be appointed by Australian ministers not British ministers, act on the advice of Australian ministers, not British ministers, and become part of the Australian system of government, no longer the British system. Britain would now appoint diplomats to represent its own interests. Australia was to be given executive and legislative independence—its link with the Empire would rest upon two pillars, the Crown and free choice.

Amery said that Bruce had been on the 'inside right' at the Conference. No doubt. In their study, *Australian Independence*, W J Hudson and M P Sharp conclude that Bruce 'helped to achieve avoidance of any explicit reference to independence, counselled against any proclamation of independence and supported such references as there were to interdependence'. Hertzog returned to South Africa a nationalist hero. Bruce went home to the 1927 opening of Federal Parliament in Canberra, the new bush capital, with the Duke of York, the future King George VI, presiding against an Australian landscape. Within three years his successor would test the boundaries of the new equality.

Labor won the 1929 election under James Scullin, a diligent, homespun and determined man. Scullin took the Balfour Declaration at its word: he decided to appoint the first Australian as Governor-General. He chose an impeccable though disliked figure. Sir Isaac Isaacs was the Australian-born

The first Australian born governor-general, Sir Isaac Isaacs.

son of a Polish Jew, a barrister, a founding father, a member of the first Commonwealth Parliament and a High Court judge for 25 years. His credentials were near perfect.

George V was not pleased. He wanted to exercise a discretion. The British Government tried to dissuade Scullin. The Opposition leader, John Latham, a tall lean legal technician and future Chief Justice, attacked the proposal as reflecting a 'narrow Australian jingoism'. His essential stance was that 'there is no reason to make a change'. Isaacs' biographer, Zelman Cowen, says: 'The argument was that it was utterly undesirable to change what had been proved since the Federation to be so good. It's the same argument in 1999 in the debate for an Australian republic.'

The issue was deferred until Scullin went to London for the Imperial Conference. In October 1930 Scullin met the King's private secretary, Lord Stamfordham, who complained that he had 'put a pistol to the King's head'. He said the move was unprecedented; the King had always been given a list of names from which to select. Scullin was unwavering. He nominated recent precedents in South Africa and Ireland. Stamfordham threw up his hands in horror: 'Do not talk to me about Ireland. This is a country of rebels.' Scullin said the Australian people would approve the Isaacs appointment. Stamfordham challenged this; the King's information was to the contrary. Would Scullin hold a referendum on the issue?, he asked. The prime minister replied 'yes' and went further—he would be prepared 'to fight an election on the issue: whether an Australian is to be barred from the office of Governor-General because he is an Australian'. Stamfordham was shocked. He insisted that the objection to Isaac Isaacs was not because he was an Australian. Scullin dissented: he said this was the real issue. The meeting ended in deadlock.

Stamfordham called into play Australia's High Commissioner to London, Richard Casey. Casey reported to Scullin that the King had his own candidate: Field Marshal Sir William Birdwood, who had commanded the Australians in the war. On 29 November 1930 the King met Scullin at the Palace.

George V made his appeal. Isaacs was unknown to him. Any Australian would have a party bias. Why change the usual procedure now? The system was working well. Scullin was unyielding; he stared down the monarch. Finally, the King told Scullin that 'I have been a monarch for twenty years and I hope I have always been a constitutional one' and therefore 'I must, Mr Scullin, accept your advice'. The Palace was resentful. Isaac Isaacs became the first Governor-General to reside permanently at Yarralumla. One of his last duties was to convey condolences on the death of the King who had tried to stop his appointment.

The irony is that the Isaacs appointment was an aberration. The Coalition returned to power in 1932 under the ALP defector, Joseph Lyons. On Isaacs' retirement, Lyons told the new King that he 'was most anxious that the next Governor-General should come from Great Britain and be of distinguished lineage'. The Palace was delighted. With only one exception British governors-general would be appointed by both sides of politics for another 30 years. The impulse ran deep—to take the best of Britain for Australia.

The 1930s were dominated by the legacy of the Great Depression. Australia's confidence was low and it clung to a weakened Empire. In 1931 Britain completed the pledge it made at the 1926 Imperial Conference—it passed the Statute of Westminster, to come into force on 11 December 1931. This was to establish the legislative independence of the dominions. It abolished Britain's right to overrule the laws of the dominions and it permitted a dominion parliament to legislate without reference to the laws of Britain. The Statute meant that, in legal terms,

Australia would be independent of the United Kingdom government and parliament. Harold Nicholson, biographer of George V, said: 'The Statute . . . solemnised the renunciation by England of an imperial mission which in the course of centuries had brought much benefit to itself, her dependencies and the world.' It was all too much for John Latham, who mounted a campaign against the Statute.

As Opposition leader, Latham encouraged the States to protest to London over the Statute. He opposed the efforts of the Scullin Government to ratify it. After Scullin lost the election, Latham became Attorney General under Lyons and opposed, initially, the adoption of the Statute. Latham's view, as outlined by Hudson and Sharp, was that 'few Australians have the illusion that Australia could maintain her existence as a completely independent state. Alone Australia is weak . . . As a member of the British Commonwealth, Australia is strong'. In August 1930 Latham told parliament that: 'In practice we, in Australia, have all the freedom that we can possibly desire.'

For Latham, race and kinship meant a trust between Australia and Britain that transcended practical or theoretical constitutional inferiority. This argument is now known as the 'if it ain't broke, don't fix it' view of politics. It has been recycled throughout Australia's history. It is an intellectual key to Australian conservatism. It was the same argument advanced by John Howard 70 years later against the 1999 republic referendum. Australia adopted the Statute under the Curtin Government in 1942, eleven years after its passage at Westminster. In effect, Britain regarded Australia as constitutionally independent from 1931 despite Australia's reluctance. The conclusion cannot be avoided: Britain offered Australia full constitutional independence in 1931 but Australia declined the invitation. The former Chief Justice of the High Court, Sir Anthony Mason, says: 'Until the 1920s, the 1930s, when you had the Balfour Declaration and the Statute of Westminister was passed in 1931 to be adopted by Australia eleven years later, Australia was not an independent nation.'

These changes, flowing from the Declaration and the Statute, also involved a new conception of monarchy which gradually took hold. They implied the divisibility of the Crown. The Queen of the United Kingdom is the same queen and lives in the same palace as the Queen of Australia but these are two different Crowns. The Queen of the United Kingdom acting on advice from her British ministers might be implementing a policy detrimental to the Queen of Australia acting on advice from her Australian ministers. Sir Garfield Barwick summarised the situation in a 1982 lecture: 'The Queen is actually, and not merely nominally, Queen of Australia. [The] law was changed in the first half of this century—not by statute but by constitutional usage and practice. The Crown became separate and divisible.'

This is a miraculous event. It is, almost, an act of faith. Like such doctrines it relies on trust as much as reason. It is a safe bet that most Australians don't understand the concept. But it has a flaw which everyone does grasp—the Queen of Australia follows a line of succession in a British family that has nothing whatsoever to do with Australia.

The people in the 1930s were even less interested in constitutional independence than they were in a republic in the 1990s. There was no popular demand for change. These constitutional debates were conducted among elites. The main conflict with Britain in the early 1930s was a row over bodyline in cricket. The fusion between nation and Empire that constituted the Australian identity still endured. The ultimate proof was at hand: the most dominant Australian leader of the century now took the stage.

Robert Gordon Menzies was a child of the British civilisation living in Victoria. He was perhaps the greatest product of the line of Australian-Britons. His grandfather had arrived from Scotland in 1854. Born in Jeparit in the Wimmera district, Menzies advanced as a scholarship boy. He was blessed with stature, voice and brains. In his first broadcast as prime minister introducing himself to the people Menzies said: 'I was not born to the purple. I have made my own way.'

He made his first visit to England only in 1935, as a 40-year-old. Menzies' diary recorded that sighting: 'At last we are in England. Our journey to Mecca has ended ... Dover: it has for centuries been the gateway of romance and high endeavour. I feel a tang in its air that no mere state of wind or weather could possibly create.' In London he was excited by 'officials, friends, the grey bulk of Buckingham Palace, the Mall, the river, the Strand, the Savoy ... at 10.30 pm I sneak out and look at Trafalgar Square and one of the Wren churches by starlight'. It was a discovery.

It was also an affirmation. As Judith Brett argues, for most of Menzies' life England could only be an imagined place for him, the heart of the literature, law and history that defined his life. When Menzies visited, finally, he saw the best and only wanted to see the best. He was confirming his imagined vision, confirming his long cherished idealised construct. But Menzies' imagined vision was merely a variation of the imagined vision that most Australians had of what they once called the 'home' country.

In his approach to the monarchy, Menzies, like Paul Keating on the republic, was a masterful story teller and myth maker. The problem with the Menzian view was its implicit denigration of Australia as a derivative and imitative society and it was this sentiment, unsurprisingly, that inspired the loathing of Menzies by Australia's intellectual class.

But Menzies was admired by the British elite and struck up a lasting relationship with the Royal Family. At tea with the Duke and Duchess of York, Menzies met the two young princesses, Elizabeth and Margaret Rose. Menzies left 'walking on air'. His biographer, A W Martin, highlights his conclusion: 'There is here a real bond between the monarch and his people that defies all the academic arguments of the so-called revolutionaries.' Menzies was not only attracted by the constitutional and romantic nature of monarchy. He made a simple political observation: it was deeply popular. As prime minister at the outbreak of World War II Menzies broke the news to the people that 'Great Britain has declared war upon her [Germany] and that, as a result, Australia is also at war'. The sentiment in parliament was unanimous. Menzies drew strong support from the Opposition leader, John Curtin. Australia entered World War II—which began as a strictly European conflict—as united as it was at World War I, yet unenthusiastic. Once again Australia was fighting for and with Britain. Alan Martin drew another parallel with the first war: 'The latter-day idea that Australia was fighting "other peoples' wars" did not occur to anyone. Nor did anyone contest Menzies' assertion that he felt he could appeal for support "because we are all Australians and British citizens".'

In his memoirs Menzies was unrepentant about the words used in his war declaration. He put the notion that, while every British country went to war, none surrendered its independent nationhood. Yet his justification revealed that Menzies subscribed to the old-fashioned idea of the indivisibility of the Crown: 'Those were the days when the Commonwealth was a Crown Commonwealth. How could the King be at war and at peace at the same time, in relation to Germany? From my point of view in 1939, neutrality for Australia in a British war was unthinkable, unless we were prepared to add secession to neutrality.' The fact today, of course, is that the divisibility of the Crown is best grasped within the war context. The Queen of Great Britain can be at war and the Queen of Australia can be at peace. Australia did not fight for the Falklands; Britain did not fight in Vietnam. The divisibility of the Crown, a concept so difficult for Menzies, is now assumed.

In 1940 Menzies, following Hughes, went to London for the war cause. He was lionised by many but had a strained relationship with Winston Churchill. Menzies, like Hughes, far from being a lapdog of the British, was a defender of Australian interests. It was his willingness to challenge Churchill that made him so attractive to many British insiders. Contrary to so much mythology, Menzies was a nationalist as well as an Empire man. In Britain he struck an effective balance, avoiding the two polarised pitfalls for Australians: the cultural cringer and the overassertive ass. But back home he succumbed and his resignation left the way, ultimately, for Curtin to become Australia's war leader.

In December 1941 when Curtin declared war upon Japan his approach was different to that of Menzies. Curtin relied upon the Balfour Declaration in a deliberate statement of Australia's independence of action, previously conceded by Britain. Yet in his radio broadcast to the nation after the declaration Curtin said that Australians would 'hold this country and keep it as a citadel for the British-speaking race and as a place where civilisation will persist'. The British racial heritage was always central to Curtin's appeals.

The achievement of Australian independence saw not the extinguishment but the evolution of our ties with the Crown. The role of the Crown was redefined, first by Menzies, then by Gough Whitlam, in separate endeavours. Menzies' solution was intensely political: he sought to popularise the Crown. Whitlam's was constitutional in essence: he aspired to nationalise the Crown. Both ideas worked, briefly, in their own time but subsequently were rendered obsolete.

Menzies' second and record prime ministership (1949–66) rested not just in the discrediting of his opponents but in an appeal to instincts deep within Australia's political culture. Judith Brett has argued that the most effective exposition of Menzies' philosophy was his 1942 'Forgotten People' speech.

> The time has come to say something of the forgotten class—the Middle Class—who, properly regarded, represent the backbone of this country ... I do not believe that the real life of this nation is to be found either in the great luxury hotels [or] the petty gossip of so called fashionable suburbs. It is to be found in the homes of people who are nameless and unadvertised, and who, whatever their individual religious conviction or dogma, see in their children their greatest contribution to the immortality of their race. The home is the foundation of sanity and sobriety.

Menzies enshrined values at the heart of his new Liberal Party. He made the home the centre of those values as opposed to Labor's class politics based in the workplace. The elements of this appeal were home ownership, family security, middle class self-improvement and a genuflection before Australia's British-based institutions at the core of which lay the monarchy.

Queen Elizabeth II bestows the order of Knight Bachelor on Sir Garfield Barwick during her 1954 Royal Tour.

In the early 1950s Menzies had a lucky break—a beautiful young Queen, Elizabeth II, came to the throne. Her coronation was an event for the ages. A re-viewing of the television broadcast transmitted to the world from Westminster Abbey is a spell-binding experience. Elizabeth II was the first reigning monarch to visit Australia. She captured the imagination of the forgotten people.

The Royal Tour of 1954 spanned 57 days and saw possibly the widest and most sustained public engagement in the nation's history. It is an event intoxicating and baffling. It showed that half a century after Federation the monarchy, or Elizabeth II, had an appeal as intense as any the Crown had enjoyed in Australia. It documented a sense of a monarchical popularity so strong that the only response from Australia's intellectual class was to retreat en masse into denial. But it is hard to argue that eight million people simultaneously succumbed to false consciousness.

Menzies saw the social significance of the new Queen: 'It is one of the most powerful elements converting them [the people] from a mass of individuals to a great cohesive nation. The common devotion to the Throne is part of the very cement of the whole social structure.' The Queen was a symbol of unity, stability and a victorious war. An affirmation of family values with the glitter of jewels. In her thesis on the tour Jane Connors notes that 'many of the people I have heard from or spoken to in the course of research tell me that they remember this event with more clarity and emotion than any other public occasion during their lifetime'. Connors reports that the Communist Party was too intimidated by popular opinion to protest the Queen. The ALP was seduced and its leader, Dr H V Evatt, struggled into tails at the Canberra banquet for the second time in his life.

Menzies' banquet speech was utterly in harmony with the public mood, yet still an insight into the skill of his monarchical projection: 'The moving truth tonight has nothing to do with high pomp or regal splendour. It is quite simply that you are in your own country and among your own people.' He called the tour a 'family reunion'. For Menzies, it was an apt label. The Queen left Sydney on a day when the temperature hit the old century mark and decorum was strained at the NSW Governor's tea party where crimson-faced guests flattened the petunia beds and drank water from garden taps.

The Queen stands with two other dominant cultural elements from the 1950s to capture the Menzian age: the dull conformity of middle class sub-urban expansion and the sense of threat from a pervasive communist peril.

Just nine years later the Queen returned. It was a Royal occasion but the magic of 1954 was lost. Australia was in transition beyond the 1950s and Menzies was losing his touch. At the Canberra reception he made an immortal miscalculation: 'I did but see her passing by and yet I love her till I die.' The Queen's former private secretary, Sir William Heseltine, said: 'I can remember there was a frisson of embarrassment and this was perhaps reflected in the Queen's own look on this occasion.' The nation had moved beyond Menzies' romance.

But the prime minister had one belated act to perform—in his twilight he appointed his old ministerial colleague and rival, Lord Casey, as Governor-General. It was now more than 30 years since Isaac Isaacs' appointment. Yet Casey was only the third Australian to hold the post—the other being Sir William McKell, appointed by Ben Chifley in the late 1940s. The century was almost at its two-thirds mark, but only now did a Coalition Government for the first time appoint an Australian to the post which had been 'Australianised' in a constitutional sense since the Balfour Declaration in the late 1920s. Casey's elevation was a turning point: it was the inauguration of the unbroken line of Australian governors-general, which has further transformed the office in a subtle but decisive way.

This is why Prince Charles was unable to become Governor-General. When I interviewed the Prince of Wales in 1994 he confirmed that the Governor-General, Sir Ninian Stephen, obviously acting on ministerial advice, had sounded him out in the early 1980s about this option. The Prince was keen. But he knew there had to be unanimous political support—and Australia had passed the stage in its history of having a Briton, even a member of the Royal Family, at Yarralumla.

Gough Whitlam, elected in December 1972, saw himself as a comprehensive moderniser. Whitlam wanted not to eliminate tradition but to invest it with contemporary flair. He aspired to modernise the monarchy. On the evening of Good Friday 1973 Whitlam saw the Queen at Windsor Castle and outlined his plan. Her new title would be 'Elizabeth the Second, Queen of Australia'. The aim was to 'naturalise' the Crown—to invest the constitutional notion of Queen of Australia with the appropriate symbolism. The Queen herself signed the bill for her new title when she visited Canberra later that year. At the Lodge the charming senior vice-president of the ALP, Jack Egerton, quipped: 'They tell us, luv, you've been naturalised.'

It is true that Whitlam's act merely extended the 1953 law of the Menzies Government which, for the first time, formally recognised the Queen as Australia's monarch. The difference, though, is that Whitlam began to popularise the title Queen of Australia. It was a neat blend of nationalism and modernism.

Whitlam promoted a new sense of cultural nationalism; he championed a more independent Australian role in the world; he completed the 1968 work of an earlier Coalition Government with a 1975 law that ended Privy Council appeals from the High Court and all federal courts. Appeals from State courts were only ended with the Hawke Government's 1986 *Australia Act*. It is extraordinary how long Australia as an independent nation allowed its independence to be compromised by permitting, in Whitlam's words, 'decisions of its courts to be taken on appeal to a court sitting in another country'.

Whitlam also sought a more prestigious role for the Governor-General. For the first time the Governor-General would be accorded Head of State status. Sir John Kerr was most interested in this innovation when he accepted Whitlam's offer to replace Sir Paul Hasluck at Yarralumla. But Whitlam and Kerr fell out when the Governor-General dismissed the prime minister. The significance of the 1975 dismissal was that it confirmed in the most spectacular fashion Australia's complete independence. The Queen was not told beforehand by Kerr of his plan. She was asleep when Whitlam was sacked and Malcolm Fraser commissioned. Kerr justified this in terms of protecting the monarchy—to have told the Queen would have involved her in Australian domestic politics and therefore compromise the Crown's impartiality. This was a sound argument as far as it went. But Kerr's decision not to inform the Palace also protected him from another possibility—that the Palace, reflecting a prudent monarch, would have cautioned delay. That would have ruined Kerr's timetable.

Sir William Heseltine, assistant at that stage to the Queen's private secretary Sir Martin Charteris, has confirmed for the first time, during an interview for the television series '100 Years', that this was the view of the Palace. 'I'm very surprised myself that he [Kerr] didn't take the advantage of [the Queen's] long experience and consult her ... We are in a position to know, I guess, how we would have advised her. But as we never had to do that I cannot say categorically what she would have said to the Governor-General. My own feeling is that she would have advised him to play out the situation a little longer ... I do suspect that in the course of another day or two a political solution rather than this drastic imposed solution would have been found.'

Sir William alludes to the Palace's real attitude towards Kerr's dismissal of Whitlam: 'I would hesitate to say that she was shocked. It would be true to say that none of us at that time thought that this was an ideal solution to the crisis. As of 11 November 1975 nobody at Buckingham Palace had expected that the crisis would be solved by the Governor-General dismissing the prime minister. It would be fair to say, however, that both Sir Martin Charteris and myself felt that it was a pity that this very drastic solution was applied exactly when it was and that a little bit more political leeway would have enabled a political solution to emerge in Canberra and that would have been a very much more desirable outcome.'

Whitlam would have won better treatment from the Queen; but the Queen was no longer a participant in the system. Australia now lived by Australian solutions administered by Australians. It is inconceivable that a British Governor-General would have sacked the prime minister; but an Australian Governor-General had the confidence to take this action. The Palace confirmed the new rules in a letter dated 17 November 1975: 'The only person competent to commission an Australian prime minister is the Governor-General, and the Queen has no part in the decisions which the Governor-General must take in accordance with the Constitution.'

The Queen was cast forever outside the Australian realm of action.

Australia, in effect, was a Governor-Generalate. The Queen was a figure-head; the Governor-General had the power. The naturalisation of the Australian Constitution was complete and confirmed. Australia was a 'crowned republic'.

It was this logic upon which Paul Keating acted nearly two decades later. Labor's first reaction to 1975 had been to blame Kerr and Fraser. Its cooler reaction was to seek to reform the power of the Senate which had triggered the crisis. After this failed because of party conflict, Labor concentrated on regaining power, the final therapy. In 1988 the guest of honour presiding over the Bicentennial celebrations with Prime Minister Bob Hawke was the Prince of Wales. Malcolm Turnbull, the subsequent leader of the Australian Republican Movement, fumed: 'Don't we have an Australian who can use a pair of scissors?'

Keating believed that Australia had reached the final stage of its national maturity—the aspiration to have an Australian as Head of State, to move from constitutional monarchy to republic. The republic, for most of its advocates, was not about being anti-British. Any such narrow and negative platform would fail. It was a reaffirmation of Australian identity; it was about Australia, not Britain; it was a declaration of Australia's uniqueness and its special mission. It was the next logical step in Australia's history of constitutional and political evolution from Britain; it was a recognition that this evolution must continue until Australia achieved, symbolically as well as constitutionally, the independence that lay dormant in its Feder-ation. It was based on a confidence that those idealistic pragmatists, Edmund Barton and Alfred Deakin, transported onwards a hundred years, would be champions of a republican destiny. Finally, it was based on the conviction that Australia ultimately would be more comfortable and united as a republic than as a constitutional monarchy with its Head of State a foreigner living in a foreign nation.

Keating advised the Queen of his plans. The Prince of Wales visited Australia, endorsed the republican debate and declared that it was for Australians to determine their own fate. The referendum was put in 1999 under a monarchist prime minister, John Howard, almost certainly Australia's last monarchist PM.

The vote was lost, just as the initial vote for Federation was lost. John Howard could perhaps have carried the republic but he lacked the belief and did not see the need. Howard acted as the descendant of the political tradition of Bruce, Latham and Menzies—a nationalist and a monarchist. He explained his position in words that could have been used by Latham or Menzies: 'I think the present system works. It is a reflection of my Burkean conservatism. I'm not going to throw out something that's given

Paul Keating offended the British press when he placed his hand on the Queen's back.

us, helped to give us, immense stability.' That conservative tradition had not yet run its course. Howard said after his referendum victory for the 'no' cause: 'To bring about that kind of change, you've almost got to allow a state of affairs to develop where there is no significant section of the population who opposes change.'

Paul Keating was typically defiant: 'I think it's important [that] when the republic comes it's celebrated, it's claimed, that we don't just wimp over the line by a vote ... and the country understands that the big psychological moment has come. I still think we can do that and it's the one trade-off for losing it.'

The moral is that the republic will be much harder to achieve than many of its adherents believed. The reason lies deep within our political culture. It should be obvious from this story: Australia was conceived and grew up as a child of the Empire.

The Crown has been at the heart of our political system. Its removal requires a redefinition of that system in a constitutional, political and emotional sense. It is not enough to hand the Crown back to London. It requires Australians to agree upon what being a republic actually means. This is an exercise in imagination and unity. Even if Australians agree on removing the Crown there is no guarantee that they can agree on a republican values system. That will require a skill for compromise that marked the Federation generation but which the 2001 generation with its self-obsessions does not necessarily possess. It is far easier in modern politics to define positions by negatives than by positives.

Australians have no ready answers to the issues involved. Does a republic merely keep the current system and substitute a presidency for the office of Governor-General? A great change with minimal change. Or does a republic mean an improved and transformed political system with a greater participation by the people? In 2001 there is no agreement on this.

The first of the three main Federation Centenary events—the July 2000 London celebrations—exposed the limitations of Australian republicanism. John Howard was depicted as tugging the forelock to Britain, a depiction not just absurd about Howard but a lie about Australia. Howard went to London as an Australia-first nationalist. It is many decades since any Australian leader genuflected to Britain. Yet the historical, outdated idea of our leaders 'selling out' to Britain seems to be entrenched within our popular culture.

Much of the opinion-making elite in 2001, like the old radical nationalists, is still partly prisoner to a republicanism defined by anti-British assertion. Australia must move beyond these chains of the past. This is an impoverished brand of republicanism. As Mark McKenna, student of our republican history, says: 'There is no future in a republic that is just about rejecting pomp and ceremony. This negative attitude is no longer enough. It is a sign of national immaturity.'

The problem with the republic is that it falls victim to its own supporters. While the republic is a weapon to fight old historical battles it is doomed. The republic cannot succeed merely as the property of the ALP, or the radical nationalist tradition, or the opinion making elites, or those who claim to be the only true patriots. The republic can only succeed as the next evolutionary step down the path of Australian independence.

This journey is far advanced. The old idea of being British is now left behind. In the process Australians are starting to appreciate better the Crown's former role as a unifying force. They are starting to realise that the republic must also be a unifying force if it is to prevail. It must bring people together.

The pretence that being pro-Empire meant betraying Australia's real interests is an orthodoxy about our history still held with passion. It is a tragic interpretation because it turns Australia's history into a caricature. It reduces Deakin, Hughes, Menzies and even Curtin to the level of craven toadies. It originates in a sense of loathing for our past. It is based on a refusal to see that Empire loyalty and Australian nationalism went hand-in-hand for so long for excellent reasons. It is a view not shared and never shared by a majority of the Australian people. It defines the republic as a rejection of the past, as a triumph against our history. But Australia has no need to repudiate its past. It has grown step-by-step with a more mature nationalism and stronger self-esteem. The republic, as this story shows, is the logical next step in Australia's ongoing evolution. Its legitimacy and its power stems from this continuity. It flows naturally from the past and it will only be carried as a celebration, not as a rejection of that history.

INTERVIEW WITH
MALCOLM FRASER

In his most wide ranging interview for 20 years, Malcolm Fraser says the Vietnam commitment was a mistake, nominates multiculturalism as his own government's most significant achievement and warns that Australia's loss of faith on immigration threatens the nation's future. With the Cold War over, Fraser is sceptical about the US alliance and fears that Australia may have to make a choice between China and America, with his own preference being Asia.

How should we see the postwar immigration program—as a visionary scheme or as a response to a need?

I think both descriptions are valid. When the scheme was introduced shortly after the Second World War, it was the Labor Government that persuaded the union movement that it was necessary for Australia's future. We'd been seven million people during the war. We were very vulnerable. A couple of bits of good fortune prevented us being invaded. The memories of the prewar years, the Depression and 30 per cent unemployment, were very much in people's minds. It was an act of political courage on the part of Arthur Calwell to get the union movement to accept a large-scale migration program from Europe. It was visionary because it had some idea of a larger, better, more effective Australia.

When you boil down the politics of the scheme, some people would say that it's fairly crude. It was 'populate or perish'. Is that an accurate view?

Well, it's a harsh view. I think it was pretty accurate because with seven million people Australia was not defensible. It was the United States' involvement in the war that prevented Australia being invaded. It's worth recalling that Britain had been at war and we had been at war for two years and five months before the United States came into the war, and if it had not been attacked at Pearl Harbor when would it have come into the war, if ever? I would say that, in today's world, with nearly twenty million people Australia is not defensible and that we really need the same sense of commitment and belief in the future to build this into a nation of 40, 45 million people, and then I believe we would start to be defensible in our own right.

The Menzies Government continued and expanded the immigration program. What does this tell us about Menzies?

Menzies was able to look at the problems of the day with a very open mind. He was a Liberal politician I believe in the true sense. People sometimes forget his own upbringing, his birthplace, a Mallee town, Jeparit. Before the war he got to the university because he was bright enough to get one of just 40 scholarships. It's a very different world today and Menzies I believe had a sense of nation-building, an idea of where this country might go in the future. He devoted a great deal of attention to international issues. He was the father of Australia's expansion in higher education and gave enormous support to Australia's universities. He knew that these things had to be done for the future. He also knew that immigration was an important ingredient in that.

When one looks back on the program from today's perspective it seems almost incredible that we took so many people and absorbed them so successfully into our community. What does this tell us about Australia?

It tells us a lot about Australia then and something not quite so favourable about Australia now. Australians did have a sense of commitment to the future. We'd had a very nasty escape during the war. The enemy came very close. Darwin was heavily bombed. Sydney had been attacked and New Guinea nearly collapsed. If it wasn't for the battles of the Coral Sea and Midway ... it was only those two naval battles that prevented the invasion taking place. Australians wanted something better. They wanted something more secure. They wanted to know that this couldn't happen again. We were prepared to do a lot to invest in the future. The Snowy Mountains Scheme was one example of that investment in the future. Nation-building in a material sense and bringing more people here in a people sense were very important ingredients of Australian policy of the day. Now nation-building in that sense is not even on the political agenda in 1999.

In 1966 the Holt Cabinet took significant steps to dismantle the White Australia policy. What was your own view of this decision?

I can remember Hubert Opperman making the speech in the parliament. It was very carefully worded and you almost had to get the speech again and say, what is this meaning? because Opperman was very cautious because of past history. Nobody in those days wanted to stir up a backlash and say, no, this is wrong. We didn't want people going around saying the White Australia policy should remain. But when you read the speech it was clear enough. It was a very important and necessary step for Australia.

What were the factors that drove the Holt Cabinet to this very significant change of policy?

It would have been driven by some domestic factors, also by foreign policy. It also would have been driven by the natural conviction that Harold Holt had in relation to these issues.

I think Sir Robert Menzies would have come from an older world. He was an older generation and he might have found it harder to come to grips with the issue in the way that Harold Holt did but Holt was a liberal in a very real sense of the term. He was contemporary in the 1960s. He had a different attitude, a recognition that the world was changing, that policies discriminatory on the basis of race or ethnicity or colour were increasingly being condemned around the world. What was happening in South Africa, all of these things, were elements which persuaded people that the policy needed to change.

So this can be seen as a change in Australia's values?

I believe so, yes. Not necessarily a conscious change except by those making the policy, because Australians I think have always been an egalitarian open people. I like to think that Australia is still regarded as a friendly country and we don't automatically look to somebody's background, colour or ethnicity when we make our friends or when we're speaking with people.

We had the boatpeople arriving after the fallout from the situation in Vietnam. For a lot of Australians this was the nightmare scenario, Asian people arriving on their shores by boat. What did you feel when this started to happen?

The dominant feeling was that we had to give these people a home, especially people who had been associated with either the Australian Embassy or the Australian Armed Forces in Vietnam. Our presence there had encouraged them to fight. Their association with either American forces or Australian forces during the Vietnam War would have made it very difficult for them in Vietnam in the immediate aftermath of the war. So I think we had a commitment, an obligation, to such people and we fulfilled that obligation.

I wasn't conscious that we were taking a dangerous decision when we took it. If you recall the politics of those times it was an issue that Michael MacKellar as Immigration Minister handled very well with a sense of discretion. He was sensitive about the way he handled it in the public mind. It never became a great issue. It wasn't a matter of division between the political parties and this of course had been essential to an effective immigration policy through the years. There was a basic acceptance by both sides of the parliament that this was very much in Australia's interest. So people came here. And I can remember on more than one occasion saying that we had taken more refugees from Vietnam and Cambodia than any other equivalent nation, having regard to the size of our population. The other two most generous countries were the United States and Canada.

I believe what we did was a major turning point because this was not just a policy that was stated, this was a policy being applied and it was applied successfully without a public backlash. I think the public acceptance was because of the way in which Michael MacKellar handled the issue, and both he and I, if it became necessary, stood ready to defend the policy in very strong terms.

When one looks back on this, it's a little bit remarkable that there wasn't a degree of public backlash.

If it was a matter of public dispute between the parties, immigration policy would have been very difficult to conduct. There were times when people said, look, we've got too many Italians here. Then once they're settled that's fine, that's accepted. Then people might say there are too many Greeks or too many people from East Germany or eastern Europe as a whole—and that never became a major issue. As each new phase in the migration program unfolded the people who'd come in the previous phase were accepted. All right, they're Aussies now. But all this is saying that there was never a great deal of public enthusiasm for particular aspects of the migration program. It was something that people accepted because the political leadership on both sides of the House were supporting it.

Do you think it also means that in some ways we were a more tolerant people than often we credit ourselves for being?

We're certainly more tolerant now than we were in the 1950s. If you go back just before the world war there'd be many people who would say that to be a good Australian you've got to be white, Anglo-Saxon Protestant and, if you're not, you'd better damn well pretend to be. Now, those days are well and truly past. Australia is a multicultural society. You can't turn the clock back. The people who walk in our streets and live in our suburbs and work in our factories and offices—we're a multicultural society in the fullest sense. Because we are a multicultural society I believe for the most part we're also a more tolerant community. We know that this is good for Australia. We know that the changes in our cities have benefited our cities and benefited the citizens who live in those cities.

As prime minister you gave very strong official endorsement to multiculturalism as a settlement policy, as a policy for the country. How important was this at the time?

It might have been the most important thing that my government accomplished. Whatever anyone might have said since, the fact that we then accepted a multicultural Australia and accepted that people didn't have to forget their land of origin or forget their affection for it to be a good Australian was enormously important in building a cohesive society. I can remember that one very significant immigrant from Italy—from a very successful family in Melbourne and the first of the family to migrate to Australia—said to me at the Lodge during a discussion or a dinner, 'You know, Prime Minister, for the first time I feel I don't need to look over my shoulder.' I thought that was really saying it all.

I think, in the longer term interests of Australia, that policy was certainly one of the more important things that my government did.

Do you think that the Liberal Party has properly nurtured and looked after the legacy of multiculturalism?

Unfortunately, the Liberal Party's political opponents have generally been better at moving into non-traditional backgrounds, into Greek, Italian, Vietnamese, other areas, other communities, than has the Liberal Party and that I believe remains true. Now, this has been broken down to an extent. But the Liberal Party organisation needs to be more vigorous in what might be called non-traditional or post–World War II immigrant areas. While the original reluctance to accept multiculturalism came from the Senate and, in relation to the Special Broadcasting Service, more from the Australian Labor Party than from the Liberal Party, there has been some reluctance in Liberal ranks to accept the idea of multiculturalism.

I make the point that it's too late to change things because we *are* a multicultural society. The review that the Howard Government established some time ago concluded that we are a multicultural Australia. We oughtn't to run away from that term and its consequences.

How seriously did you view the threat that Pauline Hanson posed in terms of the platform on which she was seeking election?

I believe that Pauline Hanson was a danger to many of the values that Australia had come to represent in a very full and open way. But I also believe that the people supporting her didn't necessarily support the policy prescriptions she was enunciating. People forget the degree of disenchantment in rural Australia, in regional Australia, with the policies of all political parties over the last ten or a dozen years. There's been several years of very poor prices. There have been five to seven years of drought. Because the country was being driven by economic rationalism, services in country areas were being reduced, everything had to pay for itself. There was a large section of regional and rural Australia that felt rejected, neglected. They believed they had very serious problems and that the Labor Party had had a go and done nothing about it, the Coalition parties had had another go and they had not acted adequately. It was this feeling of being put aside, ignored, made irrelevant, that led to the kind of support that Pauline Hanson and the One Nation Party achieved. Now governments, both State and federal, have responded. I happen to believe they have not done anything like enough to redress the balance and that in a modern economically deregulated Australia we have a long way to go to re-establish equity and fairness within the community. I took Pauline Hanson not so much as a condemnation of multiculturalism as such, but as a response to a series of economic and social policies that have led to a great deal of disenchantment throughout much of the country.

How do you judge the magnitude of the failure of Prime Minister Howard to deal with Hansonism?

I don't want to answer that directly, but if I had been dealing with it I would have said something about her policies from the moment they started to come up above the horizon. I would have said something about it much, much earlier. With my background in the countryside, I think I would have understood the motivation of many of those who did, in fact, support her and that therefore I would have realised that those who were supporting her had a real grievance. I would have tried to do something about it. I would have tried to divide Pauline Hanson from that support base right from the very beginning.

To what extent do you think that the nation-building ethos in Australia is now being compromised? Are you concerned that public support for immigration seems to be substantially eroded?

It's a significant problem. The Labor Party before the last election re-established a vigorous immigration program as central to Australia's needs. But the Coalition Government has kept the numbers down very tight. It's kept the refugee numbers down very tight and the idea of building Australia through more people and expanding our population base is not an active idea in the political scene today. Unless the political parties are going to drive immigration policy it's not really going to happen. It's interesting to note, however, that in some parts of the Australian community there are now business groups and others who are starting to argue for a much more effective migration program because they recognise that in this deregulated world a larger population base is very important for Australia.

If Australia is marginalised through this coming century, if our values are pushed aside, if we're regarded as of no consequence as a rich Western enclave on the edge of Asia, then marginalisation could pose risks for Australia's very survival. You've only got to look at the population pressures in the world. It would not be impossible towards the end of this next century for a United Nations to say, there's gross over-population in certain areas, there are other parts of the world which are under-populated, forefront amongst those regions is Australia, now Australia is going to have to do something about it. That would not be very helpful. We should not allow ourselves to be put in that position. When we look at the size of this continent, the wealth of this continent and the way we conduct ourselves in this continent, it's sometimes difficult to avoid the conclusion that in today's world, in the last ten or fifteen years, we've become more introspective, we've become more selfish, we're looking at enjoying the wealth of Australia for ourselves. The commitment to build for the future, with one exception, has really been pushed entirely aside. The exception is the advocates of a totally deregulated economy where government is much smaller than it was with lesser obligations to Australians than it formerly accepted. There are those who argue that this will build a more competitive, more efficient, more productive Australia, but that alone is not a policy, it's not a vision for the future.

What sort of population do you think Australia should be looking at as we go into the next century?

I'd like to see Australia openly aiming for a target of 40, 45 million people and reaching that target well before the end of this next century. That would be a lesser commitment than the Australians of 1945 accepted for the next 30 or 40 years. We were then seven million people. The commitment of those years built that up to almost 20 million in a relatively short space of time. If we said we're going to hit 40, 45 million people by 2050, 2060, it would be a lesser obligation. I only wish today's politicians showed the same commitment that Arthur Calwell and Harold Holt and other people showed in the late 1940s and 50s and 60s.

To achieve this, the idea of a diverse multicultural Australia is fundamental. Are Australians ready to accept that?

I believe they are but Australians aren't going to accept it of themselves. They're going to accept it if their political leaders have the courage to stand up and to argue that this is necessary for the security, for the well-being of Australia, for our capacity to advance Australian values, to participate in the region and to make this region a safer one for the future. What Australia's been doing in East Timor recently has stretched our Army to the limit. We don't have the defence forces that by ourselves make Australia defendable. Are we going to go on relying on a country that let Britain bleed for two years and five months against Nazi Germany and was then finally forced into the war as the result of a specific attack on Pearl Harbor? If we think the Americans will be readier allies for us than they were for Britain I think we're just deceiving ourselves. The Cold War days were different but that's another world. America probably would have defended us against a communist attack but I can't perceive of a danger today in which American assistance would be forthcoming to Australia.

How important is a full apology to the Aboriginal people for past injustices?

It's very important. Full reconciliation won't really occur until physical inadequacies, lack of living standard and lifestyle and such matters are overcome. But there are also matters of the spirit. For reconciliation both are important for Aboriginals.

What is your view today of that past policy of assimilation which was championed in particular by Paul Hasluck? Do you think it lasted too long?

It might have lasted too long. Some manifestations of the policy certainly did. I think policy now is to enable Aboriginals to take their place within the Australian community in their own way, preserving their culture, preserving their history; and, if they want to live in traditional ways or in areas which they own, then they ought to be able to do this. That idea of choice is a very real one.

Your government implemented a land rights law for the Northern Territory following the earlier initiative of the Whitlam Government. How hard was this initiative?

It was an issue that could have been very divisive for the government. But we handled it through discussion, compromise amongst different groups, and in the end the policy was accepted. It took some time. It took a good deal of patience and negotiation within the ranks of the government. But that's fine—the best policy often does. The land rights legislation recognised an aspect of Aboriginals' affinity with the past which up till then had been ignored. Therefore it established a groundwork for future relationships with the Aboriginal population. It was very important. In practical terms, it was also important within the Northern Territory.

Of course, the Holt, Gorton and McMahon Cabinets had declined to accept land rights before the 1972 election. How do you explain the difference with your cabinet?

It was partly because there'd been an interregnum. The coalition had run out of steam in 1972. Mr Whitlam came to power with a very different kind of government. It was a government that in a number of important policy areas changed attitudes. After some initiative by Mr Whitlam there'd been an inquiry into land rights and the legislation derived from that inquiry. I believe it would have been quite wrong to say, no, we're going to throw all this aside, we're going to ignore this. The Labor Party years 1972 to 1975 were quite important in changing the attitudes of the Coalition Government after 1975. In addition, I think that my government produced two or three of the best ministers for Aboriginal Affairs that Australia has had, Ian Viner and Fred Chaney. Their custodianship of the issues, I think, was helpful in making sure that the policy was ultimately enacted.

Is one of the lessons here that these sorts of social reforms can be bedded down more effectively if they're implemented by a non-Labor government?

That's correct if you're looking for continuity, simply because if the Labor Party introduces the reform there's a risk that a Coalition Government might come along and undo it. Now, if the parties on the conservative side are going to bless the reform then it's going to endure. This has been true of multiculturalism.

How important is the native title issue?

It's become symbolically very important, but it's an issue that probably has an impact on a fairly small number of Aboriginals as a percentage of the total Aboriginal population. It doesn't really do anything for Aboriginals in Sydney, in country towns, in the cities, a lot of whom have virtually lost their affinity with the land or their direct association with it. My personal view is that the question of the apology and the question of native title have absorbed so much time and energy of the Aboriginal leadership and of the government that other issues have been set aside which often would have had a greater impact on more Aboriginals. The symbolism is very important and until we can get the symbolism out of the way we can't get on with practical issues. We've got to find a way of advancing on both fronts.

But the government has not been forthcoming. It has not been sympathetic to the symbolic issues which are so important to Aboriginals and which have in a very real sense been pushed aside over the last few years.

A large part of the Aboriginal leadership certainly would not trust the government and the government probably doesn't trust them and it's a great pity that the capacity for an open and honest dialogue seems not to exist.

Given your record as prime minister, is it fair to assume that you would have operated differently in recent times?

Everyone knows I would have.

I wouldn't have found any difficulty with an apology. I wouldn't have found any difficulty with the use of the word 'sorry' because 'sorry' does not denote guilt. It is a recognition that something wrong happened, perhaps something grievously wrong happened, and it's an expression of very real regret that that occurred. Some people have expressed the view that if you say you're sorry you're accepting a degree of guilt for what happened. A lot of people told me they were sorry when my mother died, but they weren't guilty of the fact that she had died. The use of the word does not imply guilt.

How important is it for us, as a nation, to get this right, to get the relationship with the original inhabitants right?

It is so far one of our greatest failings. It remains a very significant challenge and one of the things that needs to be done is to dispel some of the myths about policy. For example, there's a view that governments have thrown money at Aboriginal problems and that some people have filtered off a significant part of that money for their own benefit. Now, maybe some things have not been adequately audited. If they haven't been adequately audited that's the parliament's fault. It is the fault of successive governments and that can easily be corrected. I want to take health as an example. Aboriginal health on every standard is far worse than that of the rest of the Australian community. Life expectancy, problems in childbirth, infant mortality, the sheer standard of living of Aboriginals, their homes—on all standards they fall way behind and their standards are in many respects third world. Now that is a very real disgrace.

There is a view that money has been thrown at the problem but it's not true that money has been thrown at the problem. Having regard to the fact that Aboriginals need more spending on them, there's only an extra eight cents spent on Aboriginals compared to other Australians. That is not an adequate response to the problem. This has partly occurred because people have said it's ATSIC's [Aboriginal and Torres Strait Islander Commission] responsibility. Because ATSIC had something to do with this, State departments withdrew from the area and Commonwealth departments said, we're providing money for ATSIC so that's the Commonwealth contribution. It was never meant to be that way.

In a sense Aboriginals have been blamed for the failure of the rest of the community. It should be a simple thing to lay down the responsibilities of State governments, of Federal departments and of ATSIC, and to say, this is what each of you are going to have to do to improve the situation.

The myth that most Australians would believe is that we have been generous with money. Well, the myth is false.

Looking at economic policy, in Australia there's been a long tradition of economic justice and the quest for a fair society. How important is this to the Australian character?

I would like to think it's a very important and continuing part of the Australian psyche. A 'fair go', an egalitarian society, these were things that we were proud of. They marked Australia apart from a lot of other countries. We would say that we don't have the great disparity of wealth that exists in America. We don't have the extreme wealth or the extreme poverty. A fair go was the basis of the trade practices legislation that was put through by a conservative government with Garfield Barwick as Attorney General. We spent a lot of time humanising capitalism. Capitalism left to itself means all power, all authority, goes to those with the most resources. Capitalism one or two or three centuries ago, or before the last hundred years anyway, was a pretty brutal system. But then labour laws were developed, a lot of other concepts started to be advanced, fair trade legislation, trade practices legislation, to provide a fair go for newcomers into a marketplace—trying to balance the power of the large and the small, the power of consumers against the power of producers. All of these things were part of Australia's approach and indeed much of the world's approach to the problems of equality and how to manage a capitalist society. In today's world most of this has been put aside.

Is this sense of economic justice and a fair go part of the Liberal Party tradition going back to Alfred Deakin?

Yes it is. The Liberal Party had spent a great deal of time, effort and resources in trying to make sure that we had a fair society. Menzies' speech about the forgotten people was based in this idea. He was saying that the Liberal Party is a voice not for the unions, not for corporations—they can look after themselves. It's for people who aren't organised into any specific organisation. In his view the Liberal Party's primary task was to speak for people without a voice and to establish a fair society.

Do you think that Menzies' success as a politician is often depicted too much in terms of the negatives and that there hasn't been enough emphasis on his understanding of the Australian people and on his capacity to put forward policies of stability and security?

I think you're right in that assumption, but there are two reasons for it. During those years the Labor Party had a great capacity to be divided. Those divisions forced their way onto the public stage and stayed there very openly. There were two Labor parties for quite a while and one of them was giving preferences to the conservative side of politics. But the Liberal Party has acted differently to the Australian Labor Party so far as past leaders are concerned. I can remember in the early 1970s I issued a press statement criticising those Liberals who were criticising the Menzies legacy, who were trying to divorce themselves from the Menzies years, on the basis that Menzies hadn't really understood what Australia needed. Now, if Liberals were going to do this to Australia's most successful prime minister, I had no illusions about what they might do to Fraser at some later point. The Labor Party will take what people might regard as a not particularly successful prime minister and a couple of years later turn that person into the greatest hero the world has ever known. The Labor Party is very good at that. The Liberal Party's traditional approach to these matters is not quite so comfortable.

Menzies put a great stress on the expansion and development of Canberra, tertiary education and home ownership. What do these things tell us about Menzies?

He wanted all Australians to get a fair go. When he went to university he got one of just 40 scholarships available throughout Victoria. He didn't want people to have to struggle that hard. He knew that if provisions were that tight a lot of very able people would not get to universities and he was totally convinced that a more broadly and better educated community was absolutely critical to the future of any advanced society. Those objectives tell us a great deal about Menzies because he understood what the country wanted. He was part of that vision for the future. A vision of the future which today's leaders do not speak about.

What would you identify as the important legacies in economic policy from your own period?

It was a difficult period because my predecessor in his last two budgets had increased expenditure by 46 per cent in the second last year and by 23 per cent in the year we took office. So hauling expenditure back, trying to get some balance into the Federal Government's budget, was absolutely critical. Also, those years were years of transition and years of difficulty in the international economic environment. The first oil shock and the second which came about 1980, with very substantial increases in the price of oil and great destabilisation of world economies, clearly had an impact on Australia. So re-establishing a balance was important. Also, maintaining equity was important. We sought to strengthen trade practices legislation. We sought to make taxation more competitive and fairer. I believe we did more than any other government to try and stamp out those who sought to avoid taxation, whether they be individuals or corporations.

Operating within the Australian tradition, I believe, is a fair enough description of it. I've often had discussions in times since with people like Doug Anthony, Peter Nixon and I think Andrew Peacock and others, asking them, before you got out of the parliament did you see the great wave of so-called deregulation, of economic rationalism, that was going to sweep across Australia in the 1980s and 1990s and indeed around much of the world? And they didn't really see these moves coming. If I'd been in the parliament at the time I would have wanted to handle a lot of the issues in a different way. On labour issues, where the Coalition Government is still pressing for further deregulation, how can an individual negotiate his own rates of pay with BHP? And if an individual can't do that how can an individual sign a contract which has been freely and openly negotiated? The lack of balance between the power of a large company and the power of an individual is too great.

How would you sum up the present situation? Has Australian support for the free market economy gone too far?

In many ways it has because it has moved towards greater freedom without being able to protect consumers and without being able to protect individuals. We needed trade unions because corporations behaved in certain ways. The evidence is now starting to come out that corporations behave in the same way if there's no protection from unions or industrial law.

In countries around the world people compete for capitalist investment not on the basis that they can offer a stable structure, decent corporate laws and a well-educated labour market—though these might be part of it—but by saying their labour market is cheaper than somebody else's. There is now a massive impetus worldwide to make sure that people can offer a cheaper labour force than some perceived competitor can.

What's happening to our egalitarian tradition of a fair go?

That's disappearing. The wealthy in Australia now probably compete with wealth in the United States. We're also getting an underclass who for some reason find life difficult in this new and changed world, just as there is an underclass in the United States. We're losing a sense of fairness. We're losing a sense of fair play. We're losing the whole idea of an egalitarian society.

I don't know that any one individual is to blame. Much of the promotion of the idea goes back to Ronald Reagan. But Reagan had his rhetoric and every time he signed a new piece of protective legislation he would say, thank God for free trade. So what Reagan said and what Reagan did were two very different things.

When Hawke and Keating deregulated the economy in the 1980s they attacked your government, saying they had the courage to take the decisions that you didn't take. What's your response to that?

My response would be twofold. One, we took a number of decisions that were sensible, necessary, but we did it in a rational and ordered way and with the support of industry. Philip Lynch reduced tariffs substantially over seventeen or eighteen industry areas. But because we didn't open the markets completely neither Philip Lynch nor the government got any credit for what we did. We were able to do it without the disruption which later occurred and which we were told we had to endure through the 1980s and 1990s. The second part of my argument is that in 1984 and 1985 Hawke and Keating reduced protection massively. They were doing it as part of the Uruguay Round; and trade negotiations, whether we like it or not, involve a bargain—we will let your goods in if you let our goods in. But Hawke and Keating didn't do that. They said, here we are, we're innocent, we've dropped our protection massively—now please drop yours massively. They forgot that trade negotiations involve a bargain.

They just adopted one side of the equation and the Opposition at the time supported them because they believed in free trade regardless of the kind of world we're in.

What's your view of Hawke/Keating financial deregulation, floating of the dollar and abolition of exchange control?

You can't go back to what was there before because that would impose all sorts of new difficulties. We have to live with it and do the best we can. But we need to remember that there are now a lot of people who are pretty sceptical of totally deregulated capital markets.

There are huge sums moving around all the time and even strong economies can be severely affected by changes in currency values which are speculative, much more than changes in trade capacity. These fluctuations can be far more damaging to a small economy because the fluctuations can be much greater for that small economy. It's very difficult for an Australian or a New Zealand or a Singaporean central bank to stand out against those movements if you're being attacked by speculators, as George Soros, perhaps the number one operator in these markets, has advised us.

Do you think that Australia has taken market forces and deregulation too far?

We've in part taken market forces too far, but the way we did it—reducing our tariff protection without getting access to other people's markets on an increased scale—was in my view plain silly. During the Uruguay Round we reduced protection four times more than was needed to meet all the requirements of that round. I don't think that was really sensible. My main concern with this increasingly deregulated world is that we in Australia haven't learnt to protect an egalitarian society. We haven't learnt to provide some kind of compensation, which might be, for example, increased education, increased training oppor- tunities, and therefore we've allowed a more unequal system to be introduced to Australia. We've also lost national power, national sovereignty, over a number of things. Trade practices legislation could preserve a fair market within Australia, but we have no power over the great globalised companies and they say that if we take any action that upsets them then we're in trouble. Could Australia take on Microsoft? Not a hope. The United States has tried and whether the United States succeeds has yet to be determined. So power has shifted from national governments to great globalised corporations that owe no allegiance to Australia or to any other country.

Because we believe that the world has to be deregulated our capital markets have been deregulated. We used to have rules that foreign investment was welcome if it con- tributed something to the development of Australia's economy: brought new technology, established a new factory, broadened the capacities of Australia as a whole. But in these deregulated years most of the new foreign investment in Australia has simply been buying our first class assets that had primarily been built by Australians. It might be Arnotts, which was a family name on the supermarket shelves, or it might be National Mutual, a great life insurance company which is now French. Because we've adopted this changed attitude to foreign investment, because of the deregulated capital markets, we have ended up with an unbalanced economy, with a huge balance of payments deficit which seems to build year by year by year. Our net obligations to foreigners are somewhere between four and five hundred billion dollars. All that has to be serviced before we make a cent for Australians. If you go back to 1983 our debt, external debt, was twenty-three billion. So this has been a massive change. Financial experts, the Reserve Bank, say that it doesn't matter. I'm not convinced that it doesn't matter.

I don't believe there'll be a reversion to what went before. That would be an extraor- dinarily difficult change and it's not going to happen. What we do need, what the world does need, is a way of preserving fair competition amongst those great globalised corporations. No national government's going to be able to do that. We haven't started to think of world mechanisms that might be able to achieve it but we should start thinking. We should start thinking about the loss of national sovereignty that's been involved. We should be asking ourselves whether this is good or whether it has gone too far, whether we need to strike a balance and, if so, how do you come to an adequate relationship between global power and national sovereignty. It's not even on the agenda. But it's going to be and it will become increasingly important. The toughest question is how you re-establish some kind of egalitarian society, because through all of these movements of globalised capital markets and globalised trade markets it's the great, the large, the wealthy who become more powerful, and others are pushed aside. Isn't there some concept of global equality or global fairness?—because the third world has not been able, except to a very marginal extent, to participate in this new globalised world.

You now have significant authorities saying to emerging economies, don't open up your capital markets completely. They're saying that Prime Minister Mahathir of Malaysia was in part right. He got himself out of an economic crisis by using old-fashioned nationalist tools, and they happened to work. I've participated in international conferences which have said, specifically, don't open your economy to short-term capital. If it's short term, it can go out very quickly and cause great difficulties, so don't leave it to the market. Now, this message is not really understood in Australia but it's a message that's becoming increasingly important internationally. It's one that we ought to listen to. We certainly haven't been thoughtful enough, careful enough, skilful enough in applying those changes to Australia.

There is going to be another phase emerging, I believe, quite shortly, in which people are going to want to tame those international capital markets. They're going to want to remove some of the uncertainties, the difficulties, the possibility of systemic breakdown which is very real. After the Asian crisis, people paid some attention to this. But the changes were minimal. They said, we seem to have got through it without too much trouble, the system's okay. But there are going to be more changes. We're going to need to tame the markets, the international markets.

Looking back at much of our history—World War I, World War II, combating communism in Asia— we sought support and security from great and powerful friends, Britain and America. Was this reliance on powerful friends the right policy?

It was right at the time. Australia was so small and Australian resources so small that we probably had no option. Britain, up to the end of the First World War, probably had a sense of obligation to the British Commonwealth which was a real one, even though the Second World War demonstrated Britain's incapacity to do much to help us. Because it was a war against fascism and because America herself was attacked the Americans came to be more important to us than Britain. But in the nearly 50 years since the ANZUS Treaty was signed, reliance on the United States was an adequate policy until the end of the Cold War. In my view the ANZUS Treaty would have been an effective defence against a communist attack, but I don't believe it would be an effective defence against any other kind of danger to Australia's national integrity.

So you really think our American reliance has run its course?

Not like a hot knife through butter, but I believe it is changing and changing substantially. In our own region I would like to see arrangements in which there was sufficient confidence amongst the nations of East and South East Asia, Japan and Australia to avoid the need for participation by any outside powers. For many years ASEAN ran a a successful policy by saying both to the Soviet Union and the Americans, we're non-aligned, keep off our patch. I would like to see the countries of our own region having sufficient confidence in their own relationships so that we could say to the United States or any other potential world power, keep off our patch.

I want to ask you about the Vietnam War. Was our commitment to Vietnam a mistake? How do you see it now?

Well, how I see it now is second guessing how I saw it then. I thought it was necessary. I thought what we did was defensible. It ended up not being successful and the world has changed dramatically. I've been to Vietnam several times since and have been warmly welcomed there by ministers of the government—and I was Army Minister and Defence Minister during the time of the Vietnam War. So the world is a very different one. Lee Kuan Yew would argue that Vietnam gave South East Asia a breathing space to strengthen its own co-operation and to build up its economies. He would still argue that if the Vietnam War hadn't occurred there would have been increased threats to other countries—and remember, there was an attempted coup in Indonesia which was a communist coup. It failed. That was in 1965, 1966.

But judging it all by today and judging some of the things that I now know about the United States' conduct of the war, I guess I wish we weren't part of it. I wouldn't want to be part of any military operation with the United States and would not be unless I had an Australian, a very senior Australian, right in the innermost war councils of the United States so that I would know everything that they were doing and why they were doing it.

You're suspicious of the Americans?

The idea in Vietnam, the idea to get rid of South Vietnam's leader, Diem, was an American idea and Robert McNamara—he'd been US Defence Secretary at the time—relates in his book how this occurred. The White House approved it. The Secretary of State, Dean Rusk, and McNamara were out of Washington at the time. They didn't query the White House decision when they got back to Washington. They believed that putting the decision into place was already underway. Messages had been sent to the American Ambassador in Saigon and to the CIA in Saigon. Find a general who will get rid of Diem. They found some generals who got rid of Diem and they came back with Diem's body in the back of a jeep. The Ambassador is reported to have said, we didn't mean you to kill him. Now, if America believes that it has the right to engineer the destruction of the head of state of a country with whom it is allies at war, that alone makes me very cautious about the circumstances in which I'd want to have a partnership with the United States.

So you've got regrets?

Of course I've got regrets, yes. It in the end was a failed venture.

But the issues go beyond McNamara's book, don't they?

Of course they do, but it is an exposé of the way the United States conducted its side of the relationship. Even in his book McNamara says it was wrong to do what they did. McNamara says he was wrong to be involved in Vietnam. He's expressed that regret many, many times but he never really questioned America's right to do what America did in relation to Diem. He now says it was wrong, but the right of America to act in this way he doesn't specifically challenge. If he still believes that America has this kind of right then this view of America by Americans is, I believe, of very great concern to a lot of us, or it ought to be.

This is pretty extraordinary stuff. I mean, you were Defence Minister, you had high charge of these activities and of prosecuting the war. Aren't we really looking here at a very substantial failure?

Well, at the end of it, the whole war was a failure. Of course it was. Although, in defence of Australians who operated in Phuoc Tuy Province in the Australian area of operations, they did so with enormous distinction, great skill, great commitment and, if all other forces had operated the way Australians operated, it might have been an entirely different matter, because there wasn't a problem in that province. We had what was called civic action, which was looking after the normal well-being of people, not just providing military protection.

But Menzies and Hasluck went in with their eyes open—they were keen.

I don't know how keen. A great many people learnt a large number of lessons. This wasn't going to be like the wars in the Western Desert where armies were pitched against armies. It was a secret war in the jungle which we should have known enough about because of the Japanese capture of Singapore, the failure of the troops there to be able to make an adequate stand, and because of the fighting in New Guinea where again Australians distinguished themselves, way beyond any normal call of duty. So we should have known what fighting in Vietnam would be like. We probably misjudged the extent of the commitment on the part of the Viet Cong, of North Vietnam, the extent of support that was provided by the Soviet Union rather than by China, and the lack of capacity of the South to maintain a government seen to be acting in the interests of the people of South Vietnam. That might have been the most critical element of the whole business. So there were many miscalculations. Vietnam, I believe, is going to be an economic powerhouse and within a foreseeable time frame I think it will be as powerful and effective an economy as South Korea.

After World War II one of the landmarks was the 1957 Commerce Treaty negotiated with Japan by the Menzies Government, in particular through the efforts of John McEwen. How significant do you see this particular episode?

It tells us more about McEwen than anyone else, more about McEwen than it does about Menzies. McEwen didn't believe the British when they said they weren't going to join the Common Market. He believed they'd be forced to join the Common Market and it was just a question of timing. He believed we'd lose our markets there.

So McEwen was very concerned, in a world that he judged as very protective, that we have access for our products. There was an occasion in the government party room when somebody got up and said, we don't need this trade treaty, we have our great and powerful friends. And 'Black Jack' was enraged by this comment. He jumped to his feet and said, that is just the problem because our great and powerful friends do this to us—and he went through item after item of importance to Australia which America would not buy, or Britain would not buy if they went into the European Economic Community. And as we know, McEwen won the day.

There's another sideline that I was told a long time after the event. McEwen negotiated this treaty on his own authority. He had cabinet agreement to do it but he wasn't negotiating for the government. He was negotiating for McEwen, so that if the politics of it went wrong the government would be able to say, this was just McEwen, this wasn't the government. McEwen had the courage to negotiate it on that basis even though he knew he had that potential danger. He was confident that it was right and he was confident that his capacity would enable him to win any public argument that might come.

His treaty was negotiated just ten years after the end of the war with Japan, which is somewhat remarkable given the treatment of Australian POWs by Japan. What does this tell us about domestic opinion?

It tells us that Australians were able to look to the future, that we were able to put behind past problems no matter how serious, devastating or tragic. But it says most about Australians who had been under duress in Changi or who had been prisoners of war. There were some members of parliament who started to say—when Prime Minister Kishi was coming to Australia to sign the treaty formally—that they would not attend a government reception. I'm not sure how many but some members of parliament at that time had been prisoners of war of the Japanese and one or two of them very highly decorated. Anyway, these ex-prisoners of war put out a one line press statement saying, we are all going to the reception for Prime Minister Kishi and we expect every person who is asked to do likewise. And that said it all. They knew there was no future in being concerned with past events, past tragedies. Our future depends upon our relationship with Asia. It depends upon our relationship with Japan and all the countries of the region and these people knew that just as much as we know it today.

When you became prime minister you had a particular focus on the China relationship after the establishment of diplomatic relations with China in December 1972. What sort of priority did you in fact give it?

I gave the relationship with Asia number one priority. My first official visit anywhere as prime minister was to Japan and to China, and this was quite deliberate. It was designed to send a message to Japan that we wanted the relationship to continue, to expand. It was certainly designed to say to China, all right, Gough Whitlam opened the relationship, now the Coalition Government strongly wants to build that relationship into a good working partnership for the future. It was a China in transition, everyone in their dour grey uniform. It was a very disciplined society, remarkably different from the one that exists today. I think the relationship was cemented. It was opened by Gough Whitlam, and because I came from a different party it was strengthened by my own approach.

When we look to the future, to what extent might Australia have to make a choice between America on the one hand and Asia and China on the other hand? Can we have both?

We very likely will have to make a choice. We should try, however, to conduct our foreign policy so that we *don't* have to make a choice and so that we can define our relationships with China and Asia in ways that don't really impinge upon our relationship with the United States. The Chinese relationship is of enormous importance. It's of concern to some countries in the region because China is so large. That's one aspect of a relationship that has to be worked through but China has not been an imperial power the way Britain, France, Germany, Portugal, Spain were imperial powers or even the way the United States has been and is an imperial power.

But if we had to take a choice, what is it?

The one issue that could lead to a real danger—could lead to war between China and the United States—is Taiwan, if Taiwan says it wants to be independent and if the United States breaks nearly 35 years of policy, of saying that Taiwan is part of China and Taiwan can't break away from that. If America changes its policy then the chance of getting a negotiated solution to the problems of Taiwan will just wither away and China will believe that if it wants to recapture this errant province, it must do so by military means, and it will start to build up the force necessary to achieve that. As this sort of environment unfolds, the United States could so easily say, in spite of the policy of the last 35 years we're going to support the right of Taiwan to be independent. If we had to make a choice in relation to that—if the Americans said to Japan or to us, because of ANZUS you've got to support us in supporting Taiwan—I very much hope that Japan would say no, we cannot, and I would hope that Australia would say no, we cannot. It would be an absolute disaster for Australia to support America in those circumstances. I think this is a real problem because for some time I have believed that Taiwan has made up its own mind that it wants to go independent.

So if you're saying, should we choose between America and China over this issue?, I'd be saying we should choose China. While America would expect us to offer facilities and support in favour of a military action, which I believe we ought to deny, China of course would not expect any such support and wouldn't get it. But Australia's national interests in such circumstances would depend overwhelmingly in standing aside from the problem, saying to Taiwan, look, you're wrong to have provoked this, and saying to America, you're wrong to have given support. But it's not something whose outcome we can ultimately influence, and we and other countries of the region should stand aside from it. I would hope however that Japan, Australia and ASEAN would be able to persuade the United States never to get into that position. I believe they need to be more active in telling Taiwan that what it is doing is potentially extraordinarily dangerous.

In 1975, did Australia sell out the East Timorese?

I don't believe so. It was Portugal who sold out the East Timorese. They had domestic problems. They cut and ran from what had been their colonies without leaving any kind of administration or order in place—and this wasn't only East Timor. With the wisdom of hindsight, when it looked as though Portugal was going to cut and run we all should have been saying to Portugal, take this matter to the United Nations, get a UN team in to administer the territory till a longer term future is worked out. Now, that was the mistake that was made. I think we could have had a different outcome. Certainly the 1999 year was a very difficult one. It's had the potential to establish a long-term commitment on Australia's part, but a guerilla action can be sustained without a great deal of effort and a guerilla war undertaken which can destabilise East Timor for a quarter of a century. If that comes to govern our relationships with Indonesia for the next 25 years, with other countries of South East Asia increasingly taking Indonesia's side, then it's not a comfortable outcome for Australia.

Have you got any regrets about policies you followed?

I don't believe that I could have altered policy. During the period in which I was a caretaker prime minister I was under specific commitment not to alter any policy. I was also under a specific request from our Ambassador and from the Department of Foreign Affairs to send a message to Indonesia indicating that our policy would not change. Why it was regarded as so important to send that message I don't know but a cable was sent saying that the government's policy was not going to change.

Was there any viable course of action by which Australia at the time could have stopped the Indonesian invasion?

It could only have been through the United Nations. I don't believe the United Nations would have acted. I don't believe that if it had the will to act it could have acted quickly enough. But some United Nations action should have been taken six months earlier.

What drove your policy towards Indonesia?

I don't believe anything drove my relationship with Indonesia which did not exist in relation to other countries of ASEAN or countries in East Asia including China. We need to get on with all of them. It was an approach to the region based in a belief in Australia's future. I strongly believe that it is our relationship with all the countries of the region that is going to determine Australia's future, and that this ultimately is going to be more important than our historic relationship with Britain, which I know will endure. I also believe that these relationships are more important than our relationship with the United States. I wouldn't have said that in 1975 because the Cold War was still with us but, given the end of the Cold War, I moved quickly to the position that our relationship with Japan, China, Asia, is going to be the predeterminant of Australia's success or failure in the years ahead.

What would have been the consequences in 1975 of pursuing a different policy towards Indonesia? How accurate are people when they describe the policy as appeasement?

I don't believe it was appeasement. I don't believe that we could have won a change of policy in President Suharto's time. The Hawke and Keating Governments had a very good relationship with President Suharto. My own relationship was a reasonable one. Theirs might have been closer, but I don't think I would have pursued a separate security treaty with Indonesia.

A unified Indonesia is important to Australia. We don't want an Indonesia that breaks up—with different provinces from Borneo or Sumatra breaking away and trying to establish separate countries. If that's Indonesia's future the region immediately to our north will become unsettled. Indonesia won't allow that to happen easily. The scenario of a disintegrating Indonesia is very much against our interests because it's going to have a significant capacity to destabilise the region. It's going to be of concern to Singapore, to Malaysia, to Vietnam and to the Philippines, and none of us would want that to happen.

You took a strong stand on the question of Australia becoming a republic. Can you tell us why are you a republican?

Well, time moves on. I've got a great affection for the monarchy, for the Queen. The monarchy has been good for us because it's helped to provide a sense of continuity. I just believe it's time. Australia is changing. It's growing up. It's more mature, more confident. I also believe that in this world the conflicts that can arise between Her Majesty's role as Queen of Britain and her role as Queen of Australia can become more evident.

When you look at our past century of development what, as an Australian, makes you most proud?

It has to be the way Australians relate to each other. There are blemishes, but for the most part it is an open friendly society. The quality of life in Australia is as good or better than that which exists anywhere in the world. Cities and country towns reflect the multicultural nature of Australian society. It's just a good place to be in.

Any qualifications?

I'd name two failures. One is the failure to understand adequately in government circles the nature and extent of the problem for Aboriginal communities, the need to resolve matters of the spirit, to resolve the practical matters—the standard of living, health, education and housing. This is a significant failure.

The second is dropping the idea of building Australia, of bringing people here from many different corners of the world—dropping the ball somewhere around the 1980s in relation to immigration, to building a country that will be more effective in future years.

We're saying, it's a very wealthy continent, we're going to enjoy it all and we're not going to share it with a larger number of people. Now this change of attitude is not a people failure. It's a political failure. You never would have had the policies of the 1940s, 50s and 60s coming as a result of popular pressure. It was all done because political leaders of all parties said it had to be done. Those in power do need a vision, and they need to know where they want to take Australia.

2 Rise and Fall
of White Australia

In Australia love of country and pride of race became a united faith. At Federation the most powerful single element in Australian nationalism was racial unity. White Australia was the first policy of the new Commonwealth; it was the first plank in the platform of the new Labor Party; it was the core requirement in the workplace of the new nation. To conceive of White Australia as just a policy is to misinterpret the situation. It was a policy but even more than a policy: it was the essence of national identity.

The contemporary view of White Australia as an unfortunate blot upon an otherwise impressive start to a young country is as patronising as it is absurd. No such comfortable rationalisation is available. White Australia was a restrictive policy within an expansive vision. It was the foundation upon which an enlightened, democratic, progressive Australia was built. Its racism is unacceptable a hundred years later but this racial vision was the indispensable companion to the ideals of mateship, egalitarianism, political liberalism and social unity that are lauded as Australia's glories. The surgeon has the means to dissect the human body and separate the good from the contaminated parts, but the political analyst has no such instruments and Australian polity defied any such dissection.

The two remarkable features about the White Australia policy are its near universal support and its longevity. It prevailed until the late 1960s, the two-thirds point of the century. This is testimony to the powerful economic and social logic implicit in the policy. Historians have tended either to downgrade the importance of White Australia or to apologise for its racism. But such impulses overlook its centrality in the Australian story and the fact that its values, far from being an aberration, were merely typical of its age. What made Australia different was that it was actually drafting policies for a new nation.

The Chinese community joined Melbourne's Federation celebrations with a dragon dance and by building a Chinese arch.

It was the discovery of gold in the 1850s that transformed Australia. Gold made the colonies rich and inspired a large immigration. In the decade after the discovery in 1851, Victoria's population leapt threefold. Young Chinese men came in numbers to compete with white diggers for the precious gold. The Chinese soon provoked a backlash, including rioting. In their customs, dress and way of life they were separate from the rest of the gold diggers. One of the worst of the Victorian riots occurred in July 1857, when a mob of white miners drove the 2000 Chinese off the Buckland River. The worst riot in New South Wales was at Lambing Flat, near Young, where in 1861 a mob looted and destroyed a Chinese camp. Hostility to the Chinese was based on fear of racial contamination, on working class alarm that wages would be undermined and on a sense that such an alien culture was incompatible with Australian nationalism. As protests grew, colonial legislators responded by imposing restrictions. During the 1880s there were large demonstrations and, on 3 June 1888, 30 000 gathered in Sydney's Domain at a meeting organised by the

Anti-Chinese League. Amid banners reading 'The Chinese must go', politicians pledged tougher action. That organ of Australian nationalism, *The Bulletin*, led the campaign, vilifying the Chinese in cartoons and articles but also deploying its racism in the cause of nationalism. *The Bulletin* editorialised on 2 July 1887: 'No nigger, no chinaman, no lascar, no kanaka, no purveyor of cheap, coloured labour is an Australian.' By the 1890s all colonies had laws restricting coloured immigration. In her 1923 study Myra Willard wrote: 'The development of the White Australia policy became complete during the ten years, 1891–1901.' The Constitution gave the new Commonwealth Parliament power to pass laws governing immigration. This was important not just for national sovereignty but to implement an immigration law for the new nation. The six colonies voted to federate in the belief that Australian society would be based on racial exclusiveness. At the 1891 convention the future Chief Justice of the High Court, Sir Samuel Griffith, said of the immigration power: 'It will enable them to keep out Chinese, Hindoos, or other aliens—even English, if necessary.'

The greatest champions of White Australia came from the new Labor Party. When the caucus met in May 1901 it endorsed White Australia as its first principle. Labor had no doubt about its priorities—racial unity was far ahead of socialism. Its mood was reflected by the organ of Queensland Labor, *The Worker*:

> White Australia was the greatest and the most pregnant question that has ever been placed before the Australian people . . . By the use of the ballot box, Australia would be saved from the coloured curse, relieved from strikes, be famous for having no paupers or poor-houses but be a government of, by and for the people.

The future Labor leader, Billy Hughes, said: 'Our chief plank is, of course, a White Australia. There's no compromise about that. The industrious coloured brother has to go—and remain away!'

Prime Minister Edmund Barton introduced the Immigration Restriction Bill on 7 August 1901. There was never a more important bill put before the Commonwealth Parliament nor a more defining issue.

Barton said: 'As to the undesirableness of certain classes of immigrants, I suppose we are all practically agreed . . . we are guarding the last part of the world in which the higher races can live and increase freely for the higher civilisation.' Barton subsequently explained the bedrock Australian position: 'I do not think that the doctrine of the equality of man was really ever intended to include racial equality.' For those who were interested, the intellectual justification for Australia's stance was Social Darwinism ranging from 'survival of the fittest' racial theory to a view of civilisations defined by a racial hierarchy.

In his speech Barton quoted from the influential book *National Life and Character* by Professor C H Pearson, formerly of the University of London and later Minister for Public Instruction in Victoria: 'We know that if national existence is sacrificed to the working of a few mines and sugar plantations, it is not the Englishman in Australia alone, but the whole civilised world that will be the losers.' Pearson warned that unless Australia excluded coloured races then it would go the way of South Africa and 'transform the northern half of our continent into a Natal, with 13 out of 14 [people] belonging to an inferior race'. Humphrey McQueen has said that Pearson's book sales were small but significant—both William Gladstone and Theodore Roosevelt were 'in full agreement with Pearson'.

But it was a future prime minister, Alfred Deakin, who offered the deepest insight into the motives behind the bill: 'The unity of Australia is nothing, if that does not imply a united race. A united race means not only that its members can intermix, intermarry and associate without degradation on either side, but implies one inspired by the same ideas, and an aspiration towards the same ideals, of a people possessing the same general cast of character, tone of thought, the same constitutional training and traditions ... Unity of race is an absolute essential to the unity of Australia. It is more, actually more in the last resort, than any other unity ... It was this real unity that made the Commonwealth possible.'

The parliament was agreed about the principle. The entire debate was about the method of exclusion. It was whether the method would be indirect—by using the Natal-type 50-word dictation test proposed in Barton's bill—or whether an explicit racial ban would be imposed. Britain was deeply involved in this dispute. Britain told Australia to use an indirect method of exclusion such as the Natal test and warned that Royal Assent might otherwise be withheld from the bill. There were Empire interests at stake. Britain ran an empire of coloured people from Africa to Asia and it had a strategic alliance with the racially proud Japanese.

On 20 August 1901 the Governor-General, Lord Hopetoun, asked London for a preliminary view on whether Royal Assent should be withheld from the bill. Secretary of State Joseph Chamberlain replied: 'It should, I think, be reserved if it passes in its present form.' Chamberlain's initial concern was that a dictation test in English would offend Britain's friends in Europe. The bill was amended with the substitution of European for English language.

It was the Labor leader, Chris Watson, who led the attack on the bill

This illustration entitled 'The Immigration Restriction Bill' shows a startled customs officer being confronted by Chinese, French, African, German and Indian racial stereotypes.

for being devious and hypocritical. The Labor Party and some Free Traders demanded a direct racial ban. They said that this was the only guarantee that the policy would work. Watson moved an amendment to prohibit immigration of natives of Asia and Africa. He was keen to defy the British threat on Royal Assent: 'The sooner we understand what our powers are, and how far this autonomous government with which we are supposed to be endowed is a reality, or how far it is a mockery, the better it will be for all.'

Watson revealed that, for Labor, social reasons were more important than economic factors: 'With the Oriental as a rule the more he is educated, the worst man he is likely to be from our point of view ... The objection I have to the mixing of the coloured people with the white people of Australia—although I admit it is to a large extent tinged with considerations of an industrial nature—lies in the main in the possibility and probability of racial contamination.'

Japan made strenuous representations against the bill, insisting that its racial superiority be recognised. Japan's ambassador in London, Baron Hayashi, asked Britain to intervene, saying that Barton and Deakin had made 'monstrous declarations'. Its Australian consul, H Eitaki, wrote to the Australian Government: 'The Japanese belongs to an Empire whose standard of civilisation is so much higher than that of Kanakas, Negroes, Pacific Islanders, Indians or other eastern peoples, that to refer to them in the same terms cannot but be regarded as a reproach.' He asked for the Japanese to be excluded from the operation of the law.

Deakin was sensitive to Japan's position but unswayed by this appeal. He told the House: 'The Japanese require to be excluded because of their high abilities ... they most nearly approach us and would therefore be our most formidable competitors.'

Barton knew that unless the Australian Parliament rejected a direct racial ban there would be a crisis with Britain over Royal Assent. But some Australians were ready to defy Britain. Labor's Billy Hughes declared: 'We want a White Australia—and are we to be denied it because we shall offend the Japanese or embarrass His Majesty's ministers? I think not ... I do not desire, and I do not think there are five per cent of the people of this country who desire, separation from Great Britain. But while I do not wish it, I do not fear it.' Many others felt the same. It is the proof of White Australia as the heart of nationalism. On no other issue did passions become so aroused.

For Barton it was an issue of confidence. He had given his word to London that the Natal test would be used. He signalled to the House that he could not remain prime minister if the Watson amendment was carried. He said it meant 'certain delay and possible refusal' of the bill.

Barton and Deakin carried the day: the Labor proposal for a direct racial ban was defeated 36–31. It was defeated again in the Senate. After a further delay the Governor-General, under pressure from Barton, signed the bill in the train at Adelaide en route to Perth on 23 December 1901. White Australia was confirmed; it would be enforced by a manipulated dictation test. The Barton Government was quick to put in place the administrative arrangements necessary for Australia's 'dictation test'. These arrangements were critical, since the law itself did not discriminate on a racial basis. The law, in effect, was a subterfuge. It merely provided for a dictation test whose implementation would have to achieve the racial objective.

The Secretary of the Department of External Affairs, Atlee Hunt, was in charge. On 14 January 1902 Hunt sent his first set of confidential instructions to the Customs Collectors, who were responsible for carrying out the test. 'In administering the Immigration Restriction Act, which is now in force, it will be necessary to use great care in order that no undesirable immigrants shall be permitted to enter the Commonwealth ... any person attempting to immigrate may be asked to write out from dictation and sign a passage of 50 words in length in any European language. It must be understood that the law does not insist that every intending immigrant should be asked ... tact and judgment will have to be exercised.'

This certificate exempts Roku Tanaka, a Japanese woman, from having to take a dictation test.

On what basis should judgment be exercised? Barton and Hunt ensured that a second instruction was issued verbally. According to Hunt's diary, 'Chief [Barton] decided not to put objectionable passages in written instructions but to communicate them verbally'. These verbal instructions were the heart of the White Australia policy: 'All aboriginal inhabitants of Africa, Asia and Polynesia should be subjected to the test . . . In the case of White Races, the test will be applied only under special circumstances . . . if in your opinion, the immigrant for purposes which you be prepared to state, be an undesirable immigrant, it may be better to substitute for the English test a passage from some other language.' Hunt was remorseless in his implementation of the policy. It was a diligence which reflected the will of his political masters.

There was a second law designed to entrench White Australia—the *Pacific Islands Labourers Act*. It was to end the use of coloured labour in the Queensland sugar industry and deport as many as possible of the Pacific Islanders who had been brought to Australia over the past 40 years. White Australia did not just deny entry to coloured races but went to the logical extreme of removing a whole people from Queensland. The total number of Islanders brought to Australia was around 50 000, through a combination of recruitment and kidnapping, and by 1901

A group of South Sea Islander women with their white overseer, Cairns, 1890.

nearly 9000 Islanders worked the canefields. They were known as Kanakas but today are called South Seas Islanders. The Act revealed that the new nation put racial purity before economic gain. Alfred Deakin said: 'No slave is to be allowed to tread Australian soil at all. The mere suspicion of the taint of slavery is leading to the prohibition of the Pacific Islander labourer.'

The sugar industry and many Queensland politicians saw the Kanakas as essential to the prosperity of the industry. But the results in Queensland of the first federal election revealed, in those areas where Kanakas were most employed, strong support for their deportation. Australians would not tolerate cheap coloured labour. Australian society was to be white and based on wage justice. The sugar interests were subjugated to the national vision. After the bill's passage through Federal Parliament the Queensland premier, Robert Philp, a principal of Burns Philp & Company which had direct interests in Pacific Islander labour, asked the Governor-General to deny Royal Assent—a request that Hopetoun rejected when he approved the bill on 19 December 1901.

But many Islanders fought the deportation orders and presented a series of petitions to the Queensland and Australian Governments and to the King. Many had been in Australia for some time and had established families. 'Many of us are Christians and yet some of our islands are entirely heathen and cannibal,' one petition read. But the acting PM, Deakin, was resolute: 'Islanders have been returning to their homes ever since the establishment of the traffic ... It has been universally admitted that the introduction of the Kanaka reflects no credit on Australia.' After a Royal Commission in 1906 a number of Islanders were allowed to remain; they survived on the tropical east coast, out of sight, out of mind. A total of 7068 Islanders were repatriated between 1904 and 1908. Today there are around 15 000 descendants living in Australia. Governments and the trade unions promptly enforced a policy of exclusive white labour in the sugar industry. The law achieved its aim.

The creation of the White Australia policy was the first obligation of the new Commonwealth leaders to the people of Australia. Apart from the treatment of the indigenous people no issue in our history so troubles the conscience of contemporary Australia. The typical response now is that of repression of memory since the policy is indefensible in terms of 2001 values. Yet denial of the essence of Australian nationalism is a refusal to confront our past. The nation that takes flight to escapism is hardly psychologically prepared to handle its future in Asia. So, how should the White Australia policy be seen today?

It should be seen as a policy that reflected the values of its time. The late nineteenth century was a hightide of the age of colonisation. Racial equality did not exist as a universally accepted value between nations. Much of Africa, Asia and the Middle East was under the control of European powers and did not enjoy national independence. This reality of national and international power constituted, by definition, a denial of racial equality. A separate reality is that, within Asia and Asian cultures, the idea of racial equality was not accepted. Such was the situation from India to Japan. The campaign by Japan against Australia's policy rested not in racial equality but in inequality, as its protests made explicit. Japan in fact wanted recognition of its claim to racial superiority. In this sense the values that Australians brought to their policy typified rather than contrasted with the norms of the age.

The enduring Australian values of unity and egalitarianism were promoted within the context of White Australia. Australians wanted to avoid the problems that had arisen in both the United States and South Africa. Unlike many other nations they still had the option of choosing a homogeneous society and they chose it. Deakin was explicit about drawing the lessons from the United States: 'However much we retard the remote and tropical portion of our territory, those sacrifices for the future of Australia are indeed nothing, when compared with the compensating freedom from the trials, sufferings and losses which nearly wrecked the great Republic of the West.' In his revised edition of *A New Britannia*, Humphrey McQueen said that for White Australia to be comprehended it must be seen as 'a code of civic morality'. It was a doctrine 'full of affirmative values offering much more than a negative rejection of other peoples'. He quoted the socialist nationalist writer, Vance Palmer, that White Australia was 'our chief assertion of character' and that its sacrifice would be 'the betrayal of a fine purpose'.

The economic factor was central to the policy. The Labor Party and the emerging trade unions vowed that Australia would be a high-wage nation and that meant banning cheap coloured labour. It was a self-interested stance and also a statement of the economic ideology that the new nation should embrace. Ultimately, however, the policy was driven by the vision of an Australian society: a united nation bound by a British culture. It was expressed often in racist terms and sometimes in more sophisticated language, but the motive was always the same.

Judged by these tests of unity and egalitarianism, the White Australia policy must be accounted a success. Australia was a remarkably united nation during the 60 years the policy applied and its delivery on egalitarianism was impressive. There has been a reluctance in contemporary times to evaluate the policy in terms of its essential purpose. It guaranteed a cultural unity during those decades when Australia was under severe internal strain because of war, depression, religion and class. But there were two great defects: White Australia drove a wedge between Australia and Asia, and it created a view of human rights based on colour which would demand complete revision as the century evolved.

In World War I the entire strategy of Prime Minister Billy Hughes was influenced by his White Australia convictions and his suspicion of Japan. The irony, however, is that the peace settlement drew international attention to the White Australia policy. After the war Hughes went to the Paris Peace Conference anticipating a challenge to the policy from Japan. Japan, aware of its growing power, was determined to use the new League of Nations, proposed by US President Woodrow Wilson, to push for greater international recognition. The Japanese representatives, Baron

Makino Nobuaki and Viscount Chinda Sutemi, wanted a racial equality clause inserted in the new League of Nations covenant. They sought a guarantee that nations 'will not discriminate, either in law or in fact, against any person or persons on account of his or their race and nationality'. Hughes fought this proposal with unyielding tenacity, a loud voice, and a deaf ear directed at his opponents. He saw it as an assault upon White Australia. Japan's leading scholar on the Paris Conference, Naoko Shimazu, says: 'This was a tremendously important issue in Japan at the time. There were public meetings on the racial equality proposal and the Japanese saw this as the most important demand that the Japanese Government could make.'

Hughes told the British prime minister, Lloyd George, the Americans and the Japanese that Australia would not budge. No amount of redrafting of Japan's formula satisfied him. Colonel Bonsal, of the US delegation, told his diary: 'Morning, noon and night [he] bellows at poor Lloyd George, that if race equality is recognised in the preamble or any of the convenant, he and his people will leave the conference.' The Japanese reported home: 'Hughes alone persisted along his stubborn, solitary path; he was not unsympathetic to the Japanese stand; however as representing Australian public opinion he had no alternative but to express his opposition—root and branch.' Hughes threatened the Americans that he would make trouble in their western states if they crossed him. Woodrow Wilson's main adviser, Colonel Edward House, wrote: 'Hughes insists that nothing shall go in, no matter how mild and inoffensive . . . I may as well admit it. What a man! What a man!'

Australia's position at the Paris Peace Conference was independent of that of the British, a prize won by the blood sacrifice of the war. Pressure on Hughes was intense but South Africa's Prime Minister Smuts was correct in warning that Hughes was both narrow-minded and pig-headed and likely to become only more stubborn. But Japan insisted that the issue be taken to a decision.

On 11 April 1919, in a meeting chaired by President Wilson, a decision was forced. A majority of the delegates were in favour of the Japanese amendment and 11 out of 17 delegates voted for it. But Wilson feared that the divisive racial consequences of a split affirmative vote would echo around the world. He ruled the amendment lost because the vote was not unanimous. Hughes had won. The White Australia policy was intact. Hughes proclaimed a victory, insisting that his voice had resounded across the world. But Australia had been exposed and it was left more vulnerable in Japan. Naoko Shimazu says: 'In the long run I think it did have a negative effect on Japan's relations with the Anglo-Saxon powers. From the Japanese perspective, they could say "what sort of fair and just order is it if it doesn't even accept racial equalities of peoples"'.

For the next two decades Australia's face would reflect its British–Irish heritage. In the 1920s the Bruce Government sponsored 200 000 British immigrants to Australia. In January 1934 in Kalgoorlie there was an outbreak of mob violence against Italian, Greek and Slav workers. The population was 97 per cent British–Irish stock and foreigners were treated with suspicion. The turning point for Australia's immigration policy, and ultimately for its sense of national identity, was World War II. The first war was a more cathartic event; but the second war provoked more far-reaching changes in Australia. Only in retrospect is it apparent how decisive were the changes seeded by this second war. White Australia was our first faith; but World War II left a legacy that became a second faith— that Australia had to become a large-scale immigrant nation in order to survive. This sentiment won enduring expression in the phrase 'populate or perish'.

Labor's leaders John Curtin and Ben Chifley decided that Australia's long-term survival was at risk. It was the direct result of the Japanese advance in World War II which, for the first time in Australia's European history, threatened its society. Curtin and Chifley were not prepared to run such a risk again. They concluded that Australia had to change its ways. The Labor Government devised ambitious plans for postwar recon-struction which affected the economy, society and population. Following Curtin's vision, Chifley was the principal architect of postwar reconstruc-tion. His biographer, Fin Crisp, reports that as early as 1944 Chifley wanted to bring 50 000 European orphans to Australia.

During the war there had been a strong debate within government about immigration and a view had emerged among senior public servants in support of a new approach. Historian Andrew Markus has documented the depth of this feeling and reports Curtin saying in April 1944 that he wanted to 'double and treble' the population as soon as possible. The public service advisers recognised the need to counter community hostility towards 'alien immigrants' if a new program was to succeed. Markus judges that Arthur Calwell was 'perhaps the most insistent of the immi-gration advocates'. He was also a realist. In a May 1945 pamphlet, 'How Many Australians Tomorrow?', Calwell wrote: 'We have to make up our minds now. If we want thousands of migrants we will have to liberalise our whole outlook towards non-British people and be prepared to help them become assimilated to our way of life. We cannot pick and choose as we have done in the past.'

On becoming prime minister in July 1945 Chifley appointed Calwell as Immigration Minister running a new portfolio. It was a deliberate choice. Chifley knew that Calwell was a convert to mass immigration and this was the brief he gave Calwell. It was a daunting challenge. The trade union movement and much of the Labor Party were hostile to immigration, fearing that migrants would steal jobs. The Depression was too recent a memory. Yet Labor became converted to the cause of mass immigration, one of the key conversions in its history.

On 2 August 1945, just 21 days after his appointment, Calwell made his historic announcement. The war was not yet over. It provided the climate in which Calwell was able to make as bold a declaration as any in Australia's history to that stage. Chifley's authority underwrote this vision.

Calwell told the House: 'If Australians have learnt one lesson from the Pacific War now moving to a successful conclusion, it is surely that we cannot continue to hold our island continent for ourselves and our descendants unless we greatly increase our numbers. We are but 7 million people and we hold 3 million square miles of this earth's surface.

'A third world war is not impossible. We may have only the next 25 years in which to make the best possible use of our second chance to survive. Our first requirement is additional population. We need it for reasons of defence and for the fullest expansion of our economy.'

Calwell's aim was to increase the population by 2 per cent per year which was assumed to be the maximum absorption capacity. This totalled 140 000 people and, as the natural increase was about 70 000, it meant a migration ceiling of about 70 000 each year. The magnitude of this ambition is shown by the annual intake from 1931–40, which averaged just 3200.

Calwell defined three guiding principles for his program. First, immigration would be related to social and economic needs and immigrants would be brought to Australia only where there was 'a continuous employment for them'. Calwell had to make this pledge. The program would be based upon co-operation with unions and employers. Second, Britain was the preferred target country. A program of assisted passages would be introduced for British immigrants. Calwell's dream would have been a 100 per cent British intake. But his realism told him this was never a possibility. His optimistic calculation was that nine out of ten might be British. So Calwell's third point was to bring non-British migrants from Europe and other Commonwealth nations, though criteria on such a sensitive issue were yet to be devised.

Calwell finished with an appeal to Australians to help the newcomers:

'We have been too prone in the past to ostracise those of alien birth and then blame them for segregating themselves and forming foreign communities.'

In his assessment Andrew Marcus finds that the program transcended the creation of any single man. But, 'if anyone is to be singled out, however, it should be Chifley ... it was Chifley who, knowing Calwell's views, placed him in the immigration portfolio'. The philosophy driving the new policy was a stronger Australia. That included not just defence, but national development, a better industrial base and more people. Integral to the new program was the reality of postwar production shortages and the need to bolster the supply side of the economy to meet demand. The robust, full employment economy was typified by high job vacancies across all States. This decision of the Chifley Government and its successful implementation of immigration is a milestone. Neither Chifley nor Calwell could envisage that the program they were inaugurating would help to take Australia's population from seven million to nineteen million by the year 2000. On the other hand, their declared intention was to change Australia fundamentally, to introduce a long-range program and to expand the population over several decades. The outcome, measured against their intentions, is remarkable. This decision was, possibly, the most important ever made by an Australian government since it would significantly change the nation's size and character. It was not inspired by altruism but by a deep sense of national self-interest.

Perhaps the best summary of how Chifley saw the policy is provided by Fin Crisp, who quotes some informal remarks made by Chifley in 1949 to federal and State ministers: 'There will be difficulties for many years ahead ... We know the big industrialists have confidence in the future of this country and back that confidence with their money. We, who have nothing to lose except some political popularity, can back this country as well ... Unless we are prepared to do something with it, we will not be able to justify before the world our retention of such a great country.'

It is fashionable now to see such perceptions as quaint. Yet the rise of international organisations and talk of global governance invites speculation on whether, as the next century advances, Chifley's notion might not be as far-fetched as it seems.

In Calwell's vision, however, the White Australia policy was to remain sacrosanct. The revolution in Australia's population policy would not touch the faith of White Australia. There was no suggestion that, in casting the net for more people, Australia would admit coloured immigrants in numbers. In his oral history for the National Library, Calwell said: 'I'm opposed to it [coloured migration], not because I'm opposed to the coloured people as human beings, but wherever Tamil Indians, for instance, have gone, whether it was to Natal before the turn of the century or to Singapore or to Ceylon . . . they have never become assimilated with the population.' In his public comments Calwell argued: 'Australian immigration policy is based not on racial grounds but on a desire to preserve the homogeneity of our race.' Yet this double-speak fooled nobody.

In February 1947 the Secretary of the Immigration Department, T H Hayes, commented on Indian criticism of the policy: 'The antipathy of Indians is due more to the use of the term "White Australia" than anything else. For quite a number of years the department has carefully refrained from using this term . . . [The dictation test] was in fact very seldom used, as control for entry was exercised mainly by passport requirements and in the case of non-British subjects by the landing permit system.'

Calwell saw a stronger nation as the essential precondition to upholding White Australia. The key was to provide Australia with more leverage and enable it to relate to the world on its own terms. Calwell's resolute defence of White Australia enhanced his credentials as Immigration Minister. He could implement a bold immigration program and retain complete public confidence that no compromise would be tolerated on coloured migrants. This was the politics; it was the intent; it was the theory. But it was not the final result.

Postwar immigration had consequences which its architects could not control. Calwell was always prepared to give entry in numbers to non-British migrants. But as time advanced, the essential contradiction in the policy would emerge. Australia could not thrive as an immigrant nation yet deny its intake to the independent peoples of Asia. The irony is that immigration sowed the seeds for a multiculutral society and the abolition of White Australia.

The transforming implications of the program became apparent from the start. In 1947 Calwell faced a crisis: there were insufficient ships from the United Kingdom to sustain his program of British immigration. He was forced into a drastic improvisation. On 19 June he left Sydney for a twelve week tour of the refugee camps of Europe—a trip which would give Australia's immigration program a humanitarian profile and meant that from the start it had a strong non-British component.

At the end of the war about eight million displaced persons were housed in Europe and a large number had still not been placed by 1947. Andrew Marcus has documented Calwell's European campaign. On reaching London the minister cabled Chifley that there was keen competition for the 'best migrant types' and won the PM's backing to sign an agreement with the International Refugee Organisation (IRO) to accept people from the camps. At the ceremony in Geneva Calwell declared that 'our policy has no race prejudice, all we ask of displaced persons is that they be of good faith, good character and willing to work'.

But IRO officials were told privately that Australia would be highly selective. Calwell wanted people from the Baltic states—Latvians, Lithuanians and Estonians. These were 'people who are very easily assimilated'. He wanted workers, not intellectuals. In his report Calwell said: 'We preferred the horny hand of the sons of toil.' The preference was unmarried men and women under 40 years of age. Calwell was ruthless: he was taking the cream and what suited Australia best. It was discrimination according to race, nationality, marital status, age and skills. This is how the immigration program was born. Calwell kept this process as secret as possible. But Australia's immigration officers were given precise instructions. The nation's immigration policy began as a quality control exercise. Calwell and Chifley were not just humanitarians. They were engaged in a determined nation-building exercise. The Polish newspaper in the refugee camps complained that Australia was creating a 'caste system which automatically causes the undermining of human dignity'. But it was Australia's interests that had priority. The surgeon on board a US transport ship that arrived in 1948 reported: 'The majority spoke English and German. The women in general were very good looking. Some had beautiful, dark long hair; others were platinum blonde with blue eyes, light complexion and very tall. The men were fine looking too.'

The next step, however, was all but inevitable. Australian officials had to widen their selection criteria as available numbers shrank. Ukrainians and Slovenes became acceptable by the end of 1947; Czechs, Poles and Yugoslavs were soon added. By 1949 all European races were acceptable. At this stage the intake was dominated by two categories—displaced people and free and assisted British immigrants. In the first three years of Calwell's scheme 220 000 assisted settlers arrived; six out of every ten were displaced persons. Just over a third were British and many came after the payment of a £10 fee. During the 1950s the British were the preferred settlers. The key point, though, is that the British monopoly had been broken in the late 1940s. It would never be restored. Australia had not just launched a program of mass immigration; in the process it had shattered forever the notion of drawing exclusively from Britain.

The refugee arrivals were subject to severe and unequal working conditions, part of the price of winning trade union acquiescence. They had to work for two years at government direction in jobs, selected by government, which did not displace Australian workers. The men worked

A group of migrants arrive on the Empire Brent *in 1948 to start working for Australia's post-war reconstruction.*

on railways, farms and hydroelectric schemes, while the women were typically employed as typists and waitresses. Although the trade union movement acquiesced in the matter of immigration, it was not convinced. Calwell faced a permanent struggle over the employment conditions for displaced persons. Having a Labor Government better able to deal with the unions was critical to the establishment of the program. But the Australian suspicion of foreigners ran deep. Geoffrey Bolton says the anti-foreign backlash was led by a diverse group—the RSL, the Australian Communist Party, anti-Calwell sections of the Sydney media.

But by 1948–49 immigration was an economic imperative. There were severe production shortages in the coal, iron, steel and housing industries. The government saw immigration as the only solution. Chifley said: 'So large and widespread are the benefits to be gained from success in this direction that no practicable effort can be spared.' The long postwar boom would march hand-in-hand with the immigration program.

At the same time that Calwell was opening Australia's doors to Europeans he was deporting Asian seamen who had overstayed in Australia. White Australia was not dormant; it was a driving force behind policy. In 1949 the minister introduced a punitive new law enabling him to deport Asians allowed to stay in Australia during the war emergency and who were now refusing to leave. On 9 February 1949 Calwell told the House:

'A deported Malay seaman says goodbye to his Australian wife', February 1948.

'We can have a White Australia, we can have a black Australia, but a mongrel Australia is impossible and I shall not take the first steps to establish the precedents which will allow the floodgates to be opened.' When R G Menzies came to power at the 1949 election he allowed some of the seamen to remain. But this was a mere tactical device.

The hallmark of Menzies' policy was continuity with Labor. Menzies was the final champion of White Australia and the great upholder of the Chifley–Calwell 'populate or perish' immigration program. Menzies, despite his 'British to the bootstraps' image, presided over one of the greatest movements of people of the twentieth century and thus over the cultural diversification of Australia. It is the paradox of the Menzian age. The immigration program was bipartisan and driven by an economic, security and national development ethos.

During Menzies' prime ministership from 1949 to 1966 fewer than half the arrivals were British. Italians formed the next largest group, followed by Greeks, Dutch, Yugoslavs and Germans. These people came under one condition—they had to assimilate with Australia. Immigration Minister Athol Townley said: 'The many non-British migrants who are here recognise and accept this British tradition which is the foundation and the basis of the Australian way of life.' It didn't end with Menzies. Geoffrey Bolton quotes a later Immigration Minister, Billy Snedden, declaring in the late 1960s: 'I am quite determined we should have a monoculture with everyone living in the same way, understanding each other and sharing the same aspirations. We don't want pluralism.' John O'Grady's novel *They're a Weird Mob* was a popular affirmation of assimilation, with the main character, Nino Culotta, having a series of hilarious adventures before becoming a model 'New Australian'.

Nonetheless, by the 1960s new pressures had emerged for a reform of immigration, just as they had emerged for reforms in other areas. There were several overlapping events: a growing claim from the universities and the churches that the White Australia policy was intolerable on moral grounds and could no longer be justified by a civilised society; a series of high profile cases which revealed that the policy had outlived its time; the entry into Australia of thousands of Asian students under the Colombo Plan; and the conviction among professionals running Australian foreign policy that immigration policy was incompatible with Australia's national interests in Asia.

In the early 1960s the Immigration Reform Group, a small lobby based around Melbourne University, published the influential pamphlet 'Control or Colour Bar?' urging a balanced intake of Asians. The Association for Immigration Reform was created, an unusual fusion of academic and religious sentiment. In his book *The Lucky Country*, Donald Horne attacked the racist base of the White Australia policy. A Methodist leader, the Reverend Alan Walker, branded the policy 'a denial of Christian principles', and added: 'The consistent witness of the church over a period of 50 years has gradually created a climate of public opinion which is right for change.' The author Morris West declared: 'It is my view that we are in total breach of the moral principle if we exclude people on the grounds of their race or colour.'

In 1961 a career diplomat, Peter Heydon, became Secretary of the Department of Immigration—a decisive event. Heydon, who had recently served in India, was personally aware of the damage caused by the policy in Asia and wanted to promote reform. Heydon held substantial sway with his new minister, the famous Australian cyclist, Dutch-born Hubert Ferdinand Opperman. Heydon and Opperman formed an effective partnership that would sink White Australia after 65 years.

In late 1964 Opperman put forward a cabinet submission for change: that 'consideration should be given to admitting as immigrants non-Europeans selected individually (and dependent children) in limited numbers'. The Menzies Cabinet rebuffed Opperman. Its decision, dated 15 September, said: 'The cabinet felt that the proposals could not do other, if approved, than give the impression of significant relaxation and reduction of Australia's immigration policy. The cabinet made it clear that it was not prepared to approve or permit such a result.' The principal opponents were Menzies, deputy PM John McEwen and future PM Harold Holt. Menzies told Opperman he believed the current policy was 'the right sort of discrimination'. Heydon reassured Opperman that the loss was not the minister's own fault: 'In my view if the submission had been written by the Archangel Gabriel it would hardly have made any difference.' Heydon went to his Canberra home that night upset about the decision but confident that it would be reversed on Menzies' retirement. Opperman waited for a second opportunity.

The fall of White Australia was a generational issue. Its last two defenders were Menzies and Calwell. Once their demise was signalled, the wall of resistance was broken. In his diary entry for 28 September 1965—just thirteen days after the cabinet decision—Peter Howson, a Coalition minister, records a moment with Menzies, over a nightcap: 'He hopes we will never alter the White Australia policy.'

At its 1965 Federal Conference the Labor Party voted 36 to nil to delete White Australia from its platform. The campaign was spearheaded by Gough Whitlam, Don Dunstan and Jim Cairns. The motion was moved by Dunstan. It was seconded by Arthur Calwell, who claimed that the words had been changed but the policy was the same. It was an historic moment. Labor, the greatest champion of White Australia, had turned. The old policy was doomed. In his 18 January 1966 speech to a citizenship convention, deputy leader Whitlam was able to shift towards a new ALP philosophy: a non-discriminatory, non-racial one, a prelude to the ALP's formal adoption in 1971 of a non-discriminatory policy.

And so a new era was dawning, heralded also by the retirement in January 1966 of R G Menzies.

On 14 February 1966 Sir Peter Heydon was having lunch at the Commonwealth Club. It was decimal currency day. But it had a deeper significance. Hubert Opperman rang Heydon with the news that the new prime minister, Harold Holt, only a month in the post, wanted a fresh cabinet submission. Opperman and Heydon were going to win. Holt, now his own man with Menzies gone, would be with them.

In the eighteen months since the Menzies Cabinet rejected reform the pressure had only intensified. Opinion in Asia was inflamed when a highly qualified banker who spoke perfect English, Aurelio Locsin from the Philippines, was rejected entry. This decision held Australia up to ridicule and charges of racism. Asked why he had been rejected, Locsin replied: 'Because I don't look enough like a white man.' On 7 February 1966 the two national newspapers editorialised in favour of change. *The Australian Financial Review* said: 'It is the economic implications of White Australia which are beginning to highlight the ultimate sterility of this policy.' *The Australian*, a critic of the Vietnam War, was more aggressive: 'We defend Asians in Vietnam but will not let them live here.'

Opperman's submission was almost the same. He proposed that non-Europeans be able to enter with the same status as Europeans but would be selected individually according to their suitability and their ability to integrate readily into Australia. The limit for their naturalisation would be cut from fifteen to five years. The minister would retain discretion over entry. The submission insisted that Australia's 'social homegeneity' was not in question. In short, the policy was being reformed but there would be no social impact. It was founded on a contradiction.

A deputy secretary in the Prime Minister's Department, Peter Lawler, sent a note to Holt exposing the real issue: 'Public and international criticism of the present policy is advanced as the principal reason for change. The practical consequences of the proposals must be the admission of more non-Europeans, particularly Chinese, for permanent residence . . . Admission of greater numbers would obviously erode the long-standing policy . . . If Australia's widely approved policy of social homegeneity is to be preserved the important thing is that numbers of non-European admissions be kept to an absolute minimum.'

Cabinet decided on 2 March 1966 to endorse Opperman's submission 'in broad terms'. But such agreement also meant 'that the basic principles of Australia's immigration policy are not in question'. The cabinet modified some of Opperman's recommendations. It also insisted that his more liberalised entry policy must not 'give rise to unacceptable increases in numbers'. Opperman entered the cabinet room at 4.30 pm and left at 6.10 pm. He told Heydon that 'having the PM in favour was the essential difference since 1964'.

Holt told journalists at a background briefing that 'we have all felt the policy has suffered by virtue of some of the cases which have hit the front pages of the press in Asia. I would hope that we can avoid situations of that sort in future'. There are two conclusions from this insight—that Holt was preoccupied by Australia's image in Australia and that he gave this priority because, unlike Menzies, his foreign policy aspiration was to deepen Australia's regional ties.

In an attachment to his submission Opperman had given examples of the types of non-Europeans who would be given entry in greater numbers. They included people with technical skills, proficiency in arts and science, professionals to fill undermanned areas, specialists and businessmen. On 4 March, two days after the cabinet decision, an ever alert Assistant Secretary in the PM's Department, Geoff Yeend, wrote a memo saying that

Opperman's examples were 'a far more expansive view' of the changes than were sketched in his cabinet submission. This was the cautious Yeend in action; it exposed Opperman's real tactic; and it was prophetic.

On 2 April the Heydons met Menzies at an embassy dinner. Heydon's diary recalls that the former PM said to Heydon's wife that 'he contemplated a chapter in his memoirs critical of me' but that it wouldn't be published. Heydon reflected: 'He [Menzies] is finding this change hard to take, especially as he realises it is symbolic of great changes everywhere.'

There was no public suggestion by Holt or Opperman that the principles of immigration restriction were being removed. There was, in fact, both in the cabinet documents and in public remarks an effort to minimise the extent of the change and to offer an assurance that social homogeneity would be unaffected. It was a reform that pretended to be no reform. The reason is manifest: any declaration that White Australia was being abolished would have provoked a public outcry. The issue was never put to the people. The policy was dismantled as a result of a simultaneous re-think within both parties and astute political management. Its dismantling was a 'smoke and mirrors' exercise. The trick is to understand who knew the real intention and who didn't.

In his 9 March 1966 ministerial statement Opperman presented the reforms as 'important but as not departing from the fundamental principles of our immigration policy'. He said the number of non-Europeans entering 'will be somewhat greater than previously but will be controlled by careful assessment of the individual's qualifications'. The ALP spokesman, Fred Daly, began by praising Calwell and then supported the Opperman statement, a cardinal requirement for the government. Daly said: 'We must be assured that there will be no large scale admission of workers from Asia.' Daly said the Opposition must 'accept the assurance given by the minister that there is to be no departure from the accepted and established principles'. Not all Labor MPs shared Daly's view. Kim Beazley (Snr) observed that the change 'ends the administrative practice of drawing the line at race'.

However, in his long speech Daly analysed the changes point by point and, on each point, insisted that Labor required assurances that the principles underlying the policy would stay. In short, Daly interpreted the changes as administrative tolerance intended to buttress the existing policy. So did many ALP speakers in an extraordinary debate which betrayed both Australia's traditional racism and deep confusion as to what was actually happening. This was the key to progress.

Opperman and Heydon knew exactly what they were doing. The proof lies in the results. In 1971, five years after Opperman's cabinet

Turkish migrants started arriving in 1967 after Australia signed an immigration agreement with Turkey.

submission, about 9000 non-white immigrants entered Australia, a figure which would have been rejected outright if put to the 1966 cabinet and which would have horrified many parliamentarians from both sides. Professor Jamie Mackie, a founder of the Immigration Reform Group, says: 'The 1966 changes resulted in a dramatic increase in the number of non-white immigrants.' By 1970–71 these numbers were at a level 'which even the reformers would not have dared to suggest ten years earlier'.

The White Australia policy was dismantled by stealth and by a group of politicians and public servants who struck out ahead of community opinion.

Australia had spent most of its history making two assumptions about the White Australia policy: that it was a domestic necessity or at least a dividend, and that it did not hurt our foreign relations. These assumptions were exhausted by the 1960s. The world had changed and the policy had become untenable.

The colonial age had gone or was disintegrating. The nations of Asia were independent and asserting their rights. It was no longer possible for Australia to run an immigration policy based on race and yet develop regional relations on a foundation of mutual respect. Australia had to choose between Asia and a racist immigration policy. It is at this point that a new foreign policy tradition was conceived—that Australia had to change itself to engage with Asia. Paul Keating would try to popularise this view 30 years later.

It was also increasingly clear by the 1960s that Australia was diminishing itself as a society by backing a racist entry policy. The civil rights struggle in the United States documented the true principles of a democracy. The fight against apartheid in South Africa exposed the corrosive evils of racism. White Australia had once been the central ingredient of national unity. But this was no longer the case. There had been a pivotal change based in an evolution of values. The policy was now a running sore, a divisive and disruptive ideology repugnant to too many Australians. The quality of Australian life was undermined by an official policy that asserted Australians were so impoverished they needed a single-colour democracy. White Australia was doomed once it became an embarrassment instead of the focus of national unity. That threshold was reached in the 1960s.

The Coalition Governments from 1966 to 1972 remained reluctant to remove much of the administrative structure and processes of White Australia. But the political battle had been carried in 1966. From this point the pressures grew in favour of more liberalisation. Whitlam won the 1972 election pledging to remove all remaining aspects of discrimination. His flamboyant Immigration Minister, Al Grassby, launched a necessary crusade at home and abroad to publicise and champion a non-discrimination policy. In the Philippines, when asked about White Australia, Grassby made his famous remark: 'It is dead. Give me a shovel and I will bury it.' He spoke a new language—the language of multiculturalism. This was the idea which Australian leaders would bring forward as a replacement for the White Australia credo.

The fall of Saigon in 1975 set in train events that would further transform Australia. The nation now confronted the consequences of the death of White Australia. It was one thing to abolish the policy; it was another to allow the mass entry of Asian migrants. Yet this occurred in the 1970s and 1980s under the Coalition Government of Malcolm Fraser. In 1977 and 1978 the unannounced arrival of refugees on our shores was Australia's

*In 1979 Indo-Chinese refugees
began arriving direct by air
from resettlement camps.*

lurking nightmare become reality—Asians arriving by boat. About a million people left Vietnam, and South East Asia was presented with a full-blown crisis. At one point Malaysia's leader, Dr Mahathir, threatened to 'shoot on sight' intended arrivals.

Australia's initial response to the refugee outflow in the 1975–77 period had been unsympathetic and sluggish. Gough Whitlam, in particular, had been anxious to minimise our role. But as the crisis deepened under Fraser there was a sensitive and constructive response from Michael MacKellar and Ian Macphee, his two Ministers for Immigration and Ethnic Affairs.

This became the most substantial entry of Asians into Australia since the Chinese of the nineteenth century. The solution to the refugee flow lay in an international response. Agreements were negotiated with the assistance of the United States in which refugees were held in camps in Asia in return for countries including the US, Canada and Australia guaranteeing an increased refugee intake from the camps. By the end of 1978 MacKellar had negotiated a holding operation to keep refugee boats in South East Asia and for Australia to take 10 500 refugees a year. The essence of Australia's approach was controlled entry and this needed regional co-operation to be successful. MacKellar fought to put the periodic boat arrivals into perspective: 'What we have achieved is a situation where the number of those arriving in Australia is quite literally insignificant compared with the movement of people further to the north.' He announced that Australia would lift its intake to 14 000 refugees during 1978–79. But MacKellar also began another campaign: stressing the value of Indochinese as good settlers. The government was leading public opinion but anxious to avoid a backlash. Overall, it did a remarkably good job.

Yet Australia was deeply divided. The success of the policy has obscured the extent of community concern. The refugee lobby called for Australia to take more refugees. But public opinion polls showed that up to two-thirds of people wanted Australia to take fewer or no refugees. The quality media was unflinchingly in favour of accepting the refugees. So were church, aid organisations and, with a few exceptions, the ALP opposition. When Macphee replaced MacKellar he waged a tireless campaign to encourage community acceptance of the refugees. This was a distinctly bipartisan effort, with Macphee supported by the ALP shadow minister, Mick Young.

In her assessment of this period, Nancy Viviani gives much credit to the Fraser Government: 'For Australians, Vietnamese refugee entry was the first real test of the disestablishment of the White Australia policy and a test successfully passed.' In per capita terms Australia took the highest number of refugees of any nation.

The government had worked to build community support via elite opinion, ethnic groups, the ALP and community leaders. The total number of unannounced boat arrivals was only 2059 and the overwhelming number of arrivals, about 56 000, came via regular refugee entry. These Indochinese subsequently brought out their families under the Family Reunion Scheme. A total of 190 000 Indochinese arrived in the twenty years from 1975. This symbolised and became an element in the 'Asianisation' of the annual immigration intake. From that time about a third of the intake, on average, has been from Asia.

There were several messages from this experience: that Australia had little control over the direct flow of boatpeople; that international refugee agreements were vital for Australia; that the national interest dictated a generous refugee policy; and that a bipartisan approach was essential to success. Once again, an immigration turning point had seen a broadly bipartisan stance between Coalition and Labor.

Malcolm Fraser also put in place an enduring settlement philosophy of multiculturalism. This idea was given first expression under Whitlam but it was Fraser who made it a reality. In 1977 Fraser established the Galbally Inquiry and implemented its recommendations, which created a new framework for migrant settlement. This involved ethnic associations to assist their own people, the creation of migrant resource centres, greater English language provision and teaching, better translator services, and the development of ethnic broadcasting and television. The Special Broadcasting Service (SBS) began operating in October 1980.

In his speech opening SBS, Fraser said: 'We used to have a view that to really be a good Australian, to love Australia, you almost had to cut your links with the country of origin. But I don't think that is right and it never was right.' For Fraser, multiculturalism expressed the legitimacy of ethnic culture, and he saw it as a catalyst for the integration of migrants into Australia. He presided over the absorption of the multicultural ethos into the organs of government. Fraser was probably accurate in his assessment that his support for immigration and multiculturalism 'might have been the most important thing that my government accomplished'.

The Hawke Government deepened the multiculturalism philosophy despite the recognition of its limitations. These limits were expressed in the 1988 Fitzgerald Report, which said: 'Immigration must be a two-way commitment between the immigrant and Australian society. Multiculturalism does not appear to have been a persuasive vehicle for analysis and community education about the beneficial social impacts of immigration.' It argued that the philosophy of multiculturalism was plagued by confusion and misunderstanding. It was a timely warning because the slogan had not yet won grassroots political acceptance.

The report, chaired by one of Australia's leading Asian scholars, Dr Stephen Fitzgerald, was even more prophetic in identifying the decline in the national interest rationale for immigration. The Australian people no longer saw persuasive economic reasons for immigration. The program had become too geared to family reunion, ethnic politics and multiculturalism. Indeed, multiculturalism was often presented as its justification.

In 1989 a new report from a council headed by Sir James Gobbo produced a highly balanced definition of multiculturalism: a right to ethnic and cultural heritage but only within a framework of loyalty and obligation to Australia. This balance was drawn with absolute precision. But in the late 1990s Prime Minister John Howard and his Immigration Minister, Philip Ruddock, had reservations. Howard disliked using the word 'multiculturalism'. Both Howard and Ruddock felt that the balance in the definition had been lost, with too great a bias towards the 'nation of tribes' concept.

The Howard Government commissioned its own inquiry and settled, finally, on a new term—Australian Multiculturalism. This was a further effort to refine the balance between cultural diversity and Australian unity.

During this long debate in the 1990s there had been various suggestions for an aspirational slogan, with 'many cultures, one Australia' perhaps being the most appealing alternative.

Given Australia's cultural transformation, the emergence of Pauline Hanson was a national rite of passage. Hanson was an authentic voice with deep roots in Australia's political culture. She was the final gasp of the Anglo-Celtic monopolists, the once exclusive expression of what it meant to be an Australian. Expelled from the Liberal Party during the 1996 campaign, Hanson won her seat as an independent. In her September 1996 parliamentary declaration she said: 'I and most Australians want our immigration policy radically reviewed and that of multiculturalism abolished. I believe we are in danger of being swamped by Asians ... Arthur Calwell was a great Australian and Labor leader and it is a pity that there are not men of his stature sitting on the Opposition benches today ... Immigration must be halted in the short term so that our dole queues are not added to by, in many cases, unskilled migrants not fluent in the English language.'

Hanson echoed the old Australia of racism, introspection and equality. Her One Nation party became a protest movement with populist targets—Asians, Aborigines, banks, free trade, global capital, multiculturalism, the media and the established parties. Almost everyone could find a sympathetic chord somewhere in the chorus of complaint she unleashed. Hanson became a voice for the victims of social and economic change. She was devoid of any answers or policy solutions. Her One Nation Party was a throwback in its instincts—to reverse the internationalisation of the economy and to purge the multiculturalism of the society. But such revisions were neither desirable nor achievable.

Hanson was a test of Australia's maturity. She represented an ethical challenge to Australia by injecting an explicit racism into our late 1990s politics; she represented a democratic challenge at the ballot-box to the policies that underpinned a growing and pluralistic Australia; and she posed a tactical problem for the political class over how to manage the backlash she symbolised but which transcended her own persona.

John Howard's response failed to draw the distinction between Hanson's exploitation of grievance and her resort to racial chauvinism. He misjudged the short-term damage that Hanson rendered to the Coalition. But he also misjudged the threat that Hanson's racism posed to Australia at home and abroad. By this failure Howard compromised much of his moral authority as prime minister. He also put a lesser priority on national leadership in immigration policy than did many of his predecessors.

Hanson had tapped a nerve, but she had no prospect of changing

The Woomera Detention Centre where demonstrators were protesting against the conditions under which refugees were being held.

Australia's direction. The new Australia was too deeply sunk into the social soil and the whole notion of a non-discriminatory pluralistic community was central to the national interest.

Among Hanson's opponents there was one school, best represented by Stephen Fitzgerald, who argued that Australia's engagement with Asia had to be intensified not relaxed. For Fitzgerald, Australia's progress in Asia was too superficial. He offered a bold challenge: Australia had to hasten and deepen its cultural orientation to Asia. 'The Australian commitment to Asia was not of the mind,' Fitzgerald said. 'It was not informed by deep knowledge. It was not thought out or conceptualised within an understanding of the elemental forces at work within Asian societies. It was in this sense not an intellectual engagement. This failing was a failing of government, but it was a failing across the total spectrum of Australian elites.' The gulf between Hanson and Fitzgerald is unbridgeable. It is a gulf Australia must negotiate as a nation.

There are three concluding observations that flow from the White Australia story. First, Australia has reinvented over the course of a century its racial and cultural profile. White Australia has been replaced by a pluralistic Australia. This reinvention resulted from a complex fusion of self-interest and changing values. It has been an epic example of redefinition within a democratic framework. Multiculturalism does not have the political power to replace White Australia as the embodiment of national identity, yet it is true to say that tolerance is a hallmark of the Australian identity in 2001. In Australia today about one person in four was born overseas. About 4 per cent of the population is Asian. Australia's adaptation to Asia is just beginning. It is certain to be filled with ongoing tensions about how Australians relate to each other and to the world. Yet it is no exaggeration to claim Australia as one of the most tolerant societies on earth. It is also one of the most united. White Australia has gone, yet its companion—nationalism—is stronger in the Australia of 2001 than it was in 1901. By any measure the success of this Australian reinvention is impressive.

Second, over the century Australia has increased its population fivefold. It has been an audacious exercise in nation-building, particularly since the end of World War II. Australia's decision to become a large-scale immigrant nation at this time is arguably the most important decision in our history. It was driven overwhelmingly by national interest, not altruism. Yet over time the altruistic dimension has assumed its own life. During the period of the program a total of 5.75 million people have arrived. It is nation-building on a scale that very few nations have rivalled during the past 60 years. Immigration accounts for more than half of our population growth in this time. The program was fundamental in destroying a monocultural Australia and opening up new vistas. But in 2001 support for immigration is eroding dramatically; the national interest driving the program is no longer so apparent; the combination of a more secure nation, deeper environmental awareness and economic restructuring has shaken public support for immigration and cast a shadow over its future.

Finally, Australia faces a continuing challenge in terms of defining its identity and its impact. Paul Keating offered the best formula on identity, saying that Australia was not an Asian nation nor was it a European nation: it was distinctively Australian and could only present itself to the world on this basis. The related question is whether Australia chooses to remain a young nation. That will depend on whether it chooses ongoing renewal by immigration—the contemporary Australian tradition. The fear is that Australia will turn away from immigration—deceived by its success, driven by a selfish perception of national interest and risking its marginalisation in the region. But that is still an unlikely scenario. It will only happen if Australia loses faith in the regenerative policy it has pursued so successfully for more than half of its national existence.

INTERVIEW WITH
PAUL KEATING

Paul Keating sees Australia as ambivalent about its future and as a nation too reluctant to abandon its past. It escaped from White Australia just in time; it lingered too long with the great and powerful friends, Britain and America; it was equivocal about reconciliation and unable to perceive the republic as a psychological moment to seize. Keating says the economic reforms of the 1980s and 1990s were when Labour 'smashed the mould' of the failing past and at this point Labor 'reclaimed its future'.

You initiated the debate for the republic. Is it possible to identify a particular point in time when you decided to press the button?

It was always in my mind. But it was clear to me when the Queen came to Australia in the first month or two of my prime ministership how inadequate it was for her to attempt to represent all that we were. She was here and then we had all the carry-on with the British press and what have you. And I was always rankled by the flag, always rankled by the fact that we had the flag of the United Kingdom of Great Britain in our flag, in the corner. I thought, you know, the time's come to actually put this on the political agenda. You see, the republic was an after-dinner mints and coffee conversation for 40 years. A political party has to champion these issues to make them live, has to put a live conduit on to them. And we did that in the policy speech of 1993 and it was a big risk for the Labor Party. Many members of parliament at the policy launch thought that that was the end of the election. They thought that we'd basically lost it on this issue. But it did get the issue going and of course we then appointed an all-party body to look at it. I did all the things I thought one should do in a very bipartisan way, including the model itself, in which I had the Liberal Party in mind as well as the Labor Party, to get the thing carried.

Is the question here one of bedrock faith for Australians?

I think it is. I think the spirituality of the country, its psychology and spirituality, matters. My opponents, Howard, Costello and others, would say: 'Oh, this was a distraction from the main game.' The main game was the economy. Well, I'd say: 'Given that the economy is growing at five per cent, what do you mean, a distraction?' I think the issue is central to the way we view ourselves. It says more to us about ourselves than it says to others; but by the same token, going through our region saying 'By the way, we're borrowing the monarch of another country' is too absurd in the modern age.

I mean, the main motivation for me in championing a republic in Australia was simply that the Queen could no longer represent us, all that we have created, all that we aspire to. She was an inappropriate person to represent us. It may not have been inappropriate when Queen Victoria represented us, but it's certainly inappropriate now.

After you embarked on this course of action, you had to brief the Queen, inform her, about your intentions and what you were doing. Can you describe how you did that and what was the response of the Queen?

I saw her at Balmoral. I stayed there with my wife for a weekend. We had a sort of convivial time there. But I said to the Queen that the time had come in Australia when the constitutional arrangements were no longer appropriate for us, but that Australia would have a better and more modern relationship with Britain if these constitutional arrangements were changed. And that the Queen would have perhaps a greater welcome in Australia, coming as the Queen of Great Britain, than she would otherwise seek to have as Queen of Australia. And that while Britain had become an integral part of the European Union, so Australia had to go with its geography and its history in the Asia-Pacific. I believed it was no longer appropriate for our Head of State not to be an Australian. I mean, this was all said between the two of us. We were having tea. I said to her, I thought it was very important that she break the convention and let me say, after the visit, what in fact I'd said. I added: 'To do this will remove you from the point of focus and I'll do all that I can to keep you in a personal sense, or the monarchy in Britain, away from the issue in Australia.'

How would you summarise the Queen's reaction?

I think she thought there was an inevitability about it and she said: 'Well, of course, I'll always do what the Australian people think best and take the advice of my ministers.' One would expect no less of an answer from her.

What's the message from the defeat of the referendum?

That the country is still ambivalent about its future. The country lacks political leadership, focus and direction. I've never seen a time when Australia was more marginalised in its region than now. And in part that marginalisation comes, I think, from the vote on the republic, Prime Minister Howard's remarks about being a regional deputy of the United States, and Asian perceptions over the handling of East Timor. A whole lot of things. I think when the country voted to keep the existing system, it's obviously done it tongue in cheek. It must know, as I'm sure it does, that we have to have an Australian as our Head of State. Our self-regard and our future demand no less and I think people think it was a warm-up for the real event.

I think it's important that when the republic comes it's celebrated, it's claimed; that we don't just wimp over the line by a vote, with a prime minister who doesn't want it, but rather with someone who grabs it, wants it—and the country understands the big psychological moment has come. I still think we can do that and that's the one trade-off for losing it.

I think the republic's truly inevitable, as an idea it's overpowering. I think the political parties owe it to the country to arrange to let the republic through. You might recall that I proposed at the 1996 election, that had Labor won it, we would have a plebiscite asking people: 'Do you favour a shift to a republic?' I'm quite sure that would've been answered in the affirmative. Had it been answered in the affirmative, it would've been a political instruction from the country to the political system to get a model together, and that's the way I think it'll have to go.

Let's turn to Aboriginal affairs. What did the Mabo judgment mean for you? How did you see it?

I thought that I'd be the person that would have to move on statutory land rights—that's land rights provided from the parliament. But then the Mabo judgment was handed down and it was essentially unremarkable, even though it has been attacked up hill and down dale by Tories. It was quite unremarkable. It said, of course this was not the land of no one. It could never have been *terra nullius*. This is just historically wrong. Therefore, if it was a land of someone, that someone, their customs and traditions, were as much a source of the common law as European custom and tradition had been—and in that law there's a title. It's called native title. We don't know what it is or who has it and maybe in subsequent judgments we can think about that. But essentially there is a title, native title.

I believed that matters, psychological and spiritual, are as important to reconciliation as are the nuts and bolts matters like schooling and health. There was a certain amount of politics in the High Court judgment. It gave freehold title to those who settled here since 1788 and who had a grant of interest in land from a government, and the freehold title extinguished the native title; but it gave to Aboriginals a native title to areas where they could show continuing occupation.

What we had to do was either wait twenty years for a body of case law to develop about who owned what or have the government legislate, and so I took the course of building from a clean sheet of paper what I think is the most comprehensive piece of property and cultural law in Australia, the Native Title Act. Essentially, it was to say who had the title, what it was, and how people could get it, preserving where possible existing Aboriginal rights.

Is it hard for Australians to come to grips with this issue because we've denied it for so long?

Yes, I think the basis of reconciliation is the act of recognition—not to fall for this argument about the black armband view of history or the guilt industry. There's always been a lot of guilt about Aboriginal history, European history with Aborigines. It's never done any of us any good. It was really an act of recognition that we're the ones that did the dispossessing and that we wouldn't have appreciated these things being done to us. And, even though it's late in the piece, if land was there and hadn't been alienated it should be theirs from this point. I think coming clean on the land, coming clean on the dispossession, changes the psychological balance. It breaks the cycle of despair that was around.

Your Redfern speech was a landmark, but it was very confronting for the Australian people. Why did you give that speech?

I said there that it had to be about an act of recognition. We were the ones who did the dispossessing. We're the ones that brought the diseases, the alcohol. We're the ones that did the murders. We're the ones who took the children. Either we did or we didn't. And if we did, where should the act of recognition begin? It should begin with the prime minister. It should begin with the person who has won the democratic mandate and has the political authority and, in this respect, the moral authority to say these things. So it was adding a new life to the process of reconciliation.

Just going back to the Mabo judgment itself. You said that the judgment identified what was the lie and what was the truth.

The lie was the claim that this was the land of no one. There were indigenous people here before the first European settlement. The truth was that the land was theirs, that we took it. The Court took the view that native title was subordinate to the Crown—that is, that where there had been a grant of interest in land it had extinguished the native title. But it made clear that where there was no alienation the land could still be held by Aboriginal and Torres Strait Islander people, but it was silent about the big tracts under pastoral leases. That came out in the Wik judgment, where the Court found that a pastoralist's right to graze, though the predominant right, didn't extinguish the underlying native title right.

I thought the Wik judgment was completely sound. Moral and good. And I thought one of the shabbiest episodes of Australian politics was the alacrity with which the Howard Government moved to extinguish, in the name of the States, underlying native title rights that were not inconsistent with grazing. It was one of the meanest things I've ever seen a government do.

What was your response to the conservatives who wanted blanket legislation to extinguish native title rights?

I had a lot of pressure on me from the pastoralists. They said: 'Well, if you believe, prime minister, that the judgment says or implies that any grant of interest in land, including a leasehold grant, extinguishes the native title, why don't you say so in the bill? Why don't you extinguish it?' To which I said: 'Look, this will be in the preamble. The preamble will say it's the government's belief that it's probably the Court's view that any grant of interest extinguishes native title.' But I left it open for Aboriginal and Torres Strait Islander people to take this question to the Court itself. In other words, I wouldn't pre-empt it, as

I thought they had a better than even chance of the Court finding in their favour, which it did.

I thought, if we were going to embark upon this most complex task, that we should do it *with* the Aboriginal and Torres Strait Islander people. So I tried to empower them to be part of the process. They had good leadership and Lowitja O'Donoghue gave them the leadership that mattered. We also had a process running with stakeholders, landholders, mining companies etc. And then we had a very good committee of the cabinet focused on it and an absolutely tip-top group of people in the Prime Minister's Department, headed by Sandy Hollway. And we built the Native Title Act, line by line, clause by clause, concept by concept. It took that cabinet subcommittee—meeting probably three nights a week—a year to do it.

I think once the trust is there, then things can be done. But trust is a hard thing to get together on both sides. Trust builds up like laminations, but once it's there, I think many things, more things, become possible. It's whether we want the reconciliation, genuinely want it, to happen. In my view it has to happen. Therefore this process of building trust has to be one that's not fractured.

So, is this the essence of reconciliation? I mean, is trust the essence?

I think that for these, let's call them the psychological matters, the matters of truth, it is. We set up the inquiry into the 'stolen generations'. I mean, of course, it was unconscionable for any group to take children from the parents of another group. And we've got to recognise that and know that we did that. Then there are the intractable matters about health and drug dependency and alcohol and housing, but again, we've got to bring the States into this in an ambitious way. These things are done by the States, but often the States just didn't do them.

Have the Australian people got the heart to genuinely commit to reconciliation, or is there some darkness in the soul still?

I think they do have the heart for it but they have to be led. You remember the hysteria around native title. How everyone's backyards were going to go and all of that. I mean, in the end, it went through because the political system wanted it to go through. So, I do believe Australia has the heart for it; but I also believe this, it must have the heart for it. We can't live this lie, you know, we can't simply say it's our place, not their's, and at the same time toodle off to the region and say: 'We've turned over a new leaf but, just by the way, we have no real basis for reconciliation with our own indigenes.' You know, for our own self-regard, our sense of ourselves, as well as what it means to Aboriginal and Islander people, I think reconciliation is a must for Australia.

What about the influence of Hansonism? What's your feeling about that?

I think a lot of Hansonism came from the rural decline, the decline in the countryside that had political and community expression in looking for a way out with somebody who gave them what they thought were easy answers—or worse, somebody who kept posing the questions but didn't have the answers. Political parties need depth to deal with intractable problems and the One Nation Party didn't have that depth or substance and it's foundered as a consequence.

But what about the vote against you in 1996? A lot of people would say that that vote was partly motivated by the fact that you actually did pursue these pro-Aboriginal policies.

This could be so in parts of rural Australia, could be so. But it was also a drought overlaying a rural decline. Even though we'd propped up the price of wool and we'd done everything in terms of the Uruguay Round to find markets, and we'd financially underpinned the drought, there was a great turning towards more conservative solutions. I'm not going to suggest to you that there isn't some sort of objection to what the conservatives call the 'Aboriginal industry' in these country towns and rural places. I think there is. But it's a matter of what the country wants and the country didn't endorse Hansonism at the subsequent poll, and as a force it's collapsing.

Do you think the Australian people understand that we are going to be judged internationally by our performance on this issue?

Not adequately, no. I think in a funny kind of way they can stand back and look at Nelson Mandela's career and all that it represented but not make the same connection here. But, of course, many people do. I mean, many Australians know clearly what this is all about. This is where political leadership matters. The latent goodwill is there if the political leadership wants to tap it, but if the political leadership wants to talk about black armbands and Aboriginal industries and all the rest to camouflage the truth, well, it's just going to take much longer and be much more painful.

Going to the issue of economic reform, what some people would say in terms of deregulation, support for markets, privatisation, is that this is where Labor lost its soul. What's your response to that?

In truth, it's where Labor reclaimed its future and where it underpinned, in a more useful and wider way, its commitment to egalitarianism. If you start talking about equity you've got to start with employment. Through the Labor years there was massive employment growth. We had a huge participation rate in the workforce. So many women, particularly, went out looking for work because there was so much employment through those years. Then there's the great programs like Medicare. There were the income support programs, like the Family Allowance Supplement. And the great liberating policies of education. In 1983, three kids in ten completed Year 12. In 1996, it was nine in ten—a revolution in participation in schools. And we trebled university places to take them. So, I just think it's baseless, the claim is baseless. And on top of that—higher real wages and rising living standards because prices are lower. You know, a young person will buy a bubble car today for under $20 000. This was impossible while tariffs existed. Families can get shoes and under-clothes and clothes cheaply now, that they couldn't get before.

I mean, what was Labor really, in economic terms, before 1983? As a party, it believed in regulation. It believed in regulation of the banking system. It believed in regulation of the exchange rate. It believed in tariffs. We had abysmal rates of productivity, of labour productivity and factor productivity. We had low profits, therefore low investment. We had high unemployment. I mean, what did we abandon? It's like losing an eczema. I know there's a bit of rewriting of history within the Labor movement. People who sort of class themselves as academics wouldn't get a feed in the real academic show. Tony Blair talks about the 'third way'—well, the third way, of course, was done in Australia, beginning in 1983 and all through the 80s. I'm that proud of it. I would never want to call it 'third way'. No, we came first. Ours was the only way—a good internationally competitive economy with a really kindly social wage grafted on to it.

To what extent is this really a remaking of our economic compact?

Any country that runs a co-operative model, in income determination, ends up in front. The Accord with the unions over fifteen years was essentially a co-operative model. We took Australia to the biggest economic adjustment we could ever imagine, without people losing limbs, metaphorically speaking. Australia's been through the longest growth phase in its economic history, essentially thanks to a Labor Government. The Coalition Government of John Howard is simply built on the tradition and the foundations that were provided and that's a good thing. In the end, the political process is about improving economic and social outcomes. The Accord process in Australia is the reason why we completely outstripped New Zealand's economic performance—they tried a non-cooperative process, and we tried the opposite.

Just going back to your economic reforms as Treasurer. When this was being done, to what extent were you conscious that you were pulling down an old model and creating a new model?

I always felt offended that we were regarded as not the appropriate people to manage or reset the economy. Yet we did have one half of the equation with us. That was organised labour. I wanted a much more market-related focus in our economic policy. One where we dropped this pretence about economic planning and the notion of state intervention and state capitalism. And we actually said: 'Look, this is not going to produce the goods. What's going to produce the goods are basically a proper share between profits and wages, proper macro-economic policy settings, other competitive issues, like the exchange rate etc.' I wanted to get that stamp on the Labor Party. This was the chance to get it. Now, I thought we were probably going to be, for all manner of reasons, marked down for extinction—and the only thing to do is to go for the lick of your life. Make every post a winner. And go for the big value decisions. We did that and we kept winning. We won in 1984, then we won in 1987. So the only thing to do, if the formula worked, was to keep running. And as a consequence it did change.

And the other thing is, we should never underestimate the value of the political leadership of the ACTU. It was the most enlightened leadership of its kind in any organised labour movement around the world. Thanks in very large measure to Bill Kelty [former ACTU Secretary].

If one looks back over the century, Australia devised a unique method of civilising capitalism—the idea of state intervention, protection, arbitration. In the future, with our market economy, how confident are you that we can find a way of mediation between the market and social justice?

I'll say two things about it. One, in my lifetime, capital was always king. In the lifetime of my children, it'll be the knowledge workers who are king. Capital will be freely available, much more freely available, and in venture capital it'll be like driving into a petrol station to top up. You'll be able to top up, providing you've got the knowledge to make it work. So I think there's going to be a swing back to labour, in the sense that people will command a premium.

The second thing is that with globalisation and internationalisation there's an even bigger requirement on government—to fashion domestic policy for egalitarian purposes. That is, to protect the weak and to support those in transition in an economy where permanence of employment has changed, where new technology changes the way we work and think and organise ourselves. I think there's a bigger role for government today than there's ever been. We're not in the static economies and the static economic models that we were in for most of our history, when people joined an industry and stayed there all their lives. This is all changing.

In a policy sense can Australia keep its commitment to equity and have a market economy?

It's going to be done against the context of a widening disparity in wealth, because markets are piling value on to innovation and people in non-innovative sectors are not going to get that premium. This is going to cause resentment just as impermanence of employment causes resentment. Therefore governments have got to be alert to the fact that they'll be providing more equitable policies for people in that sort of context. It's why I believe things like Medicare are so important, because they're not about the division of national income going to the top 1 per cent or 10 per cent of people. It's a policy for everybody. So these broad-brush things, like access and equity in education, access and equity in health, are the things that will guarantee equity. Superannuation's another such policy, long-term provision of retirement income and savings. They're the big-brush issues which will make the society better. You won't be able to stop the disparities. You can ameliorate them but you won't be able to stop them. But you can lift the average, lift the floor.

Some people say when they talk about globalisation that it's bad, bad for countries like Australia—that we've lost our national sovereignty. What's your response to that?

I think it's wrong. It's dreadfully wrong. Yes, we are less sovereign in some respects. We had the sovereign right to make the wrong exchange rate. We had the sovereign right to build a tariff wall, which made us poor. But are these sovereignties we really enjoyed? I don't think so. So, if one wants to pick up the premium that comes with good governance, I think one can. In other words, I don't really see that there is such a decline in sovereignty. American unemployment was as low at the end of the twentieth century as it was in the middle of the twentieth century. Real wages have been rising. Normally the stock market adds four hundred billion in value a year. In the last two years, 1999, 1998, it added four trillion. In two years it put on ten years' value. I mean, I don't think this is a cause for gloom.

What has this meant for Australia? How do you think we should look on the process of globalisation?

With optimism and for the opportunity that it brings. I mean, would we wish today to be as we used to be, a monoculture, closed in by tariffs, essentially limited to producing raw materials or semi-finished goods for the world, whereas today we are part and parcel of the age of services or information, of elaborately transformed goods. All this has come by being domestically and internationally competitive.

Concerning your period as Treasurer—is it possible for you to identify a key event, a decision, which separated the old from the new?

I think there are two things. One, letting the most important price in the economy, the exchange rate, be set in the market, free of controls, was putting a large part of our economic future in the hands of people other than the central bank and the Treasury. Two, taking down the tariff wall. What those two things gave us was an open financial market and an open goods market. Now, I think they're the two critical things.

At the same time, in the same period we doubled trend productivity. This was a very big thing. We doubled the capacity of the Australian economy to grow. Before the Labor years, 1983 to 1996, the Australian economy's capacity to grow was under two per cent. Now it grows pretty well all the time at four or above. This is a world of difference, an economy that produces twice as much wealth, spreads a lot further in profits, in prosperity, in real wages. We've now got real wage increases of about two and a half per cent a year. In ten years, that gives people a 25 per cent real increase in incomes, not inflationary increase, real increase. Now, I think, frankly, anyone who doubts the value of that is a sort of obscurantist who doesn't want to face the fact that it is a good result.

When you began to internationalise the economy, to what extent were you conscious of the fact that you were smashing the old mould?

I knew we were smashing the old mould. Once the exchange rate fell to its proper competitive value, we had to deal with the immediate price surge and price effects. All of these things came home to roost at the one time. We knew that to keep a truly low inflationary culture we had to have the competition of imports and we couldn't have that while ever we had protection.

Essentially these years were about stripping the economy down to make it more supple and internationally competitive and then pointing it to where our future was, in Asia.

How much do you think that as a people we were attached to the old ways of protection and big government? How deeply implanted were these ideas in our culture?

I think the Joseph Chamberlain policy of Imperial preference and the fact that we saw ourselves as a dominion of the British Empire greatly influenced everything we did, until the emergence of some sort of independent foreign policy in the 1970s. American revolutionary leaders wanted to be free of foreign entanglements. We went out of our way to have foreign entanglements. We had a very big foreign entanglement with Britain and the British Navy and the British Foreign Office for most of our history and then we had a very big set of entanglements with the United States. Australia's general policy had been to go searching for entanglements because that's how we found ourselves feeling comfortable and secure in the neighbourhood. Part of that was, of course, the economic entanglement.

I think fear was the underpinning of the links with Britain and the British Navy. It underpinned the White Australia policy. It underpinned support for Imperial preference and protection. I think fear underpinned the insularity that Australia had. We didn't have any international status of our own until the Statute of Westminster. That was not even ratified till 1942. A lot of people took offence at the fact that the British were trying to kick us out of home and to be on our own. Sir Robert Menzies—I've got a quotation of his—said in 1946, a period of decolonisation: 'When we have, in this absurd frenzy, cleared our powerful friends out of the places that are vital to us, we in Australia will know all about isolation. I hope that day will never come.' In other words, when the Dutch wanted to come back to Indonesia, when the French wanted to come back to Vietnam, these were the things we thought were signs of our protection—you know, the British hanging on in Singapore, etc. Fortunately, a Labor Government supported the Indonesian revolution against the Dutch, the first real mark of an independent Australian foreign policy. And we started then to realise, I think, that the way to overcome our fears was engagement. Instead of that, Menzies was talking about the frenzy of clearing our friends out of the region. In other words, he was resisting the decolonisation, which was part of the maturing of the region and gave its peoples their capacity to govern themselves in a society of nations, of which we could be part.

You mentioned the Statute of Westminster, which effectively gave Australia its legal independence. What does our reluctance as a people to embrace Britain's gift, the Statute of Westminster, tell us about ourselves in this period of the 1930s?

I think this is the influence of the First World War. It had a very disastrous influence on Australian nationalism. The great Australian wave of nationalism, which started with the move to federation, the egalitarian principles that we saw developing towards the end of the nineteenth century, the formation of the Labor Party, the confident operation of trade unions, the sense of the fair go—all of these things essentially were snuffed out with the First World War. The conservatives wrapped themselves in the flag and commandeered all that it meant. In the 1930s we still had that hangover. We still believed that we needed the protection of the Imperial navy. We needed the Imperial protection to find our way around Asia because we were the white tribe in Asia. So, when the whiter parts of the Commonwealth—Australia, Canada, etc—were let go by the Foreign Office under the Statute of Westminster, it was regarded here as not a freedom at all. You know, we were being unceremoniously kicked out of home and people here just didn't like it.

We clung to the White Australia policy for so long. Do you think it damaged our self-concept as a people?

I do. I think it prevented us from coming to terms with our geography, our sense of ourselves. I think White Australia was a far greater inhibition to us than it ever was to anyone who had to deal with it from the outside. The interesting thing is that we came close to being marginalised, the way South Africa was marginalised with apartheid. We got out of it just in the nick of time. It wasn't that long ago, you know, a quarter of a century ago.

Looking at your own approach as prime minister, what was the transition in terms of Australia's place in the world that you were trying to bring to fruition?

I had two aims in my years as Treasurer and prime minister. One was to strip the economy down to make it internationally competitive and supple, and the other was to point it to the place that mattered most to us, where our vital interests are, and that's Asia. I believed that at the end of the Cold War, when I became prime minister, all of Australia's vital interests coalesced in Asia—trade, security, cultural. If we put the question in the negative, do we have vital interests in Africa? The answer is no. Do we have vital interest in South America? No. Do we have vital interests in North America? Some. Where do we have our vital interests? Where we live, in Asia. So I saw that with the bipolarity of the Cold War going and with regionalism of a kind we hadn't seen before—for instance, the development of APEC—that all of our interests, for the first time, coalesced in Asia.

The premise is that Australia finds its place and its security *in* Asia. It doesn't find it *from* Asia. And that means an engaging and athletic foreign policy. It means a policy that has large multilateral dimensions and bilateral dimensions. It means, it meant, the development of a robust relationship with our largest neighbour, Indonesia, a robust relationship with the biggest power in the region, China, and a robust relationship with the biggest economic power, Japan.

But as a nation you can't do this unless you're confident within yourself. Do you think that's right?

I think matters of identity go right to this point about ambivalence. You can't be doubting who you are to undertake this kind of project. We need that certainty, the inner confidence and certainty, about who we are and what we've become. And this is why I believe that we can't go round the region—or to put it in the positive, we should go round the region with an Australian person as our Head of State. We should have a foreign policy which is completely our own and which is constructed to advance our interests. And we should go there off a base of social harmony in Australia. And this is where I thought reconciliation with the Aborigines was very important, apart from the intrinsic merit of it. We could say to the region: 'Well, here we are, "White Australia's" gone. We're no longer a derivative of any other country or society. We're here to play our part and we're going to treat you, the indigenous of the region, as we would treat our own.'

We are neither Asian nor American nor European. We go to the region as Australians—the only way we can go. What else can there be? It's absurd. I mean, there's no doubt that in time Australia will be a far more Asian country than it is today. But all the culture and morés and political tradition and democratic tradition are an Australian tradition that's grown up off Westminster principles. That's what we have to assert, and that's what we have to celebrate.

How difficult do you think it was for us to liberate ourselves from the 'great and powerful friends' mindset?

I think for Australia it's been exceptionally difficult. We came here, in a way, to claim the continent—the British came here to claim the continent—against the French, to add another territory to the Empire, another dominion. And from that time onwards, I think, Australians were fearful of their circumstances, so the linkage with Britain was a 'powerful friend' linkage. And that lasted, of course, right till the Second World War and then it shifted to the United States. And the United States earned that in our eyes for their liberation of the region and of us against the Japanese. But we confused things about great powers. We thought there was a monolith of communism between China and Russia. We thought that Vietnam was simply part of another communist monolith in North Asia, which we found was untrue. We clutched to great and powerful friends. All wise countries have alliances, but very wise countries find their own security by doing their own things. I think that in part the internationalisation of our economy was a precursor to a better understood decision to go out ourselves, as a people, without a great and powerful friend at our elbow, and make our way in the region.

You had great faith in the idea of a Pacific Community when you were prime minister. How important was this to your vision?

The security guarantor for Japan and Korea is the United States. This is also true of the Philippines, as, in nuclear terms, it's true of Australia. I didn't believe that we could develop, with the emerging power of China and of South East Asia, a political community without the stakeholders all being present. Therefore, the model I wished to see in place was a trans-Pacific model. That model expressed itself when we got an APEC leaders meeting together for the first time.

What was President Clinton's response to this idea?

The idea of APEC was economic co-operation in the Pacific. So when I was able to assure him that if he issued invitations we would get the political leadership of China, Japan, Indonesia and economies like Taiwan and Hong Kong together, he then made the move to initiate the first APEC leaders meeting in Seattle. He chose Seattle because it was the home of the two biggest American exporting industries, Boeing and Microsoft, and we met the leaders of those companies. So it had, for the American people, this sort of economic dimension. But for the rest of us it had a clear security dimension as well because when the President of China puts his feet under the table with the President of the United States, the Prime Minister of Japan, the President of Indonesia—all at one table, every year—it's a mighty leap forward in any sense of security and community.

How important was Indonesia's President Suharto to this whole undertaking?

Couldn't have happened without him—without his willingness, as the then leader of the non-aligned movement, to come in [an APEC leaders'] lumberjacket with an American president to Seattle.

And how important was that for Australia?

APEC is the only body we really sit in, regionally, that matters. I mean, we've been excluded from the Asia–Europe meeting. In late 1999 there was a meeting for the first time of ASEAN plus three—Japan, Korea and China—which is pretty much the old economic caucus proposed by Prime Minister Mahathir. Australia was excluded. The sole body, powerful body, that's focused on the region (outside the UN) that we belong to is APEC. So it was exceptionally important for Australia.

How do you see, now, the security agreement between Australia and Indonesia, which you negotiated with President Suharto? Was this a mistake or not?

Oh, no, no. What I wanted was not to simply rely on military-to-military relations with Indonesia—not to depend only on the Australian Defence Force and the TNI, but to go over the top of that with some state-to-state treaty of a kind pretty much with the language of ANZUS, the treaty with Papua New Guinea and also the Five Power Defence Agreement. We had strategic agreements with Singapore and Malaysia and Papua New Guinea, but not with Indonesia. In other words, for the state that mattered most in strategic terms, we had no such structure.

You might remember that Liberal Party ministers said how useful this thing was and how it set the scenery for a far better relationship between Australia and Indonesia. Then John Howard, in what I believe was rank political opportunism, said: 'Oh, it was no use to us in Timor.' Well, it was never designed for Timor, any more than it was designed for Ambon or Lombok or anywhere else. It was a structure in which to look at Australia's security and Indonesia's security in somewhat common terms in the region.

President Suharto was the only person with the willingness and the capability of delivering it. And I was willing and capable of doing it here and wanted to do it. And it was a strategic asset for us. I think that the Howard Government was recklessly indifferent to Australia's national interest in letting it just slide away, because it suited that week's politics about Timor. I mean, governments are supposed to think beyond a week or a month. I believe a prime minister's first task, very first task, is to guarantee the security of the country. Instruments of security are big, bankable assets and if John Howard thought that treaty was valueless what does he say about ANZUS? What does he say about the treaty with Papua New Guinea? What does he say about the Five Power Defence Agreement?

As prime minister, what was the tone and the balance you sought to get in the relationship with America?

The Cold War had finished, so the strategic component had changed. The enemy, the Soviet Union, had disappeared. Russia had become a democracy of sorts. South East Asia mattered much less at the end of the Cold War than it ever did before the Cold War. I think that Australia's role was to maintain the value of this cultural, political, strategic relationship which we had with the United States, extending back to the First World War, but at the same time to be a useful interlocutor—that is, a state that had a policy of its own, a view of its own, and was able to do useful things in its own right. In South East Asia we made our own way, and by building regional institutions like the ASEAN Regional Forum or the agreement on maintaining security with Indonesia, by building good bilateral relationships, Australia was doing something far more useful in US terms than simply being a strategic mendicant. This, I think, gave us a far healthier relationship with the United States—we could often disagree with them about things.

Do you think that Australia one day may be forced to choose between the United States and Asia?

I don't think that day will come. The United States is now a century into the game of being a world power and has I think learned much since the Second World War. I think that it's going to play its strategic hand appropriately. The touchstone is China and its attitude towards China—whether China will be supported to play a major role in the world.

There's been this talk around that Australia will have to choose. Well, we're never going to tie Australia to San Diego. We're here. And we've got to get along here. And that means we've got to make the US do things we want. For instance, had I won the 1996 election, I would never have let the Americans tread on Indonesia the way the IMF did at the behest of the US Treasury. I mean, I would have been on Bill Clinton's back, tearing the door to his office down. This didn't happen. The Indonesians know it didn't happen. The East Asia crisis should have been run from Canberra. It was run from Washington. It was not run from the State Department but from the Treasury through the surrogate of the IMF. We've got to make the United States—encourage it—to do things which conform to a wider view of the region than just its sole strategic view.

You deregulated the financial system and the banks. By contrast, 40 years earlier Ben Chifley tried to nationalise the banks. So how should we see the old ALP philosophy which supported bank nationalisation?

I think we should see it sympathetically—in its time, you know. I think that Chifley was too flatfooted for someone like Menzies. Menzies never had principles, he just had interests. Chifley's stewardship of the Curtin legacy was, I believe, goodhearted but flatfooted. Essentially Labor built the postwar structure and gave it to the Liberal Party, to Menzies. But in the days when the centrally planned economies were doing quite well, at the end of the war there was a sort of crisis of confidence in Western institutions. You can see why Chifley thought nationalisation was the way forward.

I think Chifley was a good person, a good Labor person, who did his very best. He never had quite the wisdom that I think Curtin had. But he probably had broader support in the Labor movement. But nevertheless he ushered in a long period of Conservative government. The Rip Van Winkle years of Australian politics. The time when we should have grown hugely, like Japan and Germany did, and we didn't. Apart from a few years in the 1960s, there were modest rates of growth, through the 50s and the 70s, where we didn't discern a place for ourselves in the world, where we got caught up in escapades like Suez, where we didn't know what our vital interests were. I mean, the losses for Australia in those years were profound.

This is the Menzies legacy?

This is the Menzies legacy, presiding over a Western economy in the salad days of postwar growth, with modest rates of growth. You know, it's not anything one would boast about.

You learnt a lot from Jack Lang. He gave you a bit of a fuel injection, did he?

He said to me—one of the few times he called me Paul—he said: 'Paul, I'll tell you this. You're a young man. When you go to Canberra, they'll all tell you you've got plenty of time. The truth is you haven't got a second to lose.' And it was dead right. It was absolutely dead right.

Labor governed during the Depression. Scullin was in power and the government failed. What sort of legacy did it throw forward? I mean, when you were Treasurer, although it was a long time later, to what extent, were you still operating with some of this behind you?

A lot. Because, you see, I was always a student of the Labor years. I had all the standard texts: *Caucus Crisis* by Warren Denning, *The Labor Daily Yearbooks*, *The Labor Daily* itself, which was the voice of Lang's government, *The Sydney Morning Herald*, always the voice of conservatism. I was very much aware, as a result of those years and the gentlemen's agreement that was then entered into to protect State debt, and also the difficult economic period in the Whitlam Government, that we had to be innovative and exemplary. Kim Beazley Senior once said to me: 'The party of social attack has to be exemplary.' For the party of economic attack it's even more true. You're dealing with the lifeblood of the economy. It was one of the reasons I kept John Stone [the then head of the Treasury] on for a year or so—I thought that a demonstrable bloodletting on the first and best known person abroad in Australian finance was not smart.

3

Land of the Fair Go

Australia offered a model to the world in its quest to civilise capitalism. If Australia's greatest claim lay in its democracy, its next claim was as a civilising mediator in the struggle between capitalism and society. It was because Australia was a genuine democracy that it had to deliver a decent living standard for its people. Australians believed in private property rights, yet this was coupled with a keen sense of public interest advanced through government and state power.

The instinct of a 'fair go' was implanted in Australia's political culture from its convict origins. The recurring debate about whether or not Australia was a classless society misses the point—the great monument of the new Commonwealth was the creation of a polity dedicated to egalitarianism. Australians endorsed the 'fair go' by deed, not just word. It was to be realised through state power for individual needs in contrast to American self-realisation through individual liberty. Australians looked by instinct to government. Americans, by contrast, had fought a war of independence in the cause of freedom against government tyranny. Australia's faith in state power was shaped by former convicts, military officers and a 'colonial secretary' mentality. In Australia land was settled not by small independent farmers but by squatters bankrolled by finance houses and holding vast estates.

The cardinal feature of the Australian faith in government intervention was its bipartisanship. Despite the class divide at the heart of Australia's party system, based on Labor versus non-Labor, both sides endorsed this philosophical foundation. As the century advanced the bipartisan edifice became a colossus. It was represented by the highest tariffs in the developed world (outside New Zealand), a pervasive judicial-based system of wage determination and industrial conciliation, a comprehensive welfare state, vast public enterprises, government-owned monopolies and rigid regulation of markets. In his classic 1932 book *State Socialism in Victoria*

Frederic Eggleston, Victorian minister and intellectual, surveyed banking, railways, roads, water supply, transport, electricity, agriculture and forests and concluded that Victoria's public services 'in proportion to the size and the economic standing of the community, constitute possibly the largest and most comprehensive use of state power outside Russia'.

Faith in government intervention became an Australian technique in its own right, described eloquently by W K Hancock. It relied upon a simple justification—'the state at the service of the individual'. The upshot was an audacious Australian experiment to create an economic order based in the utopia of social fairness. The idea and practice were adopted by the new Commonwealth in the period before World War I. They were embraced by the Liberal Government of Alfred Deakin and the Labor Government of Andrew Fisher. This bipartisanship is the key to the longevity of the philosophy; it is fundamental to Australia's remarkable twentieth century unity; it is the essence of Australia's bid to civilise capitalism.

The label 'civilising capitalism' was applied by the historian Bede Nairn to the guiding impulse of the Labor Party. Yet the early Federation story reveals that this impulse was far from exclusive to Labor—it was the dominant instinct in the economic policy of the young Commonwealth. The creation of the Commonwealth off the back of the 1890s depression was vested in expectations for a better way of life. Federation meant free trade among the States and a common market for Australia. The six colonies surrendered defined powers to the centre including trade, commerce, immigration, defence, currency, corporations and pensions. The Commonwealth was given exclusive charge of customs and excise duties, two of the main sources of State taxation. It was the first step in the relentless evolution of Commonwealth financial dominance. Australian politics was defined by the demand for political rights and economic benefits. Such demands were levied upon the Commonwealth with mounting pressure as the decades progressed.

The Commonwealth's first response to these demands was to legislate a tariff—the opening step in Australia's choice for Protection over Free Trade. This was a symbolic contest between Alfred Deakin and George Reid, between Victoria and New South Wales, and between economic philosophies of control and freedom. It determined the nature of Australian liberalism. The decision in favour of protection was the most important in the crucial 1901–14 period of nation-building. Protection was founded in the dream of national progress, the lust for economic privilege and the politician's need to win votes. But the champions of protection always sanctified the idea by altruism rather than the reality of self-interest.

Reid wears a monocle labelled 'Free Trade', Deakin wears spectacles saying 'Protection'. The Australian Commonwealth, in the form of a woman, appeals to them, 'Ah, gentlemen, won't you, to please me, put aside these provincial glasses and use binoculars? With these you will be able to sweep the whole Australian field.'

The embrace of protection was tied to the rise of the trade union movement and the Labor Party. But the initial champions of the protectionist cause came from Australian Liberalism. The key prime minister of the nation-building era was Alfred Deakin, leader of the Victorian Liberal Protectionists, lawyer, journalist, intellectual and visionary. Deakin's acute insight was combined with a subtle ability to cloak self-interest with moral principle. He saw that the new Commonwealth Parliament would come to be dominated by the party contest and he was convinced that the Commonwealth would override the States who were 'legally free but financially bound to the chariot wheels of the central government'. Deakin said of the States 'the less populous will first succumb; those smitten by drought or similar misfortunes will follow; and, finally, even the greatest and most prosperous will, however reluctantly, be brought to heel'.

The first cause in which Deakin joined battle in the new Commonwealth was on behalf of protection, the core philosophy of Victorian liberalism. For Deakin protection was a faith: 'No nation ever claimed national greatness which relied upon primary industry alone.' But it was a tactic born of necessity: 'Under Protection Victoria has reared a number of industries which are still unable to sustain the shock of free competition. High duties must be retained on these products or they perish.' Deakin wanted to ensure that Melbourne, not Sydney, set the rules of the Australian union.

Deakin's opponent was the former New South Wales premier, and early prime ministerial rival, George Reid. Reid had an economic brain and the common touch, a rare mixture. An admirer of Adam Smith, he was a cartoonist's dream—short, obese, coarse, nursing an eyeglass, doomed by a high squeaky voice and blessed with a skill for self-parody. On visiting a Perth mental asylum, a friend told Reid that most of the staff were from Victoria and the patients from New South Wales. Reid shot back: 'I can explain that. Any sensible man would leave Victoria, but only a lunatic would leave New South Wales.'

The split between Victoria and New South Wales reflected their different economic models. Sydney was a major trading and commercial centre which developed with low tariffs. Reid attacked protection with arguments that would be used 80 years later: 'It is fraught with danger and corruption. It endangers the security of capital and imperils the position of labour. It increases the cost of subsistence.' Reid fought a losing battle since the bias in South Australia, Queensland and Tasmania was also towards protection. His aim was to restrict the tariff to a revenue tariff rather than an economic policy tool.

The result of the first election in 1901 was Protectionist 32, Free Trade 27 and Labor 14. It confirmed the prime ministership of Edmund Barton, a protectionist of convenience. No party had a majority over the other two combined. This loose and unstable structure was subsequently described by Deakin, resorting to a cricket metaphor, as 'three elevens in the field'. It took eight years for the instability to be rectified. In 1909 the inevitable restructure came. Once the protection issue was settled the dividing line in politics became class power and, at this point, the old enemies, protectionists and free-traders, merged to make the party contest one of Labor against non-Labor.

In the interim, the Trade and Customs Minister, Charles Cameron Kingston, took the tariff measures through the first parliament. Kingston told the House: 'If we are to keep our own men free, it will not be by free trade. They must be protected from competition.' Taking the opposite line, Reid said: 'Woollen garments have to pay duty of 20 per cent while silks and velvets which I do not call necessities of life pay 15 per cent ... and 20 per cent on tents in which thousands of men have to spend their lives. It seems to me that this is monstrous. I honestly believe that the Victorian industries would be ten times more self-reliant and vigorous if these artificial methods were destroyed.'

Both sides insisted they were defending the interests of the working man. The debate took nearly a year and Deakin, who did not speak, found them oppressive and shameless in their detail and repetition. The result

Both the Free Traders and the Protectionists used the interests of working people, such as these men and women at the Dunlop Rubber factory, to support their cause.

was a compromise, not much more than a revenue tariff—yet the direction was set. The second election in 1903 saw Deakin lead the Protectionists following Barton's retirement and the first head-to-head Deakin–Reid election contest. The result was indecisive: Protectionist 25, Free Trade 24, Labor 25, Independent one.

This parliament saw a testing of issues with successive governments led by Deakin, Labor under Chris Watson, Reid and then Deakin again, this time with support from the Labor party. The ALP was initially split on protection for reasons captured by Reid in his appeal not to put 'burdens on every rag which the wife and child wear and every morsel of food what they eat'. Yet Labor would gradually convert to the protection cause. Reid admitted that the trend of public opinion was against him on the tariff. The decisive event in the victory of protection was Deakin's second prime ministership which began on 6 July 1905. It was underwritten by a Liberal–Labor alliance and the trust between Deakin and Watson. Watson urged Deakin to take office and settle the protection issue. Deakin, an adroit manipulator, praised Watson for his 'soundness of judgment, clearness of argument and fairness to opponents'. Naturally.

The achievement of the second Deakin ministry and the Liberal–Labor alliance was a more comprehensive protection regime and the elevation of the idea of New Protection. New Protection meant that workers would share the benefits of protection with their employers—a division of the spoils. It tied tariff protection to an obligation upon employers to provide 'fair and reasonable' wages. Profits and wages would be harnessed to the protective system.

The New Protection concept had been introduced into Victoria just before Federation. Deakin's biographer, J A La Nauze, said its inventor was almost certainly the hat manufacturer Samuel Mauger, a member of the first Commonwealth Parliament. The term began to appear in *The Age* in 1899 and it was exploited by Deakin to widen the appeal of protection. It was taken up, eventually, by a range of forces—*The Age*, industrialists, trade unions and Christian moralists. As an idea, New Protection had two ultimate consequences: it sealed the Labor Party's commitment to protection and it fatally undermined Reid's free-trade cause. Deakin presented New Protection in epic terms—as a means to achieve 'justice between class and class'. Reid's biographer, W G McMinn, described the forces eroding Reid's position: 'Labor was more impressed with the higher wages fixed by wage boards for Victoria's protected industries than with the lower unemployment rate in New South Wales.'

The key instance to give effect to New Protection was the move to protect from threat the Australian manufacturer of harvester machines, H V McKay, who employed 3000 workers based at Ballarat and Melbourne. At Federation 94 per cent of exports came from primary produce, overwhelmingly wool and wheat. The Sunshine Stripper Harvester, McKay's invention, represented a technological leap into mechanisation of the wheat harvest. But McKay's sales were threatened by the giant International Harvester company of America.

McKay was a master of political lobbying, the skill that grew hand in glove with protection. He went to the top of government to demand a more protective tariff—beating a path which Australian businessmen would follow for a century. The result was never in doubt. Deakin said of harvesters: 'They are the invention of Australian brains, the work is carried out by Australian workmen and they are doing credit to Australia wherever they are employed ... The endeavour is to protect an Australian industry against a great monopoly.'

The government decided on higher tariffs to protect the industry. But Liberal and Labor didn't merely deliver a bonus to McKay, the manufacturer. They wanted the benefits shared with the workers. Deakin stated the problem: 'If we fix the duties, why should we also not fix the wages?' Yet the constitutional power over wages did not exist. The solution, finally

This advertisement for the Sunshine Harvester appeared in the Lone Hand *in 1908.*

adopted at Labor's suggestion, was an excise duty, the equivalent of the tariff, on locally made machines, to be waived when the manufacturer paid fair and reasonable wages. That is, virtuous employers would be exempt from excise. The legislation, introduced in 1906, was a classic early twentieth century piece of social engineering.

A great Australian experiment had begun. The initial conception was a coupling between Protection and Arbitration—the two great ideas of Australia's early economic policy. Protection was faith in nation-building behind the tariff wall; Arbitration was the mechanism to redistribute the profits of protection within the community.

The Commonwealth *Conciliation and Arbitration Act* had been passed in 1904 during the second parliament. It was the greatest monument to Australian egalitarianism. The initial bill had been introduced by Deakin in an extraordinary speech: 'This bill marks in my opinion the beginning of a new phase of civilisation. It begins the establishment of the People's Peace ... which will comprehend necessarily as great a transformation in the features of industrial society as the creation of the King's Peace brought about in civil society.'

Deakin, in fact, was far less committed to the bill than Labor was. It testified to the reality of the Liberal–Labor alliance, the emerging Australian ideal of a judicial officer to regulate and limit class conflict and the ethos of the fair go. Arbitration was part of Labor's first federal platform in 1901. But the bill was secured only after a series of governments rose and fell. Watson's government—the first federal ALP ministry—fell when it failed to secure a 'preference for trade unionists' provision. The final bill was a compromise and was passed under Reid's administration. It provided for conciliation between unions and employers and, if necessary, compulsory arbitration, through a new court which would determine 'right' in industrial disputes.

There are two conflicting interpretations of arbitration: that it was designed to weaken the full realisation of working class power before it became too strong or that it was a great victory of the labour movement. On balance, both views are wrong. Arbitration is better seen as a practical yet utopian bid to manage competing class interests. Its spirit was to deny duplication in Australia of the old world's class rigidities and to prevent the entrenchment of capital–labour divisions across the towns and cities. The solution was political—the creation by politicians of new tribunals, rules and regulations. Arbitration was an heroic effort to engineer a system of social and economic fairness.

Its origins lay in the depression and class conflict of the 1890s. Much of the impetus for arbitration came from middle class liberals supported by trade unions and the Labor Party. The employers were more suspicious and often hostile. The key to the establishment of arbitration is that this 1890s spark for reform coincided with the final flowering of Victorian Liberalism—before the rise of the Labor Party forced the realignment of the parties into their modern structure.

Deakin's master stroke was to offer the inaugural presidency of the Arbitration Court to Henry Bournes Higgins. It was Higgins who presided over the H V McKay case and the effort to establish New Protection. Higgins was a middle class lawyer, radical and friend of the Labor Party. He had served in two parliaments with Deakin and had attended Deakin's wedding.

At the 1897 Constitutional Convention Higgins and Charles Cameron Kingston drove a successful campaign to include in the Constitution a federal power of conciliation and arbitration. Higgins later opposed the referendum on the Constitution, complaining it was too conservative a document. He won election to the Commonwealth Parliament as a friend of Labor, and Higgins, although not an ALP member, was Attorney General in Watson's first Labor Government. His biographer, John Rickard, wrote: 'It was as though the working class was being officially received into the corridors of power with Higgins as its guide.' A man of fierce independence, Higgins was ill-suited to party politics. He saw the

It was for this group of H V McKay workers that the great Australian arbitration experiment began with the Harvester judgment.

prospects for a middle class radical were limited at best. Higgins knew he was made for the new court and Deakin knew Higgins would adjudicate for the progressive forces. He described Higgins as a man of 'strong passions, strong prejudices and towering ambition'. On the eve of going to the court Higgins wrote Watson that he had voted the entire Labor ticket at the 1906 election.

Higgins's first case as President was the Harvester judgment. Of the applications made to him Higgins chose that of McKay as the test case. His career on the bench began by trying to define what was a 'fair and reasonable' wage within the terms of the Deakin–Watson Act. He would enrage McKay.

In this case Higgins put the idea of a civilised community before the market. He decided a fair wage would be based upon the needs 'of the average employee regarded as a human being living in a civilised community'. Higgins solicited moving evidence from the working men's wives. He sought to assess the 'normal needs of the average employee' who was expected to marry and raise a family. He took account of such needs, including allowance for light, clothes, boots, furniture, life insurance, union pay, books, newspapers, alcohol, tobacco, sickness, transport fares and others. Higgins was influenced by Pope Leo XIII's encyclical, *Rerum Novarum*, which endorsed wage justice. He found that McKay's 36 shillings a week was insufficient to pay for the necessities of life and that the minimum wage should be 42 shillings a week. Higgins's precise objection was to McKay's reliance upon the market: 'He in many cases pays no more to the workmen than the price at which they can be got.'

In his judgment Higgins declared the minimum wage to be 'sacrosanct'. It would be secured by law and employers would be unable to destroy it. The minimum would be based on the needs of the working man and not on the economic law of demand and supply. A fundamental principle of Australian life was being enunciated. McKay appealed to the High Court and won 3–2. The excise device was deemed to be unconstitutional. McKay had won the immediate battle—but Higgins would win the war.

Deakin was not surprised by the decision, since the constitutional valid-ity of the excise device had long been in question. He stressed that the government was pledged to New Protection anyway; only the means of implementation was at issue. But Deakin and the Labor Party were unable to agree upon a strategy. Ultimately Higgins resolved the dilemma. He stuck by the principle of New Protection even though the excise device did not survive. Higgins adhered to the basic wage in his decisions and helped to entrench the concept during his long 1907–21 era as President. As John Rickard says, the Harvester principle remained the rock upon which Higgins built his court: 'In subsequent cases he made even clearer the lengths to which he would go to ensure the immutability of the basic wage. The profits (or lack of them) made by an individual employer were not a relevant consideration; and although the Court might take into account the profits of which an industry was capable, this could only affect margins and not the basic wage itself.'

Higgins helped to tie the Labor Party to the Court. He was a strong supporter of unionism and the dignity of physical labour. Reviewing the history, Bob Hawke concludes: 'The Harvester judgment and Higgins are foundationally important. The philosophy was so right and so in tune with the Australian ethos that it spread, and not just through the federal juris-diction—it became embraced by the various state jurisdictions. I think it is impossible to overstate the significance of both the judgment and its author, Henry Bournes Higgins.'

The idealism and rigidity of the Higgins position were revealed in a 1909 case involving BHP and a bitter conflict at the Broken Hill mine. Higgins went to Broken Hill, criticised the directors and found in favour of the union. He said: 'I face the possibility of the mine remaining closed, with all its grave consequences; but the fate of Australia is not dependent upon the fate of any one mine, or on any one company; and if it is a calamity that this historic mine should close down, it would still be a greater calamity that men should be underfed.' BHP later went to the High Court and got some of the judgment set aside. Eighty years later the pro-market reformers of the H R Nicholls Society would revive this BHP case to discredit Higgins as a judge prepared to put the principle of wage justice before the job itself.

In the early years of the Commonwealth, Protection and Arbitration grew together in a mutual dependency. It was the third parliament after the December 1906 election that saw a further consolidation of protection. For Deakin protection was not mainly an economic device, but a philosophy for nation-building. In his book on nationalism Robert Birrell quotes Deakin's assertion that Australians 'should not all remain hewers of wood, drawers of water, shearers of wool and growers of wheat. We can find within ourselves that multiplication of employments which is the making of a modern nation'.

George Reid made a massive effort at the 1906 poll. He campaigned on 'stalking the socialist tiger' and limiting future rises in protection. Reid prepared the ground for a merger of the Free Trade and Protectionist parties. He saw that once the tariff issue was settled the real issue of politics—Labor against non-Labor—would assert itself. At this poll Deakin campaigned to save the Liberal Protectionists as the party of the centre. But it was a doomed polity. Deakin knew that a fusion of non-Labor parties was coming. He accepted it; he prepared for it; yet he dreaded it. Deakin sympathised with Labor, with whom he had co-operated. He regarded many of the anti-socialist Free-Traders as his enemy and Reid as his arch-enemy. In terms of votes at the 1906 election Reid outpolled Deakin two to one in the nation.

The election's paradox is that it saw the survival of Deakin's Liberal Government backed by its alliance with the Labor Party. Deakin's disgust for Labor's organisational wing did not extent to declining Labor's support for his minority prime ministership. Yet the realignment of the parties was now clear: Deakin Protectionists 17, Labor 26, Reid's anti-socialists 32. There were two great consequences from this result. First, there was a Deakin–Labor majority to legislate a stronger general tariff and, in this sense, the election was a pro-protection vote. Second, the Deakinite centre was being destroyed. The system was starting to polarise between Labor and anti-Labor. The Labor Party was taking votes from Deakin's Liberals. The rise of a class-based party system was irresistible.

Deakin understood the epic nature of the rise of Labor. As early as

1901, writing his anonymous column for the London *Morning Post*, he said: 'The Labor Party dominates Australian politics. It comprises only one class of those who live by their labour ... Their platform is selfish and their discipline is admirable. They constitute a caste in politics and refuse to support representatives who have not been selected from among their own number.' In 1902 he wrote of the working class: 'They alone have a political creed which inspires a religious fervour in its devotees.' He admired and feared the union movement. During the 1906 campaign Deakin summarised his own dilemma: 'With the men of experience and training and knowledge who represent Labor interests in Parliament we have been able to work, but with the machine outside which dictates to them, we have not, and could not, find it possible.'

A somewhat disheartened Deakin was surprised though relieved to survive the election. Labor leader Watson wrote to him that 'you must, I think, see the tariff through' and urged that 'you should retain office at least until the tariff is dealt with'. Deakin visited London for the Imperial Conference in the first part of 1907. On the return journey neither the New Testament nor *War and Peace* could lift his spirits.

The new higher tariff schedules were introduced into the House by the Protectionist Customs Minister, Sir William Lyne, and were debated from October 1907 to May 1908. A beaten Reid offered a spirited parliamentary defence of free-trade principles. The tariff passed all stages and, with amendments, the result was a moderately higher protective tariff. A firm platform had been created upon which future governments would built higher rates.

Deakin, with Labor's assistance, had vanquished Reid in the major policy battle of the new Commonwealth. Protection would endure for another 80 years and become a defining element of Australia. Reid was a realist and he accepted the outcome. He made it clear that he accepted the principle of New Protection but warned of the pitfalls in its implementation. Reid's defeat was a turning point. It meant that liberalism would be defined by Deakin's faith in state power, not Reid's belief in the market and liberty. It would be three-quarters of a century before Reid's free trade sentiments would be vindicated. That vindication would come in the 1980s in language virtually the same as that deployed by Reid—that protection imposed a burden on consumers and distorted the economy.

In late 1907 the Scot from Queensland, Andrew Fisher, a former miner, white-haired, slow-thinking and reliable, became Labor leader. Deakin reflected: 'Fisher has been quite as courteous as Watson so far ... There is a gulf between the Labor Party and myself but a greater gulf between Reid and myself.'

The new tariff had been legislated. The principle of New Protection had been embraced though its implementation remained uncertain. Higgins was now busy at the start of his life's work on the Arbitration Court. Deakin and Labor had exploited each other for their political ends. This Liberal–Labor alliance had established the foundations of Australia's economic polity—Protection and Arbitration. But the mutual utility was now exhausted. Deakin would not countenance Labor's more radical plans for state power. On 5 November 1908 the Labor caucus decided that time was up. It was ready to liquidate the Deakin Government. Fisher conducted the parliamentary execution on 10 November in a cordial manner. Labor had asserted its independence from Deakin once and for all.

Within days the significance of the November 1908 commissioning of the Fisher Government became clear. With Labor in power and the tariff settled, it was time for the non-Labor parties to merge. Fisher's was a minority government backed by Deakin pending an anti-Labor unity, to which Deakin now turned his mind. Relations between Fisher and Deakin, in Deakin's words, were 'cordial' and a somewhat smug Deakin consoled himself that Fisher would survive only as long as Deakin allowed him to survive.

The final obstacle to serious negotiations on an anti-Labor fusion was removed when Reid announced in Yass a week after the fall of Deakin's government that he would resign the leadership of the Free Trade party. It was Deakin's final triumph over Reid. Reid and Deakin could never work together—a point Deakin made in his London *Morning Post* column of 16 November 1908. It was known as a universal fact. But in a subsequent article Deakin said of Reid that 'Sydney will miss him sadly since he represented, as no other man has since Sir Henry Parkes, the general policy and attitudes of its majority'. It was a rare remark since Deakin, determined to write the history in which he participated, usually buried Reid.

The astute and witty Reid was replaced by Joseph Cook, a small man devoid of humour but blessed with energy. Cook, a former coalminer and prominent Labor member of the New South Wales parliament, had defected to Reid's party in the 1890s over his refusal to bow to caucus supremacy. Negotiations on a fusion began between Deakin and Cook in January 1909.

The irony for Reid is that he could only achieve his long sought aim of uniting the anti-socialist forces by sacrificing his own career. Having championed the anti-Labor cause, Reid now had to retire to allow Deakin, who had long been allied with Labor, to spearhead the anti-Labor fusion. It was a double irony.

On 12 February 1909 Deakin wrote to Cook saying that a majority of members to whom he had spoken 'think a future understanding between us desirable'. His biographer, J A La Nauze, quotes Deakin's revealing notes from this period: 'I am being faced with a crisis in my choice . . . An opportunity offers of becoming a third time prime minister with a strong party likely to be very much stronger after the next election . . . On the other hand so far as my personal wishes and aims are concerned I would infinitely prefer not to take office with the colleagues and supporters with whom I should have to work in any coalition.'

Deakin was convincing himself that he had a higher national responsibility to join with his old enemies in a fusion. Yet he seriously misjudged the extent to which he would be condemned as a hypocrite merely seeking to reclaim office.

In these notes Deakin wrote an apologia for his future actions: 'I would wish to leave at the end of the next session [1909] but for my obligation to face the special rush of great problems in 1910–12 . . . I have in a general way a better knowledge than most of those available of all the principal issues.' Deakin was starting to think he was indispensable. The hostility of *The Age* to his plans was a worry. Deakin was infuriated by the anti-fusion *Age* editorialising that overtures were being made to Deakin and declaring that 'men do not offer bribes to those they consider incorruptible'. But the political logic was overwhelming—half Deakin's party was so terrified of facing Labor candidates at the next election that they wanted a fusion to strengthen their survival prospects. As for the leadership of a merger party, both sides knew that Cook had to defer to Deakin's stature and experience.

In May 1909 John Forrest, explorer, first premier of Western Australia, and an anti-socialist who controlled his own group within the Commonwealth Parliament, brokered the talks between Deakin and Cook to secure a deal. On 18 May Deakin wrote what he called a policy ultimatum— his terms for fusion. Deakin rationalised that he was being firm, but his ultimatum was mild. Deakin and Cook met on 24 May with their representatives. It took only a few hours to reach agreement. The Liberals, conservatives, anti-socialists and old free-traders were to combine.

La Nauze recounted the events when Deakin went to report to his Liberal–Protectionist caucus. These were mostly desperate politicians unconcerned at 'the passing of a tradition which had its roots in the aspirations of the gold years'. Victorian Liberalism was being buried;

devoured by greater forces. Deakin proposed to withdraw support from the Fisher ALP Government and replace that government with the newly fused coalition. Sir William 'Big Bill' Lyne, former premier of New South Wales, protectionist diehard and member of Barton's original cabinet, rose in anger saying that to join Cook would be 'a piece of political treachery unequalled in the history of the southern world'. The vote was 11–6 for Deakin to destroy Fisher's government. Deakin briefed the party room on Cook's acceptance of a Liberal program—the tariff, New Protection, defence and federal finance. Lyne again complained and they adjourned till the next morning. The dawn did not abate the rage. Lyne now branded Deakin a 'traitor' and walked out. Deakin told the party that fusion was 'a last resort' and that it 'will not destroy the party but help it'. He asked for a vote. Eleven raised their hands. It was the death sentence for Deakin's old party—but its philosophy would endure in the fusion.

That afternoon before the opening of Parliament all the anti-Labor forces gathered except Deakin. Without dissent and with Cook's support Deakin was elected leader. He then joined the group. It was agreed to use the term 'Deakin–Cook ministry'. It was, in fact, the creation of a new Liberal Party.

When the House met on the afternoon of 27 May 1909 Deakin was master again of his domain. He had replaced Cook as Opposition leader and he had the numbers. *The Age* described his entrance: 'The galleries were full ... Mr Deakin strolled into the chamber at 2.30 pm with an easy self-confidence that others at least did not feel.' As Deakin rose to speak, Lyne roared: 'Judas! Judas! Judas!' The motion to adjourn the debate was a de facto 'no confidence' motion in Fisher's government. Debate on the motion varied between nasty and savage. Lyne spoke first, but then Labor, facing a new and bigger party about to depose it, went for the jugular. It had within its ranks the maestro for this moment. Billy Hughes sought to discredit Deakin and his new political creation. This was a speech of invective, the most famous in the history of the parliament, heavy with prospective irony given Hughes's future career.

'A national policy and every reactionary in the Commonwealth is massed behind it,' Hughes began. 'What a career his has been. In his hands, at various times, have rested the banners of every party in this country. He has proclaimed them all, he has held them all, he has betrayed them all ... The great vested interests needed a leader to protect them; and they have found one ready to their hand. He has persuaded the reactionaries, for the time being, to cover their vulpine faces with the wool of sheep.' Hughes then moved to his conclusion: 'I heard from this side of the House some mention of Judas. I do not agree with that; it is not fair—

to Judas, for whom there is this to be said, that he did not gag the man whom he betrayed nor did he fail to hang himself afterwards.'

On 1 June 1909 Deakin was sworn in as prime minister for a third time. From this day the structure of Labor and non-Labor or Liberal has defined the party boundary. At the 1910 election Deakin's new party, called the Liberal Party, was defeated by Labor: Fisher's vindication. It was the first majority national government.

Deakin's motives for the fusion haunted him for the rest of his life. Yet he acted from political logic—a logic driven by grassroots organisation and parliamentary reality. Deakin was the only leader capable of achieving a successful fusion and, in so doing, he established a new non-Labor compact under the name Liberal Party although it was not until the arrival of R G Menzies that this name became permanent.

The terms of the fusion were important. The new Liberal Party was protectionist, not free-trade. Its values were those of Deakin not Reid. It looked to state power not individual entrepreneurship.

So the defining ambivalence of Australian politics was established. Liberal and Labor both believed in the role of state power to advance individual interests. They had collaborated jointly in the architecture of the Protection–Arbitration economic polity. Yet, having created the system, these sides split asunder in 1909 and become arch-rivals in a new Labor versus Liberal party contest. That contest would be about the terms and conditions of the Australian Settlement, not the Settlement itself—not, at least, for three-quarters of a century.

The Fisher Government advanced state power and nation-building with despatch. It created the Commonwealth Bank, promoted welfare payments and strengthened conciliation and arbitration. The rise of national unions and the spread of disputes across State boundaries created fresh avenues for workers to resort to the federal court and H B Higgins. Higgins boasted about the influence of his court and was conscious of its role as a social experiment.

Taking a long view, the paradox of Australian politics is that a party structure based on class did not result in a permanently divided society. One reason is that, just as the party structure intensified class division, so the Australian Settlement was designed to reconcile class conflict. It worked but only for a while and at a price.

The Great War shattered Australia's unity, confidence and idealism. In a sense, the Land of the Fair Go never recovered. The call to revolution arose during the war. The Bolsheviks seized power in Russia and the idea of the workers' revolution gained impetus in industrial societies. Australia was split by class and religion.

The Labor Party was transformed by the Great War. It lost its moderate wing under W M Hughes, along with much of its parliamentary talent. (Hughes left to become the Nationalist Party prime minister.) Within Labor the party organisation and trade unions were radicalised and they tightened their hold on the parliamentary wing. At the 1921 National Conference the ALP adopted, in its platform, 'the socialisation of industry, production, distribution and exchange'. The age of nationalisation had arrived. It is significant that even more radical proposals were defeated by Queensland premier E G Theodore, displaying what Graham Freudenberg called his 'Napoleonic dash and Fabian subtlety'. Theodore steered Labor away from the folly of direct action, yet Labor was no longer the tame party of the prewar Commonwealth period. A new battle had begun— between capitalism and socialism.

The 1920s were dominated by the non-Labor Nationalist governments of Stanley Melbourne Bruce and heavy overseas borrowing to finance growing urbanisation: electricity, water, sewerage, roads, bridges and tele-graph. As the 1920s advanced, industrial conflict deepened between Bruce and the trade unions.

Australia was moving towards the Great Depression. As the economy faltered, income declined and, as a consequence, industrial disputes rose in number and intensity. A competent leader but devoid of understanding of the Australian character, Bruce was influenced by British industrialists in concluding that drastic changes were needed to arbitration.

In May 1929 Bruce had convened in Canberra a conference of federal and State ministers. In the face of mounting strikes, he said that the arbitration system had failed Australia. Either the Federal Government or the States must accept full industrial responsibility: the premiers should refer their industrial powers to the Commonwealth or, failing this, the Commonwealth would vacate the field except for the shipping and waterside industries. Bruce said that it was 'unthinkable' to keep overlapping federal–State jurisdictions. His frustration was understandable yet the 'unthinkable' system has endured for a century. His proposal was a death wish. As Bruce expected, the premiers refused. Federal cabinet decided to withdraw from arbitration.

Bruce had two motives: to cut wages and to secure a simplified indus-trial system. His attack on arbitration was born in frustration but it reflected a fundamental truth—the arbitration system was unable to deliver wage cuts as the economy headed towards a crisis. Bruce was searching for a circuit-breaker for the upward spiral of protection, wages and inflation. In effect, it was the first political battle of the looming depression—forced by a non-Labor government trapped by its ideology and a declining economy. But the political battle was joined. The Labour Movement and its great defector Billy Hughes would combine to destroy Bruce.

Bruce introduced his arbitration bill in August 1929. ALP leader James Scullin and the Labor Party saw the wheels of history turning towards them. Labor had the best of the argument with Theodore now ascendant and nailing Bruce: 'One man is proposing to undo the work of a generation of men.' Theodore argued the merits of the arbitration system, that the States were ill-equipped to take over from the Commonwealth, that Bruce's resort was that of a desperate man. Bruce had misjudged both the parliament and the people, always fatal. Some government rebels spoke against the bill but the manipulator of these events was Hughes, who had blamed Bruce for his removal as prime minister in 1923. Hughes ran the numbers and controlled the plotting. Bruce refused to accept that he was in mortal danger. Having won power so easily, he failed to value it properly. In a speech of invective Hughes said: 'Whatever is wrong with the federal arbitration system was wrong in November last and when the parliament adjourned in March . . . He [Bruce] has been in this, as in other things, a dilettante . . . It is not only Arbitration that is on trial today, the right honourable gentleman is also on trial.'

Hughes sought to defeat the bill. His amendment was carried by one vote and the government fell. Journalist Warring Denning described the two antagonists: Bruce 'sat through the division in his lounging, imperturbable manner' while Hughes, after the vote, paused 'with a Sphinx-like smile, in the King's Hall, to light a cigarette in a slow deliberate manner which told the discerning that he was very well pleased'.

Hughes hoped that the Governor-General would send for him. He had his cabinet list ready—and it included many ALP figures! But the dissolution was granted. Bruce went to the people and lost, doubly. His government was defeated and he became the only prime minister to lose his seat at an election. The poll on 12 October 1929 created a legend, part myth, part truth, that arbitration was Australia's most sacred political cow. Its bipartisan foundation was reinforced.

Labor had a big majority in the House of Representatives, but there had been no Senate election and it was in a 29–7 minority in the upper house. James Scullin, 53, became prime minister. The party was euphoric, but this victory was a chalice of triple poison.

The character of the Labor Government was determined by its prime minister and its Treasurer. Diligent and decent, Scullin was no match for the financial furnace he would confront. He had never previously held executive responsibility and was soon isolated in Canberra. He declined to live in the Lodge, and stayed with his wife at the Hotel Canberra as ordinary guests.

His Treasurer was E G 'Red Ted' Theodore, a man of passion and ability. Theodore had a financial brain, a business flair and moved easily from miner's shack to boardroom. Convinced of his own talent, Theodore was always able to excite enemies. Capable of drafting his own submissions and possessed of real insight, his career was engulfed in tragedy. He was forced to resign due to a corruption scandal at the worst possible time for the government's fortunes.

The Depression originated in forces remote from Australia. But Australia was vulnerable for two reasons. First, its main exports, wool and wheat, suffered severe price falls. Second, the economy in the late 1920s was more dependent than normal upon overseas capital, 70 per cent of which came here as a result of borrowing by public authorities. Yet Australia's vulnerability had a deeper dimension.

The system of enlightened state power which Australia had erected before the Great War to civilise capitalism was broken. Beneath the idealism of the 'fair go', Australia had constructed a system that misallocated resources, killed productivity and weakened private enterprise. The coupling of Protection and Arbitration had produced disastrous results a decade beyond the Great War. The system had been asked to carry too many vested interests and was now breaking down. The truth, so often denied, is that the Australian Settlement had failed even before the onset of the Great Depression. This is why the consequence of the Depression for Australia was so catastrophic in both its economic and its political aspects.

The evidence has been assembled by Australia's chief historian of the Depression, Boris Schedvin, and it is formidable. First, income per head was virtually the same in 1928–29 as it had been fifteen years earlier, before the Great War. The economy had fluctuated up and down but there was no real progress in living standards. Australia's momentum had stalled. Living standards had already become an issue before the Depression hit. This is why the people and the unions were so opposed to belt-tightening once the crunch came. It is why the political system succumbed, and it is one reason the Labor Party fell apart.

Second, protection had been shifting resources from one of the world's most efficient agricultural sectors to one of its weakest manufacturing sectors. This was the result of the high tariff. It retarded Australia's growth, productivity and exports. The Great War and the 1920s saw an intense policy of import substitution. Manufacturing grew and geared itself for the small domestic market—industrial metals, textiles, clothing, paper and chemicals leapt ahead. The expansion of textiles production was dramatic and textiles depended upon protection more than any other industry. In the 1921 tariff revision, according to Schedvin, 'rates of duty on many items were more than doubled'. At this stage British Preferential Tariff rates were 40 per cent higher than prewar and the general tariff rate had risen 70 per cent. Australia's industrialisation was desirable but it was built on a fractured foundation. For Schedvin, the 'prosperity of the mid-1920s was little more than skin deep'. By 1925 the textile industry was suffering a profit crisis, high unemployment and severe import competition.

Third, when Australian industry faced import competition it was burdened by a price inflexibility implanted by Arbitration. H B Higgins died on the eve of the Depression and never lived to see the ravages caused in part by his great experiment. Australia's wage system had been designed during an age of optimism and prosperity. It was unable to automatically adjust wage rates downwards to reflect falling world prices. That had a certain consequence—higher unemployment. In early 1930 a leading economist, Professor Edward Shann, wrote: 'Our policies of wage-fixation, tariff walls and bounties to bolster high costs have made Australian prices, loaded with indirect taxation, move in a direction that has diverged and is still diverging from the price levels of our competitors.'

Fourth, Australia had financed its social progress in the 1920s by overseas loans and government fixed-interest borrowing abroad. This distorted the balance of payments. By 1928–29 the ratio of exports needed to finance overseas payments was 28 per cent—and export revenue was about to collapse. The battle to avoid default on public interest borrowing became pivotal to Australia's Depression story.

In short, when the crunch came Australia was exposed. The edifice it had created in the name of progressive social thought had become a national liability.

Australia's response to the Depression was undermined by what Schedvin calls 'a dense layer of prejudice, personal conflict, doctrinal rigidity and antediluvian economies'. The Depression in the United States produced a hero—Franklin Delano Roosevelt. In Australia there were no heroes— just men overcome by events, dogmatists and ratbags. It is the darkest

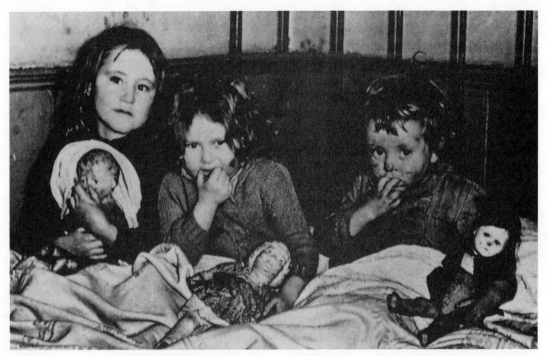

These Victorian children were unknowing victims of the Great Depression.

period of the Federation story: a time when Australians lost their way, failed to pull together and were betrayed by their leaders. The Depression was a watershed in political and economic life. It confirmed the exhaustion of one polity and sowed the seeds for a new polity. From its failure, eventually, came a better understanding of how to civilise capitalism.

The causes of the Depression were external to Australia. The Wall Street crash of October 1929 came a fortnight after Scullin's win. It hit an economy already slowing and accentuated the contraction. But the US banking crisis during 1930–33, which saw a substantial loss of confidence in the financial system, deepened the downturn. Between 1929 and 1932 world industrial production fell by one-third and world trade in manufactures by two-fifths. Australia was one of the most severely affected nations. A five year unemployment average for 1930–34 shows Australia's rate at 23.4 per cent, exceeded only by Germany among major countries. Australia's unemployment reached a peak of 28 per cent in 1932.

During the Depression in Australia there were three main economic positions. The first, the financial orthodoxy, was the dogma of Australia's Establishment and the ultimate victor. Its champions were the Commonwealth Bank represented by its chairman, Sir Robert Gibson; the representative of the Bank of England, Sir Otto Niemeyer; the private banks; and the non-Labor parties who controlled the Senate. They called for immediate and deep cuts in government spending, balanced budgets and a firm line against inflation—policies that would inflict massive hardship on the working community. Gibson reflected the orthodoxy which originated in the bank crashes of the 1890s and held that the private banks had the right to determine their own policies and that increased lending and credit expansion must be avoided since it would create runaway inflation.

Gibson was a flawed figure to hold the central bank powers then residing within the Commonwealth Bank. He misread the financial situation and believed he had a duty to override the elected government. Gibson was utterly dedicated to the so-called 'sound money' principles that would be rendered obsolete by the Depression. Equipped with an iron will and a domineering personality, Gibson defied the cabinet in the name of the national interest. He operated on the assumption that the Scullin Government had no real legitimacy and was likely to corrupt the currency. He relied upon the powers of the bank and had two allies—the non-Labor Senate and the irresponsible Labor left. Gibson's thinking would be swept away in the post-Depression revolution.

The moderate Labor position was articulated by Theodore and supported by Scullin, particularly after Theodore's return to the cabinet. This approach sought to maintain spending levels, provide a moderate stimulus to help the unemployed and the wheat industry, and expand central bank credit. It had increasing support from a small number of prominent economists. But Theodore had too many enemies: the Commonwealth Bank, the private banks, the Senate and Jack Lang.

The radical position was best represented and dominated by Lang, New South Wales premier and Australia's greatest populist. Paul Keating said of Lang: 'I learnt some things from him about political energy. If you're going to be in the business of throwing thunderbolts, you may as well try to look as much like Zeus as you can. He knew all about that.'

Lang was a Labor hero, a cunning manipulator and a great wrecker. He advocated default on external debt payments to enable a diversion of funds to the unemployed. His policy and his tactics were fundamental in destroying the Scullin Government as well as inciting his own dismissal as premier. Lang trusted nobody and most of all distrusted 'money power'. For Lang there were two classes: bondholders and slaves of bondholders.

The Scullin Government's initial response to the downturn was predictable—a resort to greater protection. From April 1930 for a year, Labor raised tariffs. It was the isolationist instinct to save profits and jobs.

The Scullin tariff was a major step in the Fortress Australia edifice. When combined with devaluation it knocked out much import competition. Yet tariffs were not the answer. Events were heading in a different direction.

For the bankers there was one issue: could Australia stay solvent? The Bank of England sent senior official Sir Otto Niemeyer to assess Australia's credit strength. At a major meeting of Commonwealth and State ministers in August 1930 Niemeyer outlined his austerity strategy: 'Australia has a maximum period of two years in which to put her house straight. I assume that everybody in this room is in agreement that costs must come down.' Niemeyer fingered Australia's dilemma: 'Australian prices are higher than British prices and have not been adjusted to the world level. [But] Australian unemployment even now is substantially greater than Great Britain's.' The conclusion was that Australia's unemployment level must rise higher.

The upshot was the Melbourne Agreement—a plan to cut production costs until primary produce exporters regained their markets and revenue. The meeting agreed to balance budgets in 1930–31 but never explained how this massive task of cutting programs and wages (which would mean electoral suicide for governments) would be achieved. The premiers didn't take the agreement seriously. They wanted merely to impress Niemeyer, the Bank of England and the London market. The Agreement would split the ALP and destroy the Scullin Government. Many Labor men never forgave Scullin for letting Niemeyer come to Australia. The agreement gave Lang the issue he wanted.

In the second half of 1930 both Scullin and Theodore were missing—Scullin was in London and Theodore had had to resign over the Mungana Mines scandal. James Fenton, utterly out of his depth, was acting PM and the former Tasmanian premier Joe Lyons was acting Treasurer. Their task was to implement the Melbourne Agreement, but the radicals in the ALP were determined to destroy it. Lang's victory in the New South Wales election on a record 12 per cent swing was the clinching event. Lang had carried all before him in a denunciation of Niemeyer, the London bond-holders and the Melbourne Agreement. The radicals had the final confidence they needed to confront the ministry and reject its policy.

The caucus met in late October 1930 over several days. The ALP Left came to Canberra to repudiate the financial orthodoxy. Fenton and Lyons failed to negotiate a compromise and the caucus passed two motions: a major credit expansion at a low interest rate, and deferment of a debt conversion. The former committed the government to a policy the Commonwealth Bank would never implement and the latter raised the issue of debt repudiation, on which Lyons fought the caucus and then left the ALP.

At the caucus meeting Lyons shouted to his colleagues: 'It is default. I tell you I will not be a party to it. I will go out of public life first.' Denning describes his departure from Canberra on the train with Defence Minister Albert Green, who followed him calling out, 'for God's sake, Joe, don't do it', as a future non-Labor prime minister was carried into the night.

The Labor Party was splitting into three groups: the Lyons faction that would defect to the non-Labor side; the radicals led by Jack 'Stabber' Beasley, a group centred mainly on New South Wales and Lang and that would form a separate Labor Party and destroy the Scullin Government on the floor of parliament; and the Scullin ministry, reinforced by Theodore's recall after Scullin's return from London.

A contemptuous Niemeyer, nostalgic for Threadneedle Street, wrote off Australia: 'The personnel all round—political, administrative and banking—is, with rare exceptions, lamentable, a circumstance which is accentuated by the marooning of the Commonwealth Government and administration on a sheep-run 200 miles from anywhere. The political leaders are listless and fragmented and quite incapable of giving a lead.' There has rarely been a better insight into the British view of Australia.

It is ironic that two of Australia's vital reponses to the Depression came from outside politics—from the Arbitration Court and the banks. In January 1931 the Arbitration Court ordered that the basic wage in terms of the Harvester equivalent be cut by 10 per cent for a twelve month period. The wage reduction was depicted as a last resort but necessary to help restore profits to the private sector. The government was appalled. It applied to have the order delayed but was dismissed by a Court more resolute than the government in confronting reality. The message was that arbitration was capable of a flexibility that many had previously misjudged.

The contribution from the banks was a devaluation but this result was attributable to the boss of the Bank of New South Wales, A C Davidson, who carried the other banks with him. There was no national policy and no leadership. But the devaluation was substantial and an important factor in promoting domestic recovery.

However, by early 1931 the final stage was approaching.

In February Theodore met the premiers to finalise a comprehensive plan. He advocated a break from traditional economic thinking and the adoption of a new and expansionary monetary policy to stimulate production and attack unemployment. It was the policy that Theodore had championed from the backbench and which Fenton and Lyons had rejected. The non-Labor premiers showed neither understanding nor interest. At this point Lang grabbed centre stage.

He stole the initiative from Theodore and shocked the meeting by calling for a suspension of external interest repayments to 'British bondholders' and a cut in internal interest rates. The New South Wales Government, he said, was pledged to the Lang Plan. It was a stunning announcement and it was Lang flying solo. His plan had been approved neither by the New South Wales cabinet nor by the caucus. It was bold but, as Schedvin said, 'it could not be carried through without at the same time bringing the collapse of the financial system of the State, and perhaps the Commonwealth'. This was tribal recklessness of an extreme kind.

Graham Freudenberg wrote: 'It was marginal to Australia's problems. Yet the Lang Plan became an article of faith for thousands and a symbol of hope for millions. It could never have saved Australia. It almost destroyed the Labor Party.'

The aim was to ruin Theodore's proposal and his career. Lang's lust for power would now encompass the destruction of the Scullin Government. In their survey of the Depression, the Australian economists E G Shann and Douglas Copland concluded: 'If the Commonwealth Government's plan [Theodore's plan] had been supported by the whole Labor Movement and the State Labour Government, its success would have been assured.' This is the critical conclusion. They argue that with such unity behind a sound policy the Labor Government would have been in a position to prevail over both the Commonwealth Bank and the Senate. An ambitious judgment.

The conference rejected Lang's plan and asked Theodore to approach the Commonwealth Bank on his proposals. But with the ALP falling apart Scullin and Theodore were doomed. Sir Robert Gibson had no intention of financing Theodore's scheme.

The Scullin–Theodore Government had been doubly repudiated—from within its own party and by its central bank. Labor was in its death throes. The New South Wales party embraced the Lang Plan. Beasley announced the formation of the Lang Labor Party and broke from the caucus with a group of six. Freudenberg recounts Ben Chifley's silent vow: 'I decided there and then to fight Lang until I had seen him out of the Labor Movement.' It was on John Curtin's motion in March 1931 that the ALP Federal Conference expelled the New South Wales branch and created a replacement Federal Labor Party in New South Wales.

With fear of a partial default by Australia in London, Scullin pressed ahead with the Theodore Plan, despite the opposition of the Senate and Commonwealth Bank. The formal collapse of government policy came in mid-April when the Senate rejected the bills. Gibson delivered an ultimatum to the government—the Bank would shortly refuse finance for government deficits. In a furious reply Theodore referred to 'an attempt on the part of the Bank to arrogate to itself a supremacy over the Government in the determination of the financial policy of the Commonwealth, a supremacy which I am sure, was never contemplated by the framers of the Australian Constitution and has never been sanctioned by the Australian people.'

The initiative now passed to the Bank and the premiers. At a May 1931 Melbourne meeting the Premiers' Plan was endorsed: spending cuts of 20 per cent, tax rises, interest rate cuts. It was the agenda dictated by Gibson, the trading banks, the Senate and the non-Labor premiers. Scullin, devoid of any other option, fought to make his own capitulation a success.

The Premiers' Plan was a victory for Gibson over Theodore. Gibson had retained a policy of deflation to keep Australia solvent, as he saw it. The prevention of external default was the driving force of the Premier's Plan, as it had been a major preoccupation since the onset of the Depression. Gibson's great ally had been the Senate, which rejected Theodore's policy. It acted as the political arm of the bank. But Gibson's success depended upon the disintegration of the Labor Party, which assisted the government's opponents. The Premier's Plan was seen as responsible and it helped confidence but, apart from the interest rate cuts, it must have hindered recovery.

The Lang forces soon destroyed the Scullin Government and forced an election. The non-Labor side under Joe Lyons returned to office for another decade. But Lang didn't last long, being sacked by the New South Wales Governor for refusing to discharge state debts and persisting in a course of action deemed to be illegal. Australia's unemployment was still just under 10 per cent when World War II broke out.

The Depression marked a triple failure. First, Australia's post-Federation model of enlightened state power had been damaged and its inadequacies exposed. Boris Schedvin said: 'As far as institutions were concerned, say the Commonwealth Bank, the Arbitration system, the protective system of tariffs, all of these were unable to respond very effectively.'

Second, the Labor Government had experienced its worst post-Federation failure. Unemployment had reached nearly 30 per cent, yet Labor infighting had prevented the implementation of a sound recovery strategy.

Third, the financial orthodoxy represented by Sir Robert Gibson and the banks involved a doctrinaire deflation that was no solution and was, in many ways, an impediment. This would constitute an indisputable case for future bank reform.

The Depression left many legacies. The overarching legacy was that new methods and policies were needed. If the story of the 1930s was

Depression and slow recovery, the story of the 1940s was that of war and a spectacular revival of the Australian model of state intervention.

There was a powerful response to each of the three failures of the Depression. First, Keynesian economics would emerge to transform the practice and politics of state intervention. Second, the next Labor Government, haunted by the Depression, would embrace a full employment strategy as fundamental to Australian polity. Third, bank reform would be tackled, at first moderately, and then as part of Australia's greatest showdown between capitalism and socialism.

For John Curtin and Ben Chifley the Depression was the defining experience of their careers. In his biography of Chifley, Fin Crisp records a moving testament offered by Chifley: 'The Depression left a bitterness in my heart that time cannot eradicate. I saw hundreds of men queued up outside the Lithgow small arms factory gate, all after one job. I cannot forget how miserable those hundreds of men must have felt when they went back each night to their families after tramping the streets all day in search of work.'

Curtin and Chifley would succeed where Scullin and Theodore had failed. They would salvage Labor's reputation and resurrect Australia's and Labor's mission to find the means of civilising capitalism.

During World War II Prime Minister Curtin and Treasurer Chifley had two objectives: to win the war and to plan the peace. The best thing about the Labor Party of the 1940s was Curtin and Chifley, two unusual talents and achievers. Before he was tempered by experience, the younger Curtin had believed in revolution and international socialism. Chifley was an Irish-Catholic train driver and unionist from Bathurst. Curtin was Labor's most respected leader and Chifley its most loved. Both men saw they had to avoid the mistakes of Hughes and Scullin: that meant keeping a united Labor Party and averting any repeat of the splits of the Great War and the Depression.

Curtin had a vision of postwar Australia, a 'second Britannia in the Antipodes'. Its ingredients were a new program of immigration from Britain, upholding White Australia, a strong industrial base, a more interventionist Federal Government and a program of postwar reconstruction. In late 1942 Chifley was given the Reconstruction ministry and appointed Dr H C 'Nugget' Coombs as director-general.

The ministerial burden Chifley carried in the 1940s was immense: Treasurer (1941–49), Minister for Post-War Reconstruction (1942–45) and, after Curtin's death, Prime Minister (1945–49). The war had broken the Depression legacy. The nation was mobilised, industrial and munitions production was expanded, women entered the work force in numbers and Federal Government controls and planning were developed in the wartime exigency. The creation of a postwar economic system was a vast enterprise but three elements stand out.

In 1942 Curtin and Chifley assumed exclusive income taxation powers for the Commonwealth by 'blackmailing' the States. The rationale was the war effort. They were backed by the High Court. Their long-range intent was to entrench the Commonwealth's financial dominance in the cause of Labor's programs. So the States were stripped of their substantive income tax powers. Some of the Federation architects would have been horrified; others such as Deakin would have expected it. Economic power was being centralised in the Commonwealth.

If there was one uniting philosophy behind the Post-War Reconstruction Ministry it was, in Coombs's words, 'the idea of full employment'. In 1944 Curtin announced the plan for a White Paper on Full Employment to outline the government's commitment to this goal.

The White Paper had to serve a variety of roles: to establish the priority of full employment; to ensure that the Depression would not recur; and to sketch the new framework to make these pledges credible. In his memoirs Coombs stresses that the paper's authors saw retention of the wartime full employment as a very difficult task: 'None of us, I think, would have believed that 30 years would pass before unemployment became again a serious concern in economic management.' The White Paper was an instrument and a symbol. It was a decisive break from the past when, in the twenty years from 1919 to 1939, unemployment had averaged about 10 per cent. It was also a compromise since the postwar reformers needed the support of the Treasury. Curtin's caution ultimately prevailed. Coombs recounts Curtin's final excisions of detail which he feared might alienate either the trade unions or the electorate—given that the people had just rejected the 1944 referendum to equip the Commonwealth with new economic powers.

The document began with a declaration: 'Full employment is a fundamental aim of the Commonwealth Government. Australian Governments will have to accept new responsibilities and to exercise new functions. Unemployment is an evil from the effects of which no class in the community and no State in the Commonwealth can hope to escape unless concerted action is taken.'

Reflecting the war experience and new economic theory, the paper said: 'The essential condition of full employment is that public expenditure should be high enough to stimulate spending to the point where the two together will provide a demand for the total production of which the economy is capable when it is fully employed.'

The third key element in the postwar system was the assumption upon which the White Paper was based—a new approach to economic management often labelled Keynesianism. Its intellectual architect was the British economist, J M Keynes, whose 1936 book quickly attracted an economic following in Australia. Coombs had the opportunity of dining with Keynes several times in a small restaurant in Clarges Street off Piccadilly. In his memoirs Coombs left no doubt about the centrality of Keynesian economics—he mentions it in the first sentence on the first page!

For all its generalities the White Paper symbolised an economic and political revolution for Australia. It was a fundamental departure. It meant that the government was proposing a newer, comprehensive form of economic intervention previously rejected. The government would robustly manipulate expenditure to generate demand at full employment. This was a dynamic view: it asserted that the economy overall should be managed to achieve defined social objectives. The new priority was demand and output rather than costs and prices. The government would operate in a counter-cyclical manner to keep employment at a permanently high level. It would be the zenith in Australia's quest to civilise capitalism.

Keynesian economics and the White Paper rejected the old economic theory that had prevailed for much of the Depression. It distilled the wisdom gained from both the Depression and World War II. Australia owed much to the remarkable generation of young public servants and economists who advised Curtin and Chifley—most of whom were retained by R G Menzies in some capacity. They were participants in an intellectual revolution that was international in scope.

Keynesianism was a natural fit for the Labor Party. In retrospect, the Theodore Plan could be interpreted as an impulse towards Keynesian economics. Fin Crisp insisted that Chifley was a 'Keynesian-of-the-first-hour'. Yet the central feature of the Keynesian revolution in Australia was its bipartisan nature. This was obscured to a certain extent before the 1949 election. But the Menzies Government post-1949 implemented and refined the Keynesian system. For 30 years unemployment would be under 3 per cent, a result the early 1940s generation hardly dared dream about. For the next generation and a half full employment became the faith of Australian politics—a triumph over the debilitating era of the 1920s and 1930s.

But Chifley was no God, just a politician who was a prisoner of his turbulent past. The postwar system was created not only by his successes but also by his failures.

Ben Chifley was a 'true believer'—not the phoney 'true believer' depicted in the 1990s media, but an authentic. He was an unusual mixture—a financial administrator who believed in the ALP platform. Chifley embodied in his career, politics and personal life the essence of laborism. He had become a railway man in a great railway town and proceeded quickly to driver's rank. When he was prime minister he admitted: 'I used to get a lot of pleasure at night with fourteen carriages behind me . . . I feel I have kept so close to engine driving that I could go back to it tomorrow.'

It was Chifley who used the phrase embraced by the party as the best summary of its aspirations: 'We have a great objective—the light on the hill—which we aim to reach by working for the betterment of mankind not only here but anywhere we may give a helping hand.' Fin Crisp said that 'Chifley's socialism was of the run-of-the-mill, loose, Australian trade union variety . . . His own temperament was essentially empirical, cautious, austere. He was for mastering particular issues, not for propounding socialist doctrines.' True, yet for Chifley the 'the light on the hill' was no abstraction; it was to be won only by political assertion. In 1947 Chifley embarked upon nationalisation of the private banks. It was the first and only attempt by the federal ALP to introduce socialism into Australia. It was possibly the most contentious economic policy decision taken by an Australian government—the ultimate effort to deploy state power for individual benefit.

In 1945 Chifley had avenged Scullin by a bank reform law which asserted two principles: the private banks were supervised by a central bank, and the central bank was responsible to the government. The structural problems that had afflicted Australian banking during the Depression were addressed to a certain extent.

But Chifley's real goal was enshrined in the ALP platform—bank nationalisation. In 1935 he represented Labor on the Royal Commission on the Banking System and in a minority report he argued for nationalisation. The origins of bank nationalisation lay in the High Court's upholding of the constitutional challenge to Labor's 1945 bank laws by the Melbourne City Council. Chifley felt immediately that the laws were now vulnerable to further challenge. It is likely that he exaggerated this danger. But Chifley would take no risks. Crisp recounts what happened next.

The cabinet met in Canberra on Friday 15 August 1947 and Chifley asked ministers to remain for a Saturday resumption. There were no cabinet documents. Chifley asked the Attorney General, Dr Evatt, to brief cabinet on the High Court's decision. Chifley immediately summed up. He said there were two choices: the government could either await a concerted attack by the private banks on the 1945 laws, or it could pre-empt the challenges by nationalising the banks. He was recommending nationalisation. Senate leader McKenna recalled that for a moment there was 'complete stunned shock' and then 'a good deal of jubilation'. All ministers supported nationalisation. It was an extraordinary outcome. Nobody opposed the decision or called for caution, delay, more examination, or even some cabinet papers on the issue. How was such a momentous decision taken so swiftly with so little assessment?

It was because of Chifley. He was not just prime minister and Treasurer but, to his colleagues, a model of competence and judgment. If Chifley was prepared to force nationalisation the party would not be found wanting. After the cabinet meeting there was a 43 word press release from Chifley: 'Cabinet today authorised the Attorney General Dr Evatt and myself to prepare legislation for submission to the Federal Parliamentary Labor Party for the nationalisation of banking other than State banks with proper protection for the shareholders, depositors, borrowers and staffs of private banks.'

Nothing more. No justification, no public relations campaign. It was a move of stubborn defiance. The impression was one of abrupt arrogance. Chifley embraced nationalisation because he was convinced that the private banks would not work within his 1945 laws. But his decision was flawed for three reasons. It was doubtful whether the High Court would find nationalisation to be constitutional; it was equally doubtful that Chifley could carry public opinion; and it was far from obvious that nationalisation was the only or best recourse for Labor in its attempts to devise effective central bank control. Chifley knew the risks. Fred Daly recalled him telling the caucus that 'we may well pay a very high price and some members may be defeated, even myself'.

The announcement reverberated around Australia like a thunderbolt. The Opposition leader, R G Menzies, said: 'It is a staggering statement. It's almost unbelievable. It sounds like a piece of petty pique for the defeat of the banking case in the High Court.' But Menzies saw the golden opportunity it presented him. He declared: 'Australians are now called to a great battle to defend their freedoms against dictatorship at home.'

The general manager of the Bank of New South Wales, T B Hesser, called it 'one of the hardest blows at liberty struck in our time'. The chairman of the Associated Banks, L J McConnan, said the aim was 'to ensure government supervision and control of financial affairs of every man and every woman'. The anti-bank nationalisation cause became a crusade carried by a coalition, both elite and grassroots, and including the federal coalition, non-Labor premiers, the banks, their employees, the business community, employer federations, chambers of commerce, farmer groups and most of the newspapers. The anti-Labor forces worked on two fronts: to defeat the move in the courts and at the polls.

The bill was introduced in the House by Chifley on 15 October 1947, with the prime minister starting his second reading speech at 8.36 pm and all galleries overflowing. The bill provided that all private banks be transferred to public ownership in the form of the Commonwealth Bank and that private banking would be prohibited. Existing bank employees were to be protected by provisions for retaining their employment, salaries and conditions of service. Chifley said: 'Australia is destined to see great developments in the coming years . . . Full public ownership of the banks will ensure control of banking in the public interest.'

Chifley, it turned out, would be sunk by two forces: the conservative bias of the Australian Constitution, and the middle-of-the-road common sense of the Australian people.

In his reply in the House, Menzies said that the key sections of the 1945 bank laws remained safe from challenge; that Chifley had no mandate for nationalisation, which should be put first to the people at election or referendum; that the profit motive was central to Australia's expansion; that Labor's blaming the banks for the Depression was misconceived; and that the consequences of monopoly banking would be dire for Australia. Menzies was hero to a new cause. He said: 'Let nobody suppose that these aspiring dictators will rest content with the destruction of the banks.'

Labor numbers in the Senate guaranteed the bill's passage and it became law. The issue went to the High Court. Labor's hope of winning was remote, a view that Evatt had held from the start. Garfield Barwick led for the banks and, in a move that was as inevitable as it was unwise, Evatt led for the government. On 11 August 1948 the court found 4–2 in favour of the banks. The prohibition of private banking was held to infringe the Constitution's s.92 guarantee of freedom of interstate trade. The High Court, in effect, had found that Labor's policy of nationalisation of industry was unconstitutional. The court was committed to the free enterprise economy and, according to its view, so was Australia. Menzies declared the result 'great news for every Australian who objects to tyranny'.

Just two days later Chifley announced an appeal to the Privy Council. Labor was asking a judicial authority based in London to overrule the

Australian High Court and permit socialism in Australia. The exercise was a monument to Labor's folly and Evatt's self-conceit. He lectured the Lords for 22 days and lost. The decision on 26 July 1949 was for the banks. The Privy Council appeal had kept the issue alive for another year, to the eve of the 1949 election. Chifley's problem was that he could prevail only by winning twice, in court and at the election.

In his policy speech Menzies pledged to repeal the law, but his overarching theme was the need to repudiate socialism. His main slogan was 'a vote for Labor is a vote for socialism', with bank nationalisation the prime exhibit. Menzies warned that the private banks were not safe if Labor was returned. He attacked what he called 'the myth of the moderate Ben Chifley'.

At the 1949 election Labor was defeated convincingly with a 74–47 coalition majority. Bank nationalisation was not the overriding issue but it was important. Evatt said: 'We lost the election on the banking bill.' Crisp said that bank nationalisation played 'the crucial role' because it galvanised the anti-Labor parties as rarely before, at a grassroots level, and guaranteed them hefty campaign coffers. The Menzies Government introduced a bill to provide for a new Commonwealth Bank board. It was a moderate measure which Labor fought to the end. When Labor secured the bill's defeat in the Senate, Menzies used it to secure the 1951 double dissolution election which was fought on communism and which delivered Menzies control of both federal houses.

Chifley was exposed, ultimately, as a true Labor man but out of touch with the Australian outlook and the strength of the private enterprise ethos. In 1949 people rejected petrol rationing, bank nationalisation and Labor's depiction of wartime controls as socialist virtues. The moral is that when Labor relied upon common sense it was successful but when it succumbed to ideology it was rejected.

Menzies saw the deeper significance of this issue for Australians: the link between nationalisation and their own private property rights. It is, in fact, the link between capitalism and liberty—a link Australian socialists underestimated. Many Australians saw a potential threat to their own life implicit in the creation of a government owned and controlled bank monopoly. While Australians wanted state power used for their benefit, they also knew the risks in its over-extension.

There had been a sense of Chifley fatalism about the nationalisation move. Labor had been outmanoeuvred hopelessly in the courts and on the hustings. There were three lessons: that Labor best governed by focusing on middle-of-the-road brands of government intervention; that the public valued the economic and moral benefits of free enterprise; and that the nationalisation issue was exploited by Menzies not to repudiate

THIS IS THE YEAR of CRISIS!

1949

THESE ARE THE ISSUES -

This election pamphlet brings home the economic issues that influenced the 1949 election.

government intervention and state power but to position himself as its most successful champion. This was Labor's real defeat.

It was impossible at the time to perceive the magnitude of the 1949 election as a turning point for Australia. However, it delivered the golden age of postwar prosperity to the Liberal Party. The Curtin and Chifley governments of the 1940s had prevailed in war and had created the postwar structure. These legacies, though, would be enjoyed by the Liberal Party and mobilised by the skills of R G Menzies. The 1949 poll was the 'make or break' election for Menzies. At this point he would either triumph or be dismissed as the biggest disappointment in Australian political history. Paul Keating said: 'We built the postwar structures and gave it to the Liberal Party, to Menzies.'

The sheer length of Menzies' 1949–66 rule and his seven election victories mean there are many Menzies—they encompass the earlier failed wartime leader, the anti-communist manipulator, the Queen's man, the free enterprise champion, the full employment specialist, the State Aid reformer, the university expansion architect, the colonial age nostalgic and the Vietnam commitment instigator. Menzies has been too big and long-lasting to make an integrated assessment an easy task. Most analysts prefer to offer one or another of the Menzies stereotypes.

There is another enduring contradiction in many accounts of the Menzian Age. Despite the orthodoxy that Australia prospered under Menzies there is a disposition to insist that this progress, somehow, someway, had virtually nothing to do with Menzies himself. It is almost as though the economic prosperity occurred in a different sphere from that occupied by the prime minister. Yet this same prime minister is typically depicted as utterly dominant within his government.

A feature of Menzies' 1949 victory was the arrival within Liberal ranks of ex-servicemen from World War II—a youthful generation, hardened in war and confident in peace. A total of 48 new Liberal and Country Party MPs were elected and 70 per cent were war veterans. Menzies' biographer, Allan Martin, says the average age of new Liberals was 43 and twelve were under 30 years. They were eager for political action, with deep ties to middle class aspirations.

Much of Menzies' success lay in the disintegration of the Labor Party after Chifley's death and Labor's near total failure to manage the domestic and foreign policy consequences of the Cold War. The Cold War was not just a battle abroad between communism and democracy but a battle at home—an issue on which Labor's loyalties and emotions were fractured. It is true that Menzies was highly skilled at exploiting Labor's divisons. It is also true that his own constructive policies have been underestimated in assessments of his government.

In his first broadcast to the nation as prime minister, Menzies said: 'I tell you that in the oldest and truest sense of the word we know that a Minister is a Servant. We are and must be the servants of all of you. I want to make it perfectly clear to everybody listening to me tonight that we shall esteem it our simple duty to do justice to all Australians, to cultivate good relations between employer and employee, to regard the great Trade Unions as our co-operators in the production of industrial justice, to make ordinary men and women feel that Government is their friend and not their oppressor.'

Menzies' words have been dismissed as shibboleths by his critics for too long. Yet they contain much of his power and his appeal.

Menzies fell within the old Deakinite Liberal tradition. He lived in a different age, but he believed in a form of progressive politics. This is why he wanted the new party bearing the name Liberal. Menzies was dedicated to the notion of public service. He put great store by integrity and process.

He had no purge of bureaucrats upon his victory and, in particular, he retained the service of Dr Coombs, upon whom he relied. Menzies valued his public service advisers and usually took their advice. He ran a remarkably stable cabinet and his ministry was remarkably scandal-free. He delegated to his ministers and didn't try to run every aspect of government. Menzies made a considerable effort to explain his policy in a clear, simple and powerful fashion.

His view of government was measured and utilitarian: it should keep out of people's way unless it was helping them, which was its main function. Menzies had an unrivalled capacity to discern the mood and aspirations of middle Australia. He achieved a better balance than any of his predecessors had, between free enterprise and state intervention. That was clearly the view of the people. Menzies had the wisdom not to hog the stage nor to succumb to mindless activity. The famous complaint of his critics—that he presided over events but didn't know what was happening—is a tribute to his skill. His era was marked by certainty and predictability, qualities much appreciated after Depression and war. His technique, generally, was to delay changes until the public was ready for them. It is idle to believe that our longest serving prime minister did not possess special political qualities or to pretend that his tenure does not offer a commentary upon the Australian character.

As Allan Martin has written, Menzies was a man of his time, which is true for most of the prime ministership. It is an explanation for his success and an explanation for the subsequent criticism he has generated. Menzies had little inclination to address the role of women. He was determined to keep White Australia. He showed no interest in Aborigines or concerns about their past or future. He was unable to find enthusiasm for a changed and dynamic Australian role in Asia and was scarcely interested in Asia. His mind and his heart were anchored to an old world of colonialism, Empire and chums.

In policy terms, Menzies brought to its finest pitch the Australian technique of civilising capitalism. There is no question: he managed this longer and better than anybody else. Unemployment hovered around 1.0–1.5 per cent. Home ownership grew. The role of the Commonwealth Government expanded, with spending rising from 14 to 18 per cent of GDP. Menzies was dedicated to the growth of Canberra as a city and the capital. Arbitration and Protection, the foundation Australian institutions, were upheld and advanced. The application of Keynesian economics reached its zenith. The welfare state marched forward. Public enterprise from Qantas to TAA to the Commonwealth Bank was supported. The move beyond sectarianism was recognised with funding of private schools.

Menzies' expansion of the university system based upon the 1957 Murray Report was an initiative that helped to transform Australia. Upon his retirement Alan Reid called him a 'cautious reformer'.

There is no doubt he was lucky. Governing in a Western democracy in the 1950s or 1960s was usually a stroke of luck. But the postwar expansion, as it continued, bred a political complacency and that was true in Menzies' case. As demands for economic change mounted the pressure point, once again, was Protection.

It was under the Menzian legacy that Fortress Australia reached its pinnacle. The latest in a long line of protectionist politicians was the most formidable, John 'Black Jack' McEwen, Menzies' deputy and Country Party leader. McEwen was a legend. Given great discretion by Menzies, he left his imprint on Australia's economy. Alan Reid said of him: 'McEwen had the aloof dignity of a patrician, a Corsican-like devotion to the pursuit of vendettas, an imperious ambition and a peasant's suspicion of both colleagues and opponents. He trampled over the top of those who got in the way of his advancement.'

McEwen remained after Menzies' retirement and ran commerce and trade policy for a total of 21 years. He was honest about his tactics: 'I would say that the man who is incapable of inspiring fear in his opponents does not amount to a row of beans.' McEwen represented the most formidable combination in Australian history of protectionist faith and political clout. It is no surprise that under McEwen Australia's protection levels reached their peak.

But McEwen also provoked a backlash—a tide of many currents that would eventually sweep his edifice away. The revolt began slowly and originated from different sources; but there were three principal elements.

First, the new chairman of the Tariff Board, Alf Rattigan, was pledged to tariff transparency: he wanted the economic effect of the tariff documented so that the citizens and taxpayers of Australia would know what the cost was and who paid. This was a critical step. The entire success of protection to that point had lain in obscuring its real impact. Rattigan's campaign to determine the cost of protecting certain industries and of protecting manufacturing overall would lead directly to the demise of protection. Once these figures were put on the table of Australian democracy the system would be politically unsustainable.

Rattigan fought as bruising a battle with McEwen as any that Canberra has witnessed in the past half century. Rattigan reformed the methodology of the Board, the results revealed vividly in its 1969–70 annual report: 'The average rates of effective protection available to individual Australian manuturing industries ranged from 0 to 120 per cent. The average rate for manufacturing industry as a whole was 46 per cent. This average rate of effective protection is equivalent to about $2700 million per annum.' This referred to the total cost of the manufacturing if all the protection had been fully utilised, compared with the same scale of manufacturing and no tariffs. The $2700 million figure was greater than all governments then spent on health, education, defence and social welfare combined. The consequence was inevitable—the politics of protection were transformed.

The second element was the power of the free trade idea. A generation of Australian economists led by the Australian National University's Professor Max Corden showed conclusively that the costs of protection outweighed the gains. An informal three way alliance of bureaucrats, journalists and academics exerted an influence on the political debate. The idea began to take hold within the political realm that protection had been a liability from which Australia must be liberated. People began to analyse the tariff in terms of the penalty it imposed. The notion of freer trade became linked to a dynamic economy—the point made by George Reid decades earlier.

The third element was the engagement in the battle of those interests and causes opposed to protection. The Country Party's own base was in revolt because the export sector bore the cost of the tariff. The National Farmers Federation was formed, eventually, in 1979 to resolve the issues that McEwen's successors had failed to confront. The Treasury fought aggressively against McEwen and prevailed after his departure. In the interim there was a poisonous struggle between McEwen and Treasurer Billy McMahon which saw McEwen veto McMahon's prime ministerial claims after Harold Holt's death.

The solo campaign which the Liberal backbencher Bert Kelly waged against tariff would be reinforced in the late 1970s by the emergence of a free market lobby headed by John Hyde. But the real key was the conversion of ALP leader, Gough Whitlam. Whitlam saw that tariffs were misallocating resources on a vast scale—resources he wanted for his historic program of social advancement. Whitlam became a low tariff man. The wheel had turned full circle.

Elected ALP leader in February 1967, Whitlam saw himself as a modernist in terms of party, policy and country. He aspired to modernise and expand the ALP faith in government intervention. Whitlam's 'program' of better education, health and welfare services was buttressed by programs for arts, culture, women, Aborigines and immigrants. The philosophical unity within his program was equality of opportunity and Federal Government funding and planning. Whitlam confirmed the enduring status of Nugget Coombs by installing him as a special adviser. But Whitlam took counsel from Rattigan and saw the low tariff position as part of his modernist persona.

Whitlam's 1972 policy speech deserves a special place in this story. It began to transcend the 'civilising capitalism' phase. This speech assumed that the task was accomplished. Its assumption was that the secret to economic growth had been unlocked. The long postwar boom had convinced Labor that growth was a permanent feature of Australian polity. The Labor pessimists of the Depression had become the Whitlam optimists of the 1970s with a late injection of baby-boomer enthusiasm. Labor's tragedy is that, having lost office in 1949 at the start of the long boom, it regained power in 1972 when the boom was about to expire. However, Whitlam didn't know this. His 1972 'program' was to be funded from that apparently magic source of strong taxation revenue—'fiscal drag' as the critics called it.

Whitlam's policy speech was a blend of utopianism, Keynesianism and rationalism. It genuflected before the 1960s ideology that every social program could be solved by government intervention and more money. In retrospect Whitlam's program appears more naive than idealistic. It occupies a special place in our history as a people: the high tide of the Australian faith in government. This impulse would never appear again with such intensity. It was the glory and the folly of the Whitlam era.

One of the many consequences of Whitlam's middle class background was his 'low tariff' policy. It is hard to imagine a leader from the union movement adopting this outlook in 1973. The mid-1973 25 per cent tariff cut was classic Whitlam 'crash through or crash' politics. It arose not from the economic situation at the time but from Whitlam's reform dogmatism. The *Australian Financial Review* hailed the decision as 'a vast step towards national maturity' but warned correctly that protected businessmen and trade unions would attribute any rise in unemployment in coming years to the tariff cut.

It was Whitlam's ill-fortune to govern during the rise of 1970s global stagflation precipitated by the first OPEC oil shock. The long boom ended in 1974, just after Whitlam's narrow 1974 re-election. Inflation and unemployment rose dramatically. The Whitlam Government was plunged into a series of economic management crises which spelt its certain doom. The external challenge was compounded by internal ineptitude during 1974–75 when massive lifts in federal spending saw the size of government expenditure swell to more than 30 per cent of GDP, its highest ever.

The 25 per cent tariff cut was the most substantial single assault on protection, but it provoked a backlash. Malcolm Fraser prevailed as a champion of disciplined orthodoxy in the Menzies–McEwen mould. Fraser won in 1975 promising to 'turn on the lights' but he lost in 1983 amid a world economy being transformed and a dawning recognition that the old Australian solutions had reached the end of their shelf life. The Fraser recession of the early 1980s shattered confidence in the orthodoxy, with unemployment rising to 10 per cent.

The 1983 election proved, in retrospect, to be a turning point. It delivered to power a talented Labor Government led by Bob Hawke and Paul Keating. Hawke was the most popular leader in Australia's history and Keating had an unrivalled will to power. They came to office with fewer preconceptions and a more open mind than any ALP government since World War I. Hawke and Keating broke from Labor's past.

They said that Labor's obligation to its supporters was to create a governing mentality. Hawke and Keating were not interested in any brief reformist rush. They came with two keen instincts: that Labor must become the party of economic management superiority, and that it must purge its hostility towards the market.

They brought a pragmatic intelligence to the issues of the day, a receptiveness to their economic advisers, and a penchant for cutting deals with business, unions and media bosses; and, unlike the Whitlam Government, they were prepared to abandon Labor's tradition in order to meet externally imposed challenges.

The 1980s saw a revolution in the international system. Hawke and Keating operated in an environment in which the Bretton Woods system of fixed exchange rates had collapsed in 1971. The Australian dollar had been tied to sterling, then the US dollar, and then a currency basket in what was a managed exchange rate. But the rapid integration of global financial markets driven by technology meant that huge volumes of capital could be transferred at high speed. Implicit in this process was a strengthening of global markets and a weakening of national governments. It was a world quite different from that in which most of Australia's major policy decisions had been made.

Hawke and Keating looked at the changing global tide and set their sails. At each point they were responding to events and crises. In the process they largely demolished the cornerstones of the Federation Settlement and the role of state power at the centre of Australian polity. The fascinating feature of these Hawke–Keating decisions is that they were largely bipartisan. This reflected, above all, the influence of John Howard on coalition economic policy during the 1980s.

The practical and symbolic decision which heralded the new order was that taken by Hawke and Keating in December 1983 to float the Australian dollar and abolish exchange controls. This had many consequences. It meant that markets would set domestic interest rates and exchange rates and that markets would be able to move capital freely in and out of the country. It was, literally, the triumph of the market. It was a leap towards the internationalisation of the economy and of our consciousness—a formidable psychological step whose full magnitude became apparent only much later. Hawke and Keating decided that governments could no longer defend the exchange rate but should use the currency as a weapon of economic adjustment. Once this decision was taken it was clear that financial deregulation would never stand alone. It would promote further deregulation in other parts of the economy—product, trade and labour markets.

Their second epic step was to put Australia on to a free course and terminate the century of protection. This was another revolution in economic identity. Hawke and Keating saw that Australia, as a medium-size economy, had to integrate itself as successfully as possible with the world. The government cut protection in two stages, in May 1988 and again in March 1991 when Hawke announced that the general tariff level would be reduced to 5 per cent by 1996. In the highly protected areas, tariffs on cars would be cut to 15 per cent and on footwear, clothing and textiles to around 25 per cent.

These reforms reflected several assumptions: that Australia would grow faster as an open rather than a closed economy; that in a more competitive world Australia had to move quickly to put its economy on a competitive basis; that Australia had been on the path of relative economic decline and that a fundamental change was needed; and that an open economy would integrate Australia into Asia with both financial and political dividends.

This second step was seen by Hawke and Keating as representing a change of national direction and as a cultural declaration that the old Fortress Australian psychology was dying.

The Liberal Party supported these decisions. Just as the embrace of Protection in the first decade of the century was achieved by a Liberal–Labor alliance, so the switch to free trade at the century's end was made on the basis of an implicit Labor–Liberal understanding.

The third major reform lay in the adjustment of economic policy to a more globally competitive outlook. This had many manifestations. Its progress was often abrupt, uneven and inconsistent. It was begun by Hawke and Keating and continued by John Howard's government elected in 1996. The unfinished agenda encompassed the entire economic picture. The unifying theme was a move towards a more market-oriented economy.

This included labour market reform, with a shift away from the power of the Arbitration Court towards an enterprise-based wages system—a higher priority under the Howard Government. But this area of reform remains the central political challenge. Protection and Arbitration rose together. The issue now, with the shift to free trade, is how Australia adopts a more market-based wages system.

The other elements in the reform agenda were fiscal consolidation, begun by Keating, abandoned in the recession, and pursued with success by the Howard–Costello government; taxation reform, tackled initially by Labor but effected by Howard who introduced the Goods and Services Tax with offsetting income tax cuts; privatisation, which Labor implemented by compulsion not as an article of faith, with the sale of icons such as Qantas and the Commonwealth Bank, but which required Howard to press the ultimate case with Telstra; and deregulation of domestic markets and the introduction of competition policy.

Howard was the first pro-market reformer to lead the Liberal Party, just as Hawke and Keating formed the first pro-market ALP government. But the policy transition was turbulent in every sense: an early 1990s recession as the monetary authorities struggled to understand the deregulated economy; the backlash manifested in the success of Pauline Hanson's One Nation Party at the 1998 election; and a pervasive unease within the community about the loss of job security and the fear that a market economy would terminate Australia's egalitarian ethic.

Paul Keating was unmoved about the need to change direction: 'What was Labor really, in economic terms, before 1983? It believed in regulation of the banking system. It believed in regulation of the exchange rate. It believed in tariffs. We had low profits, therefore low investment. We had high unemployment. I mean, what did we abandon? It's like losing an eczema.'

But it was easy to forget that the Hawke–Keating Cabinet had put a premium on equity in its transition to an open economy—an accord with the unions, revival of Medicare, a targeted welfare system, award-based superannuation, expansion of family support, and a tax tradeoff of lower rates for a closing of loopholes. Indeed, equity was presented as part of the Hawke–Keating agenda of economic liberalism—an aim in its own right. The bigger question, of course, is what instruments will be used to maintain equity now that Protection, Arbitration and state power are in retreat.

The judgment a decade and a half later is that Australia's change in national direction has been vindicated by its 1990s growth performance. With annual growth late in the decade around 4 per cent, Australia was boosting its national income faster than most other industrialised nations.

The Reserve Bank Governor, Ian Macfarlane, pointed out that the 1990s growth cycle had lasted longer than either the 1970s or 1980s expansion. In his 1999 Chris Higgins Memorial Lecture, Macfarlane analysed Australia's performance compared with OECD nations for each of the five decades in the second half of the century. He said: 'While economic growth in Australia was lower than the OECD average over the 50s and 60s, it was higher in the 80s and 90s, with the biggest advantage in Australia's favour occurring in the 90s.' For the decade of the 1990s, including the recession, Australia's average growth was 3.3 per cent compared with 2.1 per cent for the rest. The same trend is apparent when analysing income per head. Macfarlane said that the 1990s was 'the only decade in which Australian GDP per capita has grown faster than the OECD average and by an appreciable amount'.

The results are conclusive: while Australia grew strongly during the Menzian Age, it was still in relative decline compared with its customers and competitors; stagnation reached in its peak in the Fraser recession, with Australia facing the challenge of global catch-up; and the 1990s has been Australia's most successful decade for comparative economic performance. Australia's avoidance of the late 1990s Asian financial crisis further testifies to this point.

Macfarlane argues that the main factor in this improvement lies in the structural changes of the past seventeen years: financial deregulation, tariff cuts, labour market deregulation, privatisation, competition policy, low inflation, and fiscal prudence. In short, the transition from state intervention to economic liberalism. It is the belated triumph of George Reid over Alfred Deakin.

It is a mistake to think that nirvana has arrived. Surveying the situation, Boris Schedvin said: 'I think the new Australian economy is about halfway there. The signs are encouraging. The real cause of concern is the lack of progress in replacing all of those commodity exports that have suffered over the last 20 years: wool, wheat, gold, minerals. We have not yet diversified the economy sufficiently to have a robust export sector that will carry us forward without excessive reliance on overseas savings. We still have a lot of hard work to do to make sure that we have a robust balance of payments for the 21st century.'

A variation on this theme was the Year 2000 debate on whether Australia had the right policies to develop its IT economy, and the entrepreneurial culture to reap commercial gain from high technology. The dollar slumped alarmingly in late 2000 in a warning of the sheer volatility of the globalised age.

The historic step-up in Australia's economic results was undermined by a sense of national angst. The longer the 1990s expansion ran the more concern was vented about its negatives. Australia's future was in tension with its past. The essential issue was whether such success was destroying the 'land of the fair go' and whether the basis of Australian egalitarianism was being dismantled. It was whether the national mission of civilising capitalism had been surrendered to the lure of the marketplace. The conundrum in the late 1990s seemed to be one of a nation both richer and more unhappy.

Australia now confronts a new series of issues: How far will the new individualism run? How compatible is the market economy with a successful community? What is the redefined role for government? Can Australia still honour its tradition of civilising capitalism?

The first lesson for the future is that the market will continue to deliver dynamic and unequal outcomes. This was the conclusion reached by Professor Ann Harding, director of the National Centre for Social and Economic Modelling, in her 1990s research. Harding's finding is initially optimistic: that the Federal Government, through welfare payments and a progressive tax system, was instrumental in largely or totally nullifying the market-driven inequality that emerged in the 1982–96 period. But how realistic is it to think that such offsetting action will be maintained?

The danger in rising inequality is that more people will sink into demeaning poverty, that equality of opportunity will be undermined, and that a new feudalism will emerge with an overclass living a life decoupled from the rest of society.

The second lesson is that the change 'downside' has a cultural dimension—a dimension identified by US analyst Francis Fukuyama and branded the Great Disruption. He wrote:

The culture of intense individualism, which in the marketplace and laboratory leads to innovation and growth, spilled over into the realm of social norms where it corroded virtually all forms of authority and weakened the bonds holding families, neighbourhoods and nations together. The technological change that brings about what economist Joseph Schumpeter called 'creative destruction' in the marketplace caused similar disruption in the world of social relationships. It would be surprising were this not true.

For Fukuyama, modern capitalism thrives on the breaking of rules. The question for the future is whether the social unravelling will continue or whether it will reach equilibrium at another level of economic prosperity.

The question that Australians will be forced to confront is: What do we mean by egalitarianism; is inequality a bad thing and, if so, why? For economic liberals the answer is obvious: provided there is a strong social safety net—to prevent people from going backwards—the transition from a dulling equality to an incentive-driven pluralism is desirable. John Howard says: 'Providing those at the bottom are protected and looked after, disparities between, I guess, the middle, upper middle and higher still groups don't matter quite so much.'

For the ALP and social democrats, the answer is somewhat different: it is that government must find new ways to honour its historic commitment to social justice. This is Kim Beazley's view. But it won't be easy, as Paul Keating recognises: 'We won't be able to stop the disparities. You can ameliorate them but you won't be able to stop them. But we can lift the average. We can lift the floor.'

The old-fashioned Deakinite Settlement no longer works. Yet this model had a cultural legitimacy based upon the Australian belief in the fair go. The new policies, the updated version of George Reid's liberalism, depend more upon Australia's aspirational values.

Boris Schedvin remains an optimist: 'Our future didn't lie with reliance on internal market processes. It relied on an increasing nexus with the international system. That change must be linked to the Hawke–Keating period. It is in the process of overturning the Australian tradition and, by overturning it, will give us more opportunities for the future. It's not a rejection of egalitarianism.'

There is a new challenge for government—making the open economy work and giving the community a stakeholding in its benefits. The task will require leaders as visionary as those of a hundred years ago who designed the 'civilising capitalism' model. It is a necessity because Australia is a compulsory-voting democracy. The vote of a battler has the same value as that of a millionaire. The people will vote against the globalised economy unless they are given a stake in its dividends. This is the new challenge facing Australia's governance.

INTERVIEW WITH
BOB HAWKE

Bob Hawke nominates Gallipoli as the moment when people began to think of themselves as being Australians and World War II as the decisive event in Australia's coming of age. He sees the postwar immigration program as Australia's greatest achievement and offers a powerful defence of the epic changes that his government made to Australia's economic direction.

Looking at Australia's political development over the last hundred years, most people agree that we won our independence in a series of gradual steps. Is it possible to identify when Australia really became an independent country?

If you had to take one point, I would say it was Pearl Harbor, December 1941, and what flowed from that. My illustrious predecessor John Curtin later made a statement—I think perhaps the most important statement to come out of the mouth of any Australian prime minister. He said: 'I want to make it clear that, without any pangs as to our traditional ties, our kinship with the United Kingdom, Australia looks to America.' After that, it was never going to be the same. It involved the beginning of a complete reorientation of Australia's views.

Why is John Curtin such a revered figure for you?

I revere Curtin for a number of reasons. One, he was a man ahead of his time. I remember reading his speeches made in Federal Parliament during the time of the Great Depression. He was pre-Keynesian in his perception of the need to spend your way out of the Depression. Secondly, he was a man of very considerable courage, both in the conduct of his personal life—he was an alcoholic and he gave up alcohol to discharge the duties of leadership of the party and then of the nation—and in taking on his own party, particularly over the question of conscription for the armed forces. He had been one of the leading lights in the First World War fight against conscription. But he realised that in the challenge facing Australia in the war against Japan it was necessary to throw over old positions. He had a hard fight and he took it right up to the party. Thirdly, he was a man of very considerable foresight. Most importantly, he had a vision beyond the war. He wasn't fighting to win the war so as to restore the old Australia. He wanted to see a new, better, fairer Australia, and during the darkest days of the war he gathered together some of the best minds in the country under the leadership of 'Nugget' Coombs in the Department of Post-War Reconstruction. He was, in the depths of war, planning for a new and better Australia. So those reasons, together with his capacity to feel and understand the Australian people, lead me to the judgment that he is the greatest prime minister in Australia's history.

One of the themes in our history is that we came from British stock, we looked to Britain for a very long period of time. Do you think we were too slow in moving away from the shadow of Britain's influence or do you think we essentially got it right in terms of the rate at which we grew up?

You can never say in politics that you've got every part of it exactly right, either in substance or in timing. But having said that, I find it difficult to be critical of the path or the timetable. After all, if you look at the period until the Second World War, the economic facts were that our welfare was very much wrapped up with Empire preferences. The major investor in the country was Britain and our people overwhelmingly came from Britain until the end of the war. So it was inevitable in economic terms and in demographic terms that the ties would be close. Curtin saw that if we were going to survive, or maximise our chances of survival in the Second World War, we had to reorient towards the United States. He did that eloquently and efficiently in terms of the personal relationship between himself and General MacArthur. We moved into the postwar period and, of course, under the leadership of Bob Menzies there was more of a concentration on the ties with Britain. That was the nature of Menzies and I'm not criticising him. With the economic realities of the development of the postwar period, and as we moved into the 1960s and 70s with the rise of the Asian dragons, it was inevitable that Australia would gradually shift from its close relationship with the United States. Britain moved towards Europe in the early 1960s and cut the ties and the preferences with us. It was natural in those circumstances that we were going to emphasise our own self-interest.

Are the Australian people essentially republican in their hearts, despite the 1999 referendum defeat?

I believe that a significant majority of Australians are republican in their heart, but they are at the same time a cautious people. They were unhappy at the division that existed. I think a lot of Australians genuinely—although in my judgment mistakenly—wanted to have a direct say in the election of the president. But I don't have any doubt where the majority of the Australian heart and mind is.

I think the republic is inevitable. I said that in the Boyer Lectures in 1979. Now, you'd be a bold man to bet your money on what year it was going to happen. It won't happen under a Liberal government. If Labor wins the next election in 2001, which I think is a reasonable assumption, then it will be a question of how Prime Minister Beazley wants to go about it. There is a possibility I think that he could associate his first election as prime minister, in 2004 presumably, with a question on the republic, so I can't see it happening before 2004.

As a long-serving prime minister, you dealt with the Queen. How would you describe her attitude towards Australia, and how hard do you think the republican debate has been for her?

The Queen's attitude to Australia is a very positive one. One thing about the Queen is that she takes her position as Head of the Commonwealth extremely seriously. I had the opportunity of speaking with her on many occasions during my prime ministership. Her knowledge of each member of the Commonwealth is quite outstanding—not the tourist knowledge but knowledge of the people, the Constitutional set-up, the economies and the political situation. She has a genuine interest in this country. As far as her attitude to the debate about the republic goes, I think she was unconcerned. I mean, she understands that the overwhelming majority of the members of the Commonwealth are republics. It doesn't affect our allegiance to the Commonwealth. Nor, I suggest, would a vote for a republic be a vote of no-confidence in the Queen; rather, a vote of maturity for our own country. I don't think she would have been at all upset had the vote gone the other way.

What impact did the White Australia policy have on your own political development?

I was born as a son of the manse and, from my earliest recollections, I was inculcated with the belief that all men and women are equal, irrespective of race, creed or colour. That's been deeply ingrained in my psyche. I was moved to join the Australian Labor Party—when I first went to university in 1947 in Western Australia—as much as anything through my sense of excitement at the immigration program being initated by the Labor Government. I went out of my way at university to make students from overseas and particularly from Asia feel at home. I established the International Club at the university because I found abhorent the 'ghettoisation', if I can use that ugly word, of people from what was then Malaya and Ceylon, and from Singapore and India. They were sort of living alone in their own places and were not mixing much, which I thought was sad for them and sad for Australian students. In my personal relations, having them at home and going to their places, I was not easy about the White Australia policy. When I became active at the national level and as I was coming up in the Labor Party, I identified with those, particularly Don Dunstan, who showed leadership and I was part of the push to remove that policy from the books of the party.

How should we see the postwar immigration program and how should we evaluate it in terms of its contribution to this country?

There is nothing more important in the history of Australia than the immigration program. At the end of the Second World War we had a population of seven million people, overwhelmingly Anglo-Irish stock. In that program initiated by the Labor Governments of Curtin and Chifley, and carried on by the other side of politics, we have brought to this country almost the equivalent of that population of seven million. Over five and a half million people have come as immigrants and well over half a million under refugee and other humanitarian programs. So you had the population at the end of the war, and almost the equivalent of that has since come from more than 140 different countries. In the history of the world there has in my judgment never been any other country which, in such a short time, has so peaceably and constructively changed its composition, and in a way which has been economically beneficial and also enriching us culturally. Australia today is an infinitely better country because of it. One of the marvellous things has been that we have retained the very best of our British tradition, most particularly the system of parliamentary democracy and the rule of law. We have enriched our country immeasurably by bringing in the traditions, cultures habits and practices of so many others. Marvellously, these six million who have come, plus their children, have embraced what I see as the essential ethos of the Australian character, which built up over that period of 160 years before they came. That ethos is basically what I would describe as the 'fair go'. It was part of the thing they found attractive about Australia and they embraced it. So we imbued our growing and enlarged and enriched population with the best of our own past.

What were the dynamics that drove the demolition of the White Australian policy?

I think it's fairly simple. In the 1960s, the United Kingdom went into the Common Market. We had then to start to turn our attention to other markets. That coincided with the emergence of the strong Asian economies. Japan was starting and it was quite clear to anyone studying these things that Asia was going to be more important to us in economic terms. Now, by definition you are not going to be able to have a worthwhile productive economic relationship with a region if you regard their citizens as second class human beings, as not worthy equally with people from Europe to become citizens of this country. There was this fundamental convergence of changing economic realities together with a moral view that we could not take our place proudly in the world if we were saying that non–whites were inferior human beings.

How deeply were you attached to the idea of multiculturalism when you were prime minister?

I felt a profound attachment to the concept of multiculturalism. We had opened our doors to people from 140 different countries. We wouldn't have been as economically strong and we wouldn't have been as culturally diverse and enriched if these people hadn't come to make Australia their home. I mean, just take the fundamental things like our eating habits. When I grew up, basic Australian tucker was chops and eggs, sausages and eggs, roast lamb, corned beef; but we enlarged our range of what we enjoyed eating and what we enjoyed drinking. I can remember as a young person, you thought those who drank wine were plonkos. But we developed an appreciation of wine and we had different forms of cultural entertainment arising from the contribution these new people were making. I had this feeling that Australia was just changing for the better and that we should glory in the fact.

Recently we've seen the emergence of Hansonism. What sort of threat does this pose to the social diversity you're talking about?

Hansonism posed a very significant threat. I believe it is diminishing, but I know from my own experience after she went into parliament in 1996 and from my frequent visits to Asia that there was a deep, genuine widespread concern throughout Asia that this woman was saying something for and about Australia which was unacceptable. I spent every available minute that I could making the point that she didn't speak for Australia. Of course, the high point of Hansonism came in 1998 with the election of so many of her people to the Queensland Parliament. That was very disconcerting. But I believe that her influence is dissipating for a number of reasons. I predicted that once they got some significant representation they would fall apart because they had to take positions. Her national level of support, as far as you can tell by the polls, would be about 2 to 3 per cent. They have shown themselves to be inadequate. They have shown themselves in many senses to be corrupt. I think that credit must be given to a wide range of people on both sides of politics who have stood up and fought the good fight in exposing them for the evil they represent.

You took an initiative at this time in relation to Hanson: you wanted former prime ministers to combine with John Howard to make a statement.

I took the view that it would be useful if all living prime ministers, past and present, made a statement. It had the advantage of political balance because it was Whitlam, Hawke, Keating and then Gorton, Fraser, Howard, a perfect balance. I didn't present John Howard with a fait accompli, because I didn't think that was either fair or sensible. I ascertained that Fraser and Whitlam and Keating were supportive. John Gorton refused and that didn't worry me so much. But John Howard declined and his reasons, I thought, were inadequate. He gave two reasons. One, that if we were to do this, it would give her more publicity. I answered that with: 'John, she is a fact of life, she's there, it's something we have to deal with.' The second reason, I thought, was more inadequate. He said that in these Asian countries they had racial discrimination and we weren't alone in people having these sorts of attitudes. I said: 'Well, that is true, there are racial attitudes and discrimination in Asian countries. But it's Australia which we're concerned about. We must do our best to eliminate that perception in our country.' But John, for reasons that recommended themselves to him, declined to sign.

Do you think the prime minister misconstrued the damage that Hanson was doing to Australia in Asia?

I definitely believe that the prime minister did not understand and was not properly informed about the extent of the damage that was being done to Australia's interests by Hanson. I was a frequent visitor to Asia, and wherever I and Blanche went, this was always raised with us. It was a matter of very, very real concern and, as far as I was concerned it came into two categories. First and most important was the moral issue. It was just morally wrong. As I said, if one Asian child in a school ground was humiliated as a result of this sort of phenomenon then it was not only a tragedy for that child and their parents—but all Australians, I believe, were diminished by that. Secondly, there were the economics of it. At that stage, 60 per cent of our exports were going to Asia. Asians were constituting more than 50 per cent of our tourists. We had something like 150 000 Asian students in this country and that was enormously important in terms of establishing future links. So on both moral and economic grounds it was wrong and bad for Australia.

Looking back, how do you see the floating of the dollar and the other economic reforms introduced by your government?

I see them as necessary. Remember the setting. We came to office early in 1983. The world through the 1970s had undergone a fundamental transformation with the oil crisis and then the spectacular growth of the Asian economies and increasing globalisation. It was no longer tenable that Australia could entertain the thought of maximising its opportunities by closing itself off. We had to internationalise the Australian economy. If we were going to be arguing as we did in the international councils for liberalisation of world trade, which was absolutely vital to a nation like Australia, then we had to set our own stable in order. We had to combine a lowering of tariff barriers with increasing competitiveness in our own economy. That meant opening up our financial system. It meant floating the dollar. It meant changing work practices in Australia. All those things had to happen if we were going to give Australians the maximum opportunity of participating in and benefiting from this world economy which was becoming more and more integrated. I think you'd have to say that it would be difficult to find a period—other than in the war time, and that was a unique situation—where you got such a dramatic transformation of Australia's economic base.

We were about internationalising the Australian economy for a very simple reason. We were a population of 17 million people and the realities of the world were that we would become a shrinking economy. In per capita terms Australians would be worse off unless we took steps to maximise our opportunity of being part of the global market. We couldn't do that unless we changed our practices.

What do you say to critics who said you sold out, sold Labor principles down the drain? What's your response to that critique?

In my less academic moments I say bullshit to those who make that criticism. When I get a bit more refined I say—when I hear this epithet 'economic rationalism' thrown at me—I ask a simple question: 'Did you want us to be economically *irrational*?' Is that the way you should go—be economically irrational? We did take some tough economic decisions which in an immediate sense hurt some people. But in respect of those that were hurt, particularly in terms of reducing tariff barriers, we put in place schemes of retraining and relocation. I have a fundamental view, and had it as prime minister, that you cannot justify economic changes on the basis of the public interest if the public as a whole does not look after those who are immediately hurt by the changes. I mean, it's immoral to do that. You've got to make the changes, and to the extent that they have some adverse impact you have to try and make provisions to help people, either by welfare payments or retraining or relocation.

And what do you believe has been the result of those decisions in terms of living standards for the Australian people?

I suppose the best case I can put in favour of what we did is that there has been a recognition by our political opponents that the present strength of the Australian economy owes a great deal to those decisions we took when we were in office. In other words, Australia would not be as competitive now if we hadn't made those decisions. In the period we were in government, and it has continued, the annual rate of increase of exports of manufactured goods was 16 per cent. Nothing like that had happened before. Because we made these changes Australian manufacturers were able each year to increase their exports of manufactured goods, so we were diversifying the Australian economy. We were no longer going to be in a position where we were totally subject to fluctuations in the prices of primary products and mineral products. The more you can lift your manufacturing base and your service industries, the exports of service products, the more you're a diversified economy. The proof came with the Asian downturn.

The purpose of reducing the tariff barriers was to make the Australian economy more open. We couldn't any longer justify a situation where you kept every enterprise going—whether they were making shoes or some form of clothing which meant that 99 per cent of the Australian people were paying very much more for things they consumed—in order to keep particular jobs. What you had to do was to make the economy more competitive so that, as you did that, opportunities for employment would open elsewhere.

What would have happened to Australia if we hadn't taken these decisions?

There is no doubt that if we hadn't taken those decisions that we did after 1983 the Australian standard of living would have declined remarkably. We wouldn't have had the stature on the international stage that we had to affect what was happening in the rest of the world. I don't want to overstate Australia's position. We're a small country but it is universally recognised that the Cairns Group was a very significant factor in bringing about a successful outcome to the Uruguay trade round.

You've got to have a more market-orientated economy, because if you think that you can simply build tariff barriers and have some sort of command-type economy—well, just look around the world. It never worked anywhere and it wouldn't work here.

I think we made changes which did turn the direction of Australian economic activity. If you look at the independent economic assessments by academic economists within Australia, in international organisations like the OECD, the IMF, the World Bank, there is a judgment that those decisions—floating the dollar, internationalising our financial markets, lowering tariffs, reforming work practices—that all those things did change the direction of the Australian economy for the better.

In a sense, the critical question is whether one can reconcile a more market-orientated economy with an egalitarian tradition.

There is absolutely no reason why you can't create a more efficient economic system and maintain your compassion for the less fortunate and those who are not directly benefiting. On the contrary, if you are increasing your levels of economic growth, and we are, then you do have the capacity to look after those who need assistance. There is no conflict between economic growth and compassion for the needy. It's a question of will, political will.

You're very strong on that point, but a lot of people think there is a conflict.

Well, a lot of people are wrong. If in fact you have taken steps to increase the size of the cake, which we have and that's happening, then the division of the cake is something which requires, as I say, political will. But if you have got more cake, then you have a greater capacity to look after those who need it.

How much were you, as prime minister, influenced by the reform experience of the Whitlam Government, in particular that government's economic management or mismanagement?

The experience of the Whitlam Government was certainly one of the factors in our thinking. Let me say, at the outset, I think the Whitlam government did a number of magnificent things in the social and educational field and externally. But when the history books are written, under the category of economic management they won't rate highly. There were a lot of mistakes made. I was determined that this government that I led in 1983 was not going to be a short-term government. I mean, if you are going to change the direction of Australia for the better you can't do it in one term. It requires time and we were determined that we were going to be effective economic managers.

I want to take just one example here. How did you see the 25 per cent tariff cut?

I supported it but I was very critical of the way it was done. There was zilch consultation with the trade union movement and I think that was stupid and one of the reasons why it was so controversial. Was it counter-productive? I don't want to go that far because, you know, it was done and in economic terms I think that was a plus. But you are going to make these things work better if you take into your confidence the people who are going to be affected. That was the contrast between the 25 per cent cut where there was no consultation and what we did, because we sat down and talked with the unions, representatives of the workers who would be affected by the cuts, and while they weren't too happy, nevertheless we were able to broadly take the trade union movement along with us. We also talked to employers who were going to be adversely affected. So it was a great deal of consultation and the setting up of plans for retraining, relocation and assistance. I think it's just a matter of common sense that it's going to work much better if you do it that way.

You devoted a lot of your life to the study of the wage-fixing system, the unique Australian system of wage arbitration. How important has the system of arbitration been in terms of maintaining the egalitarian traditions of this country?

I think the Australian wage system historically has been a basic reflection of and buttress to the egalitarian concept. I mean, you go back to the 1880s before Federation and it wasn't just the unions who were talking about the concept of a 'fair and reasonable' wage; the employers, particularly in Victoria, had a protectionist view and they said, the only way we can pay fair and reasonable wages is if we have protection. So there was an alliance of interests. That was reflected in the inclusion in the constitution of Section 51(xxxv), which gave you the arbitration power, and you had the Conciliation and Arbitration Court established in 1904 and then you had the Harvester wage award in 1907. So from very early on you had the concept of 'fair and reasonable' wages embedded into your constitution and into your legislation and then into your tribunals and into your practice. I think it reflected the Australian ethos very much and it's really why it's survived so long. Now, this doesn't mean that a system that worked well for a long period of time should never be changed. We changed it to some extent. The basic thing was that as you move more to collective bargaining or enterprise bargaining, there has got to be a facility within the tribunals for safety nets. I'm committed to that concept, because if you allow the unfettered forces of the market to operate without the state being prepared to set safety nets, then you are going to have a very unstable society ultimately.

How important were the Harvester judgment and the role of H B Higgins in establishing the system's foundations?

They were fundamentally important in establishing a system of industrial arbitration and conciliation and fairness in the system of rewards. I think the measure of the judgment's importance was that when it was done people didn't realise just how widespread it would become. But the philosophy was so right and so in tune with the Australian ethos that it spread not just through the federal jurisdiction, but then became embraced by the various State jurisdictions. I think it's impossible to overstate the significance of both the judgment and its author, Henry Bournes Higgins.

Higgins was an austere man and a fair man. He was no wild radical. He was a man who was meticulous. It's very interesting reading the judgment [which examines the needs of a man, wife and three children for food, rent and clothing, in order to set a basic wage]. It was a very meticulous exercise.

A lot of the policies you introduced reversed the labour tradition in terms of . . .

I dispute that. I reject the criticisms that we repudiated Labor philosophy. I took the view that the fundamental of Labor philosophy, and certainly the reason why I was a member of the Labor Party, was that it was about fairness and it was about trying to grow Australia in a way which looked after the most vulnerable. That's my concept of Labor philosophy and I think we were true to that. It's ridiculous to suggest in a rapidly changing world that all you've got to do is repeat the things that you did in another era which was unrecognisably different from this one.

Looking back into history, there have been some efforts by the Labor Party to implement its platform which proved to be spectacularly unsuccessful, such as Chifley's effort at bank nationalisation. How do you see that?

I have great admiration for Chifley and I've spoken about my admiration for Curtin. These were great men. I've used the phrase that when I became prime minister I stood on the shoulders of the giants of the past, and that's not just rhetoric. These were great, great men. But great men can make mistakes and I think the attempt to nationalise the banks was an emotional reaction and not sensible economic policy. It certainly wasn't sensible political policy and wasn't essential to Labor philosophy.

Do you think, when you look back through Australian history, that too many of our leaders have played the politics of confrontation and that this has undermined the best in the country?

I think there has been far too much confrontation in Australian politics. I preferred consensus. At a meeting of the Federal Executive, just before I was leader, I wrote down on the back of an envelope three words and said, this is what we should go into the 1983 election with— Reconciliation, Recovery and Reconstruction. That represented what I believed had to happen. The first was Reconciliation. Remember, in 1983 when we came to office the country was riven. We'd had the constitutional events of 1975, then a virulent anti-union policy under the Fraser Government, and we had city against country. The first thing that had to be done was to try and bring them together. That's why we had the Summit conference and I think it worked, and out of the process of Reconciliation we moved to consensus. I don't think we would have been able to reform the Australian economy unless we'd had that background and that approach.

As a son of the manse I had a father and mother who imbued in me a belief in the intrinsic value of every human being. My father said to me that a belief in the fatherhood of God necessarily involves a belief in the brotherhood of man. He said the one follows logically from the other. I've always held that there is a basic responsibility of one person to the other, a relationship of one person to the other, not just in a direct personal sense or in the community, but in a nation as a whole. What I was trying to say at the Summit was that workers have a legitimate interest in improving their standard of living. Employers have a legitimate interest in growing their businesses. Those dependent upon welfare have a legitimate concern to get a share of growth and to be protected. It's much more likely that each of those legitimate interests is going to be satisfied if we co-operate rather than fight one another. So it was a moral as well as a pragmatic view that I had.

I think one of the emotional highlights of your prime ministership was the trip to Gallipoli for the 75th anniversary of the first Anzac landing. How did you feel, presiding there above the beaches that morning?

I had a great sense of pride, not personal pride but pride in my country. There we were; the dawn was coming up. We were sitting waiting for the veterans, all in their nineties, to come up and be part of the ceremony. And on the side of the path were all these hundreds of young Australian backpackers. As the old men came up, the young Australians embraced them and they embraced them back and it sort of reinforced just how much we as Australians owed to those men for the tradition they established. It was a very moving moment. Then, in an equally moving moment when the ceremonies were over and we were going to have the eats and drinks, the Turkish veterans came in from the side and they and our old blokes went to one another. You watched them as they went towards one another—there was this sort of hesitancy, and then a rush to embrace. It was *very* moving.

I believe that Gallipoli was a major turning point in Australia's history. In 1915 we were only fifteen years old as a nation. People tended to think of themselves as much as being New South Welshmen, Victorians and so on as being Australians. What did Australia mean? It really hadn't jelled by that stage. I think Gallipoli did a hell of a lot to get into the minds of Australians that we were *Australians*. I mean, it was Mission Impossible, and when you went there and saw the place—my God, Australians have got much they shouldn't thank Churchill for. We've also got some things we should thank him for. But when you went to the beach and up the hills and then went in the trenches and saw where the action had taken place—the courage of these blokes and the mateship they displayed on this Mission Impossible was something that really did constitute a high turning point in our history.

So, to be there 75 years later and see the way in which these young Australians recognised what they owed as Australians to these men was something very special.

How would you describe the essential premise of your approach to foreign policy?

Some time before I became prime minister in 1983 it was crystal clear that Asia was going to be more and more important to us. And at a press conference I held on international affairs in my first week or so, I said that the future of Australia was going to depend upon us becoming more and more enmeshed with Asia. Remember, in 1983 we were still very much in the depths of the Cold War. The threat of Soviet hegemony was very real. You had Soviet bases in Vietnam. You had an arch of Soviet influence going from Angola through the Middle East and across Asia. In that context the relationship with the United States remained profoundly important and I did everything I could to strengthen that. But it was fundamentally important to me that Australia move from a position of just being seen to be an adjunct, an accessory, to the United States and to some extent Britain. For too long, except in the Whitlam period, there had been this view that you exhausted the exercise of foreign policy by looking to see what the United States and Britain were going to do and then put up your hand and follow. I wanted to build the United States relationship, because of the threat of the Soviet Union, but to make it clear to our American friends that we would do things and say things about which they may not be happy if it was our judgment that it was the right thing to do—for example, the South Pacific Nuclear Free Zone, disarmament issues and relations with Vietnam as the 1980s went on. We took initiatives in all those areas and our friends in the United States were significantly less than happy, but it was our judgment. We had to look at things and make decisions in terms of Australia's interests. If it upset the Americans, too bad, but we did that within the framework of keeping the alliance strong, because it had to be.

How important was China for you?

Profoundly important. I took the view, and I've not changed it, that China was going to be extraordinarily significant in our region and in the world. It's now 1.2 billion people, a fifth of the world's population. At some stage in this century, it will have in absolute terms the biggest economy in the world. When the Chinese do get to that point they'll just be resuming a position they have had for most of the last 2500 years. So it's very important to have a sensible relationship with China, and in economic terms there's a lot of possible synergies there.

It seemed to me very important to develop an understanding relationship with them in the sense that they have a different political system to us. Things happen in China that are not in accordance with the way we would do things and, of course, in 1989 I was terribly upset about what happened then. The truth is that as a result of that whole period—not just what I did: it started with Gough Whitlam, Malcolm Fraser to his credit kept it going, I accelerated it and Keating kept it going—as a result of that long period Australia developed an extraordinarily good relationship with China. When the Howard Government came in they did some silly things which jeopardised the relationship, but to the credit of this government they recognised the mistakes and so the relationship has been repaired.

In talking about Australia's relations with Asia you use the word 'enmeshed with Asia', and that of course implies a degree of intimacy. How do you regard the word?

Enmeshed means that you are interconnected. I wanted to see that, and not just in economic terms. I wanted to see it also in increased cultural relations, sporting relations, increased tourism from Australia to China. I wanted Australians to get to know Chinese people. I wanted Chinese to get to know Australia. So enmeshment simply was interconnection in many ways, not just economic. I wanted to see the process—not just with China, but with the region in all the ways I've talked about in regard to China. We were never going to be and we're not Asian but I wanted the Asian people, the Asian governments, to understand that we wanted to be, as far as possible, involved not only bilaterally but in multilateral organisations in discussions which were going to be helpful to them as well as to us. We wanted to have Asia seeing Australia as a country which was not just physically close to them but was aware of the challenges they faced and which wanted, within our relatively limited resources, to help them. I had the view that the more we were enmeshed with their development and their understanding of us, the more there was in the future going to be an understanding on their part of Australia's interests. I think the enormous number of Asians coming here for education is important. I don't think you can overestimate the importance of having people going back into Asia who have been educated here and hopefully well treated by Australians.

Does Australia have to choose between America on one hand and Asia on the other?

Australia doesn't have to choose between America and Asia. I mean, this concept that it's a matter of choice is stupid. When I was prime minister I didn't have to choose between America and Asia. I had a strengthened relationship with China but I was able to talk directly to the Chinese leadership and explain why our American relationship was there: we have our friendship with them but we have our friendship with you. Decent friendships are not defined by geography.

You said we're not an Asian country, but obviously we are part of the region. Do you think that we can successfully combine these two characteristics?

I've got no doubt that we can. You don't have to be theoretical about this. We've done it, and not just in my period of government. I never tried to say to the Asians that we are Asian. It would be an absurdity to say we are Asian—we are not. May I say I'm pleased that we are getting an increasing proportion of our population who are of Asian origin; I think that's great. But you've got to understand that 'Asia' is a term invented by Europeans. There is as much diversity within Asia as there is between Australia and a lot of Asian countries.

What's your view about the process of reconciliation with Aboriginal people? Are you an optimist about this or do you believe it's going to take us a long time as a nation?

Ultimately I'm an optimist. I think the process has been set back under the present government. But let me say this: the reasons for optimism are, firstly, as far as the Australian people are concerned I think there is goodwill there; secondly, on both sides of politics there are people of goodwill on this issue; thirdly, within the Aboriginal community there are some outstandingly able people of goodwill. And fourthly, and I don't think enough attention is paid to this, within the mining industry there are people of goodwill who have sat down with the Aboriginal representatives and in every major mining State and in the Northern Territory there are significant agreements in place which allow exploration and development of our mineral resources in co-operation with the Aboriginal people. For non-Aboriginal Australians, it is vital to understand the fundamental importance of land to the Aboriginal people. It's not just a question of prior ownership, which in itself is important, but that the land is intrinsic to their beliefs and their gods. We've got to understand that and act upon that basis.

Your government decided not to legislate for national land rights. Was that a sound decision or do you have regrets about that?

It was a difficult decision and it was taken in the context that there was not yet, at that stage, sufficient understanding on the part of some electorates, particularly in Western Australia. An enormously virulent campaign had been waged over there which made people in a suburb of Perth think that their houses were going to be taken over, and it required, I think, more time. I only wish that Mabo could have come on my watch.

We talked about the great tolerance of the Australian people, but is there a problem in their hearts when it comes to the Aboriginal people?

The last words I said as prime minister were when we were hanging the Barunga portrait in Parliament House on the 20th of December 1991. I said [to the Aboriginal people present], in regard to reconciliation, that I hope that we will move to have embodied in a treaty a reconciliation between us; but I finished up saying, but what is important is what is in your hearts.

You would have to say honestly that you would like to feel there was more passion amongst non-Aboriginal Australians about the issue of our responsibility to our fellow Australians, the Aborigines. I think there are, you know, tens and tens of thousands of good people who have that passion. It's not broad enough yet, so there's more work to be done. But I am optimistic that we'll get there.

I said I would personally like to see a treaty. I tried deliberately not to make the position too difficult by saying, 'that's what it is'. I established the reconciliation process and to their credit the Opposition became part of that. You've got to have the right attitude in enough of the Australian people for a treaty to become a reality, and there's still a fair bit of work to be done on that.

4

Unfinished Business

In the beginning was the Dreamtime. The Aboriginal peoples came to Australia across water in a story lost in the mists of antiquity. Aboriginal civilisation was largely untouched during an unbroken history estimated at 50 000 years and perhaps much longer. That is 2000 generations, in comparison with the eight or ten generations of European civilisation on the continent.

When Britain's most famous naval explorer, James Cook, sighted the Aborigines he wrote: 'they may appear to some to be the most wretched people upon Earth, but in reality they are far more happy than we Europeans.' In January 1788 the first Governor of New South Wales, Arthur Phillip, raised the Union Jack at Sydney Cove and took possession of the land in the name of the British Crown. The doctrine of *terra nullius*—that nobody owned the land—was assumed.

Yet from the start the settlers and soldiers were interacting with the Aborigines, a people with their own customs, extended families, social law and spiritual beliefs. Phillip laid the foundations of a colony but his failure was the resort to violence in this opening European–Aboriginal dialogue. The unfolding encounter would be marked by mutual incomprehension, misunderstanding and the destruction of much of Aboriginal society. There was no acknowledgement of British conquest of the indigenous people; no act of submission; no treaty to govern the relationship. British sovereignty equated with Aboriginal dispossession.

One of Australia's most prominent anthropologists, John Mulvaney, says: 'When Europeans came here, the Aboriginal population was probably half a million, if not more. By the time of Federation it was probably down to a hundred thousand or less. This was mainly caused by introduced disease. The Aboriginal population was very susceptible to European-induced diseases. Even common colds, measles, whooping cough, things of that kind, virtually decimated them because they had no resistance.'

Ten weeks after Federation, on 19 March 1901, a pioneering

This colour etching entitled 'Old Race and the New' of an elderly Aboriginal woman leaning on the arm of a young white woman was published in 1875. It is an unusual commentary on race relations.

anthropological expedition left Oodnadatta to document the conditions of the Aborigines in Central Australia. It would produce the first sound and moving footage of Australian Aborigines and it travelled through land where the encounter between Aborigines and Europeans was only 30 years old. This was the Baldwin Spencer and Gillen expedition. It would offer anthropological confirmation of the political judgment made by the Federation architects—that the native savage, the victim of the 1788 arrival, was doomed.

English-born Walter Baldwin Spencer, foundation Professor of Biology at Melbourne University, was a diligent scientist imbued with the values of his time and certain of the superiority of European civilisation. His colleague was Frank Gillen, a rogue, a reckless sharetrader, former post and telegraph master at Alice Springs and a defender of the Aborigines against brutality. The pair were accompanied by and dependent upon two Aboriginal men, Erlikilyika and Parunda.

Gillen, a Central Australian veteran since his arrival in 1875, was sympathetic to the Aborigine. He had mastered two dialects of Arrente and was regarded as an initiated member of the Arrente tribe. But Gillen was a pessimist about the future of the Aboriginal people: 'Boiled down, the whole policy of the department should have two objects, firstly, to collect and record the habits, customs etc and secondly to make the path to extinction—which we all agree is inevitable and rapidly approaching—as pleasant as possible.'

The expedition travelled through Alice Springs, then known as Stuart, which had a white population of about a dozen and three breweries. After the overland telegraph came the pastoral industry, which would transform Aboriginal life and become dependent upon unpaid Aboriginal labour. This was frontier territory. No arrests were made before the late 1880s, dogs and revolvers proving highly efficient.

The expedition spent nine months in central and northern Australia. The party documented a traditional culture and created a heritage for the Aboriginal people. Despite his sympathy for the Aborigine Baldwin Spencer, like Gillen, believed that in contact with the white man he was 'doomed to disappear'. John Mulvaney says: 'They thought the Aboriginal people were going to die out absolutely. Of course, they and many others at the time only thought of people who were fully tribal, fully traditional. Once intermarriage took place with other races they thought this was degenerate.'

For Aborigines, Federation in 1901 meant nothing and gave them nothing. The Constitution refused to acknowledge the Aboriginal people, let alone provide for them in the new nation. This contrasts with both the United States and the Canadian Constitutions which contained provisions relating to the indigenous people. There are many commentaries on our long debated and carefully drafted document but this absence is the moral vacuum at the heart of the Constitution and the Australian nation. The reason for it was that the founders believed the Aborigines were a dying race. The Constitution was premised on the death of the original inhabitants, a conclusion arrived at by observation and by scientific faith in Social Darwinism. *The Bulletin* welcomed this grim prospect: 'There is no valid reason why the nigger should not be wiped out by— let us say—natural decay.'

The Constitution mentioned Aborigines twice, merely to exclude them from the census (s. 127) and to exclude them from the Commonwealth's power to 'make laws for the people of any race . . . for whom it is deemed necessary to make special laws' (s. 51(xxvi)). These exclusions remained until removed by a constitutional referendum in 1967. Responsibility for Aborigines was left with the States, most of which had discriminatory laws of varying harshness. The conclusion is unavoidable: there was no sense, no recognition, whatsoever that Aboriginal dispossession or the injustice had to be addressed or rectified in the new Commonwealth. However, the Constitution did not deny Aborigines rights of citizenship and it did not deny them the right to vote.

The denial was an altogether more deliberate and disreputable affair. In 1902 the Commonwealth Parliament passed a law to provide for a uniform franchise in federal elections. Australia, an enlightened democracy, passed an enlightened law—it gave the vote to all men and women, married or unmarried, aged 21 and over. Australia was the second nation to provide for female suffrage. But during the debate the bill was amended to deny Aborigines the vote. Australia was a liberal but racist democracy. This repudiation of political rights ran into most aspects of citizenship law over the next several decades. The injustice was removed only in 1962 when the Commonwealth Parliament finally gave Aborigines the right to vote, thereby wiping one of the most odious laws from its statute books.

The Government Senate leader and future High Court judge, Richard O'Connor, had introduced the franchise bill on 9 April 1902. It extended the vote not just to women but to Aborigines. It was a victory for Australia's pioneering feminists and campaigners for women's suffrage. O'Connor said: 'I think that we might treat this question of the position of Aboriginals under our electoral laws not only fairly but with some generosity. Unfortunately they are a failing race.'

There was strong opposition to O'Connor's position from Western Australia. Senator Alexander Matheson, a wealthy businessman and English aristocrat with a perfect dress sense and marked English accent who had migrated to the west in 1894, moved an amendment. It was to strike down the Aboriginal franchise. Matheson told the Senate: 'Surely it is absolutely repugnant to the greater number of the people of the Commonwealth that an Aboriginal man, or Aboriginal lubra or gin—a horrible degraded dirty creature—should have the same rights, simply by virtue of being 21 years of age, that we have after some debate today decided to give to our wives and daughters. To me it is as repugnant and atrocious a legislative proposal as any one could suggest.'

In a powerful and eloquent attack on the amendment Richard O'Connor adverted to Aboriginal dispossession, an unusual concession to truth. His speech is an historic epic—a benchmark against which the young nation must be measured and found wanting. O'Connor said: 'It would be a monstrous thing, an unheard of piece of savagery on our part, to treat the Aboriginals, whose land we were occupying, in such a manner as to deprive them absolutely of any right to vote in their own country, simply on the ground of their colour and because they were Aboriginals.' Yet this is exactly what the parliament proceeded to do.

At first and briefly O'Connor carried the day. Matheson's amendment was defeated 12–8 in the Senate. The bill now went to the House of Representatives. The debate was short and shameful.

After the principle of female suffrage was agreed the Labor leader, Chris Watson, said: 'I want to submit for the consideration of the committee the question of whether it is a wise thing to enfranchise all the Aboriginal inhabitants of Australia.' Watson's fear was that Labor would be disadvantaged. He argued that in Western Australia and Queensland there were many Aboriginals whose votes would be manipulated by their employers and delivered to the anti-Labor side. In reference to these two States he said: 'There are thousands upon thousands of Aboriginals. In some electorates they positively outnumber the white people. In Western Australia I understand Aboriginals are very largely indentured to squatters. They are practically the slaves of those squatters . . . they would not dare to attempt to exercise their votes in defiance of the wishes of their masters.' In North Queensland, Watson argued, 'uncivilised blacks' could be brought in to 'turn the tide at an election'.

Watson was followed by the Victorian pro-Labor independent, H B Higgins, later hailed as the father of arbitration and an Australian champion of social justice. He moved to deny Aborigines the vote. 'It is utterly inappropriate to grant the franchise to the Aborigines or to ask them to exercise an intelligent vote,' Higgins told the parliament. 'I do not think that there is any constitutional obligation on the committee to provide for a uniform franchise for the Aborigines.'

Under s. 41 of the Constitution the Commonwealth could not strip voting rights that applied at the State level. Western Australia did not recognise Aboriginal voting rights; Queensland all but denied them; such rights existed in the other four States and Aborigines in these States had been entitled to vote at the first federal election in 1901, though most did not. Only a limited number were enrolled. Higgins's amendment was consistent with s. 41 and its effect was to deny the federal vote to any Aborigine who did not yet vote at the State level.

The Barton Government accepted the Higgins amendment. A future Governor-General, Sir Isaac Isaacs was a strong supporter of it: 'The Aboriginals have not the intelligence, interest or capacity to enable them to stand on the same platform with the rest of the people of Australia . . . How, for instance, would these blacks vote on the question of a white Australia?'

The former premier of Tasmania, Sir Edward Braddon, quickly despatched the argument about dispossession: 'We are told that we have taken their country from them. But it seems a poor sort of justice to recompense those people for the loss of their country by giving them votes.'

The Higgins amendment was carried 27–5 and the bill was recommitted to the Senate. A humiliated O'Connor concealed his embarrassment with sarcasm: 'The prospect of our giving the franchise to the half-wild gins living with their tribe seems to have startled some of our friends in the other house. I very much prefer the bill to be carried in the form in which

Local Aboriginals were involved in a re-enactment ceremony during Sydney's Australian Commonwealth celebrations in 1901 despite the Constitution not acknowledging them as a people.

it left the Senate.' But O'Connor said regretfully that the amendment was needed to save the bill. The Senate voted accordingly.

In their book *Citizens Without Rights*, John Chesterman and Brian Galligan argue that this franchise law was the basis on which denial of citizenship rights to Aborigines became entrenched. They said: 'Had O'Connor prevailed, Australia's Aboriginal people might have been saved from 60 years of deprivation of basic citizenship rights, the consequences of which are still clearly visible.'

In a sense there was worse to come. Sir Robert Garran, the Commonwealth's most influential legal adviser for the first three decades (as head of the Attorney General's Department and then Solicitor-General), consistently offered a restrictive interpretation of s. 41 to successive governments. Garran's view was that 'a right under s. 41 ... does not entitle any person to vote whose name is not on the Commonwealth electoral roll'. Under Garran's influence the Electoral Commission denied federal enrolment to any Aborigine not entitled to vote in a State election before 1902.

In effect, the 1902 law had sent a signal to politicians, lawyers and the public—that Aborigines were of little worth. It encouraged a policy of exclusion and discrimination towards them at federal and State level. It was the Constitution that largely ignored the Aborigines and assumed that they were doomed. But it was the Commonwealth Parliament that decided they would be denied basic political rights before they became extinct.

In 1911 the Commonwealth acquired control of the Northern Territory from South Australia. This meant it had responsibility for a quarter of the surviving Aborigines. At this time in the Territory men outnumbered women in a 4:1 ratio which meant that Aboriginal women were in demand and sexual access was either presumed or negotiated with payment in alcohol or opium. Baldwin Spencer was appointed briefly as Chief Protector of Aborigines. This position had legal authority for near total control of Aboriginal life—children, marriage, employment.

In his July 1913 report Baldwin Spencer provided a comprehensive survey of the condition of the indigenous people:

> The Aboriginal is, indeed, a very curious mixture; mentally, about the level of a child who has little control over his feelings. He has no sense of responsibility and, except in rare cases, no initiative. His memory in many cases is wonderful. When once he has seen any place or any particular natural object he knows it for all time.

Baldwin Spencer recommended large-scale reserves as the only way of preserving tribal Aboriginal life. But those Aborigines who had gone to the towns 'have long since become degenerate and have lost all their old customs and beliefs'. Once the traditional culture had been broken the Aborigine had lost his way.

The report identified a serious expanding problem:

> No half-caste children should be allowed to remain in any native camp, but they should all be withdrawn and placed on stations. So far as practicable, this plan is now being adopted. In some cases, when the child is very young, it must of necessity be accompanied by its mother, but in other cases, even though it may seem cruel to separate the mother and child, it is better to do so, when the mother is living, as is usually the case, in a native camp.

The idea took hold at an early stage: part-Aboriginal children were seen to have a chance to find a place, although an inferior place, in white society.

The 'half-caste' children were relegated to special homes or compounds. It became a Federal Government practice to separate part-Aboriginal children from Aboriginal society. The justification in all official documents is clear: the welfare of the child. This was both a racial policy and a welfare policy. In terms of the contemporary Australian debate the claim that it was only a welfare policy cannot be sustained—nor can the claim that it was motivated just by race and not the welfare of the child.

On 12 September 1911 the acting Administrator of the Territory had written to the Minister for External Affairs recommending that all half-caste children be assembled in an institution. 'No doubt the mothers would object,' he wrote. 'But the future of the children should I think outweigh all other considerations.'

The Bungalow was established for this purpose at Alice Springs in 1914. It was three corrugated iron sheds. Each child received one blanket a year. Instruction was provided by the matron, Ida Standley. She wrote to the External Affairs Department in Canberra on 21 June 1915: 'It affords me great pleasure to forward you some specimens of work done by half-caste children at Alice Springs ... the little half-castes have possibilities of a future.' The Northern Territory Administrator was proud of the Bungalow and wrote the Minister on 27 November 1914: 'These half-castes, quadroon and octoroon children have been brought together and are now accommodated in a building erected under the supervision of Senior Constable Stott, Protector of Aboriginals. The erection of the building has cost only 25 pounds.'

However, some visitors from outside the Territory were shocked. In 1924 M H Ellis in the Brisbane *Daily Mail* reported: 'This is an institution which must make everyone who sees it burn with indignation. It is more than a scandal. It is a horror.'

Removal of part-Aboriginal children was conducted on a legal basis. The main authorising instrument was the Aboriginals Ordinance 1918, which replaced an earlier 1911 law. Under this new ordinance the Northern Territory Director was authorised at any time 'to undertake the care, custody or control of any Aboriginal or half-caste, if, in his opinion, it is necessary or desirable or in the interests of the Aboriginal or half-caste for him do so.' The Director had immense powers—he was the legal guardian of every Aboriginal and he could enter any premises to take a person into custody without consent.

The issue here is not legal. It is moral, racial and social. The practice of removal clearly reflected the values of the age. The purpose of removal was written into the law—the welfare of the child.

In his August 2000 Federal Court judgment, Justice O'Loughlin ventilated some of the critical issues. To what extent did this practice constitute a federal policy of removal of part-Aboriginal children? Was it selective and on the basis of the child's interest? Was it a 'blanket' removal policy irrespective of circumstance and without assessment of the child's interest? How much was it based on coercion? These issues are still being contested and Justice O'Loughlin identified some of the key historical decisions.

In 1928 Queensland's Chief Protector of Aboriginals, J W Bleakley, was commissioned to inquire into the situation of Aborigines in the Northern Territory. He recommended that 'all half-castes of illegitimate birth, whether male or female, should be rescued from the camps, whether station or bush, and placed in institutions for care and training.' The government accepted Bleakley's recommendation in a media release of 14 July 1930, with the exception that the responsibility for education of the part-Aboriginal children who had been removed would rest with the government and not with the missions as suggested by Bleakley.

Official documents from the 1930s reveal the basics of the policy which were summarised by Justice O'Loughlin: since 1911 part-Aboriginal children were taken from native camps; the policy mainly applied to illegitimate children with a full Aboriginal mother and white father living in tribal conditions; they were reared and educated as a government responsibilility; the purpose was to enable them to find a place in the life of the white community; the view was that, left in the camps, they would be treated as outcasts; in the early decades there was scant reference to parental consent and no evidence to indicate that consent was a requirement or priority. The practice evolved over time and by the 1940s greater weight was given to parental consent.

In the early days of the policy the two main homes for part-Aboriginal children were at Darwin and the Bungalow. In the 1930s the head dormitory girl at the Bungalow was Hetti Perkins, whose tenth child would become a courageous fighter for his people. Charles Perkins, who died in October 2000, said of the Bungalow: 'The dormitories were pretty rough to live in. Everybody slept in rows, like in prison, and the food was all served up in a harsh manner as though you were all in prison and you ate what you had in front of you and you don't ask for anything more, and my mother was, you know, trying to keep everybody organised and keep the morale up and everything, and so it was pretty tough going for all of us.'

The values underpinning the policy would be unacceptable in the year 2000. The removal policy occurred in the long age of dogmatic paternalism. The worth of family connection, the mother–child bond and the emotional deprivation of child separation were severely downgraded or ignored as factors to be taken into account. The pervasive assumption and

A group of Aboriginal women and children at Bungalow, Alice Springs.

arrogant justification were that removal would be in the child's best interest. Many children were scarred for life; others lived better than would otherwise have been the case.

The policy was implemented against a changing backdrop reflected in two events—the last Aboriginal massacre in the Territory, and enshrinement of assimilation as a powerful guiding philosophy for the future.

In the 1920s and 1930s Alice Springs was still a frontier town. Mounted Constable William George Murray was the local policeman. A first-rate shot and a Light Horse veteran from Gallipoli, he thrived in the outback. In August 1928 he organised a search party to track down the Aborigines responsible for the murder of a dingo trapper, Fred Brookes, killed by the local Warlpiri, 14 miles from Coniston Station.

Murray later admitted that his expedition had killed 31 Aborigines, including two women. Murray arrested two of the Warlpiri for killing Brookes. At trial they were found not guilty. The journalist and writer Ernestine Hill reported an exchange during Murray's cross-examination:

Annie Lock with a group of Aboriginal children.

'"But you didn't shoot to kill, Mr Murray?" It was at Darwin that a judge of the Supreme Court asked that question. Straight and clear, came the answer he was not expecting—"Every time."' The Aborigines claimed that more than 31 were killed and a lay missionary, Annie Lock, said: 'The natives tell me that they simply shot them like dogs and that they got the little children and hit them on the back of the neck and killed them . . . instead of 31 it was over 70.'

Prime Minister S M Bruce was forced to hold an inquiry. Two police officials, A H O'Kelly and P A Giles, and Murray's superior, J C Cawood, presided. They found that 'the shooting was justified' and that there was no evidence of a massacre. The official finding said: 'Each of the witnesses . . . emphatically stated that the shooting was absolutely necessary to save their own lives . . . no provocation has been given which could account for the depredations by the Aborigines and their attacks on white men in Central Australia.'

It was a whitewash. Murray was cleared and demands for his removal were rejected. The white power structure was rarely able to confront the need for justice on the basis of equality before the law. After all, the Aborigines were seen as inferior and had been denied full citizenship rights.

As for the Warlpiri, they retreated from their traditional lands after the killings. The recompense would take 50 years—when Justice Toohey accepted their claim under land rights law.

Despite the violence and disease it was obvious by the 1920s that the Aboriginal people had triumphed over the European belief that they would die out. The more elementary view of Social Darwinists had been defied. The Aborigines, despite the destruction of their society, would survive the encounter with the white man. It was at this point that the white man formalised a new theory to manage this outcome. The symbol of this process was the April 1937 inaugural meeting of Commonwealth and State officials responsible for Aborigines, which formulated for the first time an agreed national policy. It was summarised under the heading 'Destiny of the Race': 'That this conference believes that the destiny of the natives of Aboriginal origin, but not of the full blood, lies in their ultimate absorption by the people of the Commonwealth and it therefore recommends that all efforts be directed to that end.' In order to realise this objective, State government efforts should be 'towards the education of children of mixed Aboriginal blood at white standards and their subsequent employment under the same conditions as whites with a view to taking their place in the white community on an equal footing with the whites'.

Assimilation was being enshrined at the heart of policy. The meeting affirmed the current practice in relation to part-Aboriginals but gave a firmer philosophical basis to the policy. The aim was to prepare those Aboriginals who were able to take their place as 'honorary' whites. In relation to 'full blood natives' the policy was either assimilation over a longer period or, for the 'uncivilised native', the establishment of inviolable reserves. The assumption was that assimilation was doing Aborigines a great favour—they would be given entry into white society. Over the decades the policy would evolve and be refined. Its greatest exponent was the principal Aboriginal affairs administrator, and intellectual of the Menzian age, Paul Hasluck.

As a journalist Hasluck reported on the plight of the Aboriginal people. His MA thesis was on native policy in his home state of Western Australia—his argument being that the idealism of the early settlers in trying to civilise the Aborigine had been lost by successive generations. When Hasluck became Minister for Territories in 1951 he aspired to reform. 'From the start,' he said later, 'I had urged that we should replace the idea of protecting the Aborigines with the idea of advancing their welfare. I sought a system under which the Aborigines were recognised as Australian citizens and were regarded as having the same status and rights as other Australian citizens.'

The reality had been far harsher than such theory conceded. The child removal policy had continued in the Northern Territory and was notable for a 1949 incident involving a patrol officer, Ted Evans. Evans filed a report about his removal of five children by plane from Wave Hill, referring to 'the grief and fear of the children resulting in near hysteria in two of them'. Acting on this report the Government Secretary, R S Leydin, wrote to the Administrator warning of the need for ministerial approval of such a policy and for arguments to justify it. By the early 1950s there was concern and debate about the nature of the policy and its application.

After Hasluck became minister he found that opinion was divided within the Territorial administration about the child removal policy but that 'in southern church circles and among those sympathetically concerned with the plight of Aborigines there was a strong continuing advocacy of giving children "a chance in life"'. Justice O'Loughlin's judgment in August 2000 offers a detailed account of Hasluck's 1952 policy decisions about child removal. Hasluck decided that children could be removed on the grounds of neglect, the need for medical care or at the request of the mother. Children could be removed in other circumstances provided that 'a painstaking attempt has been made to explain to the mother the advantages to be gained'. The younger the child was at the time of removal the better. While maternal consent was desirable, it was not essential.

In a minute of 12 September 1952 Hasluck wrote: 'The test to be applied is simply what action is likely to be conducive to a happy future for the child. I do not want a hard and fast rule.' He favoured a transfer out of the Northern Territory to suitable institutions and private homes.

Aborigines had survived but their culture would die. The assumption now was a form of cultural Darwinism. In his 1988 book *Shades of Darkness*, Hasluck revealed his still prevailing belief: 'I believe that in the long run, perhaps several generations ahead, the vestiges of an Aboriginal society, in spite of many ingenious attempts to find a new cohesion, will gradually fade away, but there will still be Aborigines in Australia.'

Hasluck fought the apathy within the Commonwealth Government towards Aboriginal issues. After twelve years as minister he was proud of his achievements and the improvement in living conditions. He saw the tragic life of Aboriginal painter Albert Namatjira—a man trapped between two cultures—as confirmation of the validity of his assimilation policy. For Hasluck assimilation was not just a theory but an empirical matter; it was based upon the 'observation by anthropologists of the crumbling away of Aboriginal society and culture'.

However, assimilation was driven by a deeper impulse: the Australian idea of racial unity. The embrace of the White Australia policy at Federation was not primarily about economics. It was about identity. Australia chose to define its nationhood in terms of cultural homogeneity and racial

Paul Hasluck with a family in front of new Aboriginal housing.

unity. Aborigines would not be allowed to break this mould. They would be required to conform to the mainstream. The contrast often drawn in the 1950s and 1960s was with segregation. In August 1959, addressing an audience of scientists at the ANZAAS conference, Hasluck began by saying that Australians had rejected the idea of segregation. In 1963 he said: 'There shall be no racial group living within its own closed boundaries of land completely segregated from the rest of the Australian community.' It was because there were many Australians, particularly in country towns, who wanted and practised segregation that assimilation was often seen in ambivalent terms by conservatives. Despite the lapse in practice, it represented a repudiation of the South African racial model.

The reality, though, was that the Menzies Government was reluctant to show leadership in tackling the extent of discrimination against Aborigines. Charles Perkins recalled the early 1960s situation: 'If you went into a dress shop, if you were a woman, well, you just don't try the dress on. And if you did try it on, you buy it, regardless whether it fitted or not. In a delicatessen or, you know, a milk bar, a restaurant, if a white person came in, you've got to give up your seat. If they haven't got a seat you stand back. And if they're at the counter, even if you're there first, you've got to let them be served. Everybody accepted that. And the same with swimming pools and picture theatres. You go down the front straightaway.'

But the Menzies Government did move to correct the injustice of 1902, the denial of voting rights. This followed a campaign by sections of the Australian Labor Party for many years. In 1962 the government introduced a bill to ensure that all Aboriginals and Torres Strait Islanders had the right to vote at federal elections. Enrolment would be voluntary but, once enrolled, compulsory voting would be enforced in the normal way. The government acted on a select committee report which said: 'The Aboriginal people are increasing in numbers. Changes have occurred in the customs of the great majority which ensure, in the words of one of our witnesses, "that they will never tend to die out again".'

In the debate a future Aboriginal Affairs Minister, Peter Howson, said there was no need to apologise for past failures. Kim Beazley Snr said the bill would rectify the situation in Queensland, Western Australia and the Northern Territory where the vote had been taken away. Hasluck said that 25 years earlier when he had advocated the Aboriginal vote he had been 'laughed out of court'. He hoped the Aborigine would feel a pride in his ancestry but 'learn to be proud of the fact that he is an Australian'. Overall, there was little sense of outrage at the magnitude or length of the denial of political rights now being rectified. The change to the law was unanimous.

The next year, at the 1963 conference of federal and State ministers, the official policy was defined in these terms: 'Assimilation means that all Aborigines and part-Aborigines will attain the same manner of living as other Australians and live as members of a single Australian community . . . observing the same customs and influenced by the same beliefs, hopes and loyalties as other Australians.' The notion of a common destiny was powerful but it had consequences which the political elite had not fully comprehended. A mood for dramatic change was now building.

An effective lobby group of largely non-Aboriginal activists had emerged to campaign for Aboriginal rights. The moving spirit was the feminist Jessie Street. In 1958 a new organisation was created—later known as the

During the Freedom Ride through western New South Wales, Charlie Perkins took on local authorities who refused to allow Aboriginal people to use a town swimming pool.

Federal Council for the Advancement of Aborigines and Torres Strait Islanders (FCAATSI)—which called for constitutional reform and equal citizenship rights. The ALP Federal Conference in the late 1950s adopted a motion seeking the removal of constitutional discrimination as policy. Hasluck was reluctant to respond to these moves and preferred to emphasise practical action. The most powerful focus on Aboriginal injustice came with the Freedom Rides through New South Wales country towns in the early 1960s, pioneered by Charles Perkins with student support. The Freedom Rides would dramatise for the rest of Australia the extent of racism and segregation institutionalised in country towns. By the mid-1960s there was a push from political activists, the churches, the ALP and a new group of Aboriginal leaders for major reform.

In 1965 a delegation of Aboriginal leaders came to Canberra for a meeting with Prime Minister Menzies. It was a brief encounter between two alien worlds. Menzies for most of his prime ministership had displayed little interest in Aboriginal affairs. A young Faith Bandler was one of the activists and recounts what happened: 'He [Menzies] had no idea there was such suffering in this country, no idea whatsoever. He listened very carefully and then later he said, "Well, come and have some tea in the ante room." He started off by offering drinks and he said to Oodgeroo, who was then Kath Walker the poet, and whose work he had read, "What will you drink?" She said, "Well, Prime Minister, if you lived in Queensland and offered me a drink, you'd be put in jail." And he hesitated and I could see, we could all see, he was quite shocked—this woman who had created these beautiful poems that he'd read was deprived of having a drink. Totally illegal in the State she came from. And I remember very clearly, he threw his head in the air and said, "Well, I'm the boss around here", and she had some alcohol with us. It was very revealing.'

But the Aboriginal delegation did not convince Menzies. On the removal of Aboriginal discrimination, like the abolition of White Australia, Menzies was unmoved.

The proof of this came when in 1965 Attorney General Billy Snedden took to cabinet a submission for a referendum to remove the two discriminatory provisions of the Constitution. Menzies agreed that s. 127, which excluded Aborigines from the census, should be deleted. It was agreed that this was offensive and an embarrassment. But Menzies drew the line at deletion of s. 51(xxvi), which said that the Commonwealth could make laws for any race excluding the Aboriginal people. Snedden argued that if the cabinet was to be credible in removing discrimination it should also tackle the s. 51(xxvi) anomaly. But Menzies' main public service adviser, Sir John Bunting, urged caution, asking: 'Is the government yet ready to take a far-reaching policy decision of this kind?'

This constitutional amendment had a great potential. Once the Commonwealth had the power to pass laws in relation to the Aboriginal people then the path would be open for the Commonwealth to assume a degree of direct responsibility. Snedden made it clear that this was not the political intention and that the policy status quo would prevail. His argument was tactical: unless the referendum was seen to be credible, it might actually be defeated.

The cabinet took a grudging decision in favour of a referendum to remove the census exclusion alone. Menzies told parliament it would be too dangerous to abolish the s. 51 provision. He saw such a move as an attack upon assimilation since the resulting power would 'enable the parliament to set up for example a separate body of industrial, social, criminal and other laws relating exclusively to Aborigines'. For Menzies the undesirable result would be that Aborigines 'would be treated as a race apart'. The Coalition, mercifully, decided not to put the narrow referendum it had endorsed, and the substantive change had to wait until Harold Holt succeeded Menzies.

In February 1967 the Holt Cabinet accepted the essentials of the Snedden submission as advanced by the new Attorney General, Nigel

Bowen. But it was with the proviso that, if the referendum was successful, the States would retain responsibility for the administration of Aboriginal affairs, though the Commonwealth would have 'a role of policy participation'. That is, in practical terms very little would change.

As the years have passed, the 1967 referendum has become a much misunderstood event. Indeed, so severe has been the misunderstanding that it is often wrongly reported that the referendum gave Aborigines the vote and it is almost universally assumed that the referendum gave Aborigines citizenship rights—when it did nothing of the sort. The tendency, as Bain Attwood and Andrew Marcus point out, has been to invest the referendum with a deeper meaning that is inconsistent both with its constitutional impact and with Holt's campaign.

The inescapable conclusion from the cabinet papers and public statements is that the government saw the referendum not as the path towards a new policy but as a means of correcting 'misleading' impressions about racial discrimination in Australia. The question as to what the referendum was and how it was seen at the time is central to explaining the remarkable 'yes' vote.

Holt's referendum campaign was well intentioned but weak. There was no plan or vision for the Commonwealth to pursue Aboriginal advancement after the new power had been mandated. The strongest line Holt offered in his speech launching the 'yes' campaign was that the two provisions in question were 'completely out of harmony with our national attitudes and modern thinking' and had 'no place in our Constitution in this age'. In the Coalition's mindset the referendum was actually a vote for the policy status quo. It was about proving that Australia did not discriminate against Aborigines, removing grounds for international criticism of Australia and, in terms of practical messages, giving Aborigines a fair go.

Peter Howson says: 'I don't think we had looked at it . . . that it was going to be such an historic point. I think it was really looked on at that time as something . . . that was just putting to rights a situation that was, had been, anomalous.'

However, the referendum was partially hijacked by the more ambitious outlook of the ALP and of FCAATSI. Their aim was to inject greater meaning into the vote and to put Holt under pressure to respond to its success. In the words of Attwood and Marcus, FCAATSI 'misrepresented' the campaign by suggesting it meant that the Commonwealth would assume responsibility for Aboriginal affairs and adopt major new programs. Labor's shadow minister, Gordon Bryant, said that 'the referendum would not solve everything but it would be a start on a national problem'. Attwood and Marcus explain that FCAATSI was astute in depicting the

Celebrating the 1967 Referendum victory.

elimination of the census provision as affecting political status. It called for a 'yes' vote so that Aborigines would be regarded 'as Australian citizens by right'. This rhetoric would endure. But the Holt Cabinet had bigger fish to fry, as two different referendums were put on 27 May 1967. The other referendum was to amend s. 24 so as to break the nexus that required the Senate to be approximately half the size of the House of Representatives. This was more contentious, and it was contested. The impression was that the government ran the proposals together in the hope that the momentum for the Aboriginal referendum would also carry the nexus referendum. Such hopes would be dashed.

The Aboriginal referendum result was stunning. There has never been anything like it. In a nation that usually rejected referendums, the 'yes' vote was 90.8 per cent. Only 9.2 per cent voted 'no'. While the opposition in rural seats was higher, the 'no' vote was still only 13.1 per cent in rural Australia. This was hardly an urban–rural divide.

It was the sentiment of a more innocent, less politicised age. It was a goodwill vote; a vote for Aborigines to be treated as equals, to be given a fair go. But in no way was it a repudiation of assimilation. The Aboriginal affairs scholar, C D Rowley, said the vote was the expression of 'a changing public opinion' and a general feeling 'that something was wrong'. There are, however, two conclusions to be drawn.

First, the referendum raised expectations enormously among Aboriginal leaders and the ALP. The vote was used in subsequent years as a basis for campaigns for Aboriginal initiatives and land rights which were never the legal issue at the 1967 referendum. The mandate of 1967 was consistently exaggerated by its champions, who imputed views to the Australian people that they had never expressed in the referendum vote itself. This sowed the seeds for misunderstanding in future years.

Second, the referendum, far from offering a basis on which to settle Aboriginal policy, guaranteed that the real battle was about to begin. It exposed the gulf between the Holt Government running largely on the status quo and progressive opinion which saw the referendum as a call to action. It is not too much of an exaggeration to say that the difference was between those who saw the referendum as an end and those who saw it as a beginning.

Harold Holt established a Council of Aboriginal Affairs with Dr H C Coombs as chairman. But it became a time of frustration and bitterness. Coombs was disillusioned, particularly with the startling lack of commitment displayed by Liberal prime ministers John Gorton and Billy McMahon before the 1972 Coalition defeat.

However, the 1967–72 period was dominated by a revolution within the Aboriginal leadership. A new idea would take hold arising from the historical view of Aboriginal dispossession and the claim by Aborigines of land rights based on traditional association. This was no longer a quest for equal rights; it was a declaration of Aboriginal rights. Henry Reynolds has argued the historical depth of the land rights case. But in political terms it arose abruptly, and quickly became a divisive yet irresistible force.

In August 1966 the Gurindji and their families walked off the giant Wave Hill pastoral station in the Northern Territory demanding equal pay. Wave Hill was owned by a British company, the Vestey Corporation. The strike was led by the head stockman, Vincent Lingiari, and it would change the course of Australian history. It resulted in a collaboration between the Gurindji leaders and non–indigenous Australian activists that created the land rights movement.

The Arbitration Commission had ruled in 1966 to extend the pastoral award to Aborigines but only after two years. Aboriginal leaders were outraged at the delay. In fact, the economic impact of the decision would later prove to be disastrous for Aboriginal employment. The Gurindji made their camp at Wattie Creek and soon won support from trade unions, the ALP, much of the southern media and, in particular, Frank Hardy, writer, communist and pro-Aboriginal activist. Hardy went to the Territory to assist the Gurindji campaign. From the start he drafted demands which made the campaign more political than industrial.

In his analysis of the strike Bain Attwood documents the centrality of Hardy's role. In an unpublished letter to *The Australian* in September 1966 Hardy wrote: 'Vesteys do not own this land ... The land of course is Crown Land controlled by the Federal Government but the rightful owners of it are the Aboriginal tribes.'

In Hardy's long dialogue with the Gurindji, in particular with Lingiari and Dexter Daniels, they talked about the Gurindji past, their claim on the land and their desire to run the station. The Gurindji could not write and Hardy became the draftsman of their demands. Bain Attwood finds that Hardy did not merely represent their story but was involved in making the story with them. It was Hardy who wrote the famous April 1967 petition to the Governor-General, Lord Casey: 'We, the leaders of the Gurindji people, write to you about our earnest desire to regain tenure of our tribal lands ... of which we were dispossessed in times past. Our people have lived here from time immemorial and our culture, myths, dreaming and sacred places have evolved in this land. Many of our fore-fathers were killed in the early days while trying to retain it. Therefore we feel that morally the land is ours and should be returned to us.'

The Federal Government rejected the petition outright. Yet the situation at Wattie Creek had to be addressed.

The Gorton Government's Minister for Aboriginal Affairs, W C Wentworth, initially proposed to excise eight square miles at Wattie Creek, for use by the Gurindji, from the Wave Hill lease of 6158 square miles. The Northern Territory pastoralists and cattle producers were enraged. An attachment to the cabinet submission contains letters in which they claimed: 'The proposal is communist inspired ... [it] represents a new form of segregation which would hinder assimilation since it is not based on viable economic activity.'

The National Party Minister for the Interior, Peter Nixon, controlled much of the government deliberations. The final decision was to offer the Gurundji no excision whatsoever but an area for a township on the Wave Hill commonage away from Wattie Creek. The cabinet felt that any other concession would have breached its assimilation policy. The cabinet rejected Wattie Creek precisely because, in Wentworth's words, 'the Aborigines have chosen it for themselves'. The issue was identified in the cabinet papers—it was whether to adopt Wattie Creek as a precedent for 'making Aboriginal groups independent and self-supporting' or whether 'such enclaves could lead to segregation'. Ministers knew that once the precedent was established it would lead directly to the pastoral properties where some of the traditional links were strongest.

The cabinet was governed by fear and a crisis of imagination. Its refusal to the Gurindji became a milestone: it intensified the pressure for land rights and was decisive in tying the Labor Party to this cause.

The last third of the twentieth century would reveal two paths towards Aboriginal land justice. The Gurindji took the political course, but the Yolngu people at Yirrkala went to the courts and set in train another revolution.

The Yirrkala in Arnhem Land, one of the most remote parts of Australia, having failed to obtain redress from the mining company Nabalco or satisfaction from the Federal Government, took legal action. They sought, in effect, land title over the mining area and damages from Nabalco. It was an historic step—a claim for land rights that pre-existed the British assertion of sovereignty. In 1969 the Commonwealth made representations that the case be dismissed but a Northern Territory Supreme Court judge, Justice Richard Blackburn, decided to hear the case. It would become the prelude to Mabo.

In 1971 Blackburn found against the Yirrkala people in what is now best seen as a legal defeat and a moral victory. Blackburn upheld the constitutional orthodoxy and, in so doing, revealed its flaws. He said: 'I am very clearly of the opinion upon the evidence that the social rules and customs of the plaintiffs cannot possibly be dismissed as lying on the other side of an unbridgeable gulf . . . If ever a system could be called "a government of laws and not of men" it is that shown in the evidence before me.' But Blackburn, despite being convinced of an Aboriginal spiritual link to the land, took the traditional view of the common law. He said there was 'no capacity within Australian common law or property rights to recognise any indigenous rights to land'. In Blackburn's view, 'no doctrine of common law ever required or now requires a British Government to recognise land rights under Aboriginal law which may have existed prior to the 1788 occupation'.

Reflecting on the matter the former Chief Justice, Sir Anthony Mason, presiding at the time of the Mabo case, says: 'Much of Justice Blackburn's judgment accorded with the High Court's ultimate decision in Mabo.' In effect, Blackburn helped to establish the foundation but was unable to make the final great leap. That would take the judiciary another 21 years. In the interim a visionary politician would accept the challenge.

In his 1972 policy speech Gough Whitlam identified a new but enduring benchmark for the nation: 'Australia's real test as far as the rest of the world, and in particular our region, is concerned is the role we create for our own Aborigines . . . Australia's treatment of her Aboriginal people will be the thing upon which the rest of the world will judge Australia and Australians.' A week after taking office Whitlam asked Justice Edward Woodward, who appeared for the Yirrkala, to conduct a Royal Commission into the granting of Aboriginal land title. Whitlam said the 'one ambition' for which he wanted his government remembered was delivering 'justice and equality to the Aboriginal people'. No prime minister had ever spoken in this way before.

In 1975 the government concluded new leasehold arrangements with Vesteys and on 16 August Whitlam flew to Wattie Creek, now bearing its traditional name, Daguragu. In a symbolic meeting with Vincent Lingiari he declared: 'I solemnly hand to you these deeds as proof, in Australian law, that these lands belong to the Gurindji people.' Taking advice from Dr Coombs that in 1834 an Aboriginal chief had poured some earth into the hand of John Batman on the site of Melbourne, Whitlam repeated the act: he poured the sand into Lingiari's hands as a token that this was now tribal land.

Woodward brought down his final report in July 1974 and a series of bills were introduced in 1975 to provide for land rights in the Northern Territory. The Whitlam Government was dismissed on the same day that two of the key land rights bills were to be introduced into the Senate. Aboriginal leader Patrick Dodson says: 'A national government was prepared to look at how land might be returned to the Aboriginal people. That was a transforming sentiment in this country for Aboriginal people.'

To the surprise of many, the Fraser Government proceeded with the bills after making some amendments to them. Malcolm Fraser faced strong reservations from the Coalition parties and the Northern Territory Government, but held firm. The law enabled Aborigines to own previously reserved land and to claim vacant Crown land where a traditional association could be demonstrated. Aborigines could veto mining unless the government overrode the veto in 'the national interest'. The law provided that the primary vehicle for ownership would be Aboriginal Land Councils, not smaller groups based upon clan.

Fraser represented a dramatic break from Coalition policy of the years before 1972. Looking back on his decision Fraser says: 'The Coalition had run out of steam in 1972 and Mr Whitlam came to power with a very different type of government. I believe that it would have been quite wrong to say, "No, we're going to throw all this aside, we're going to

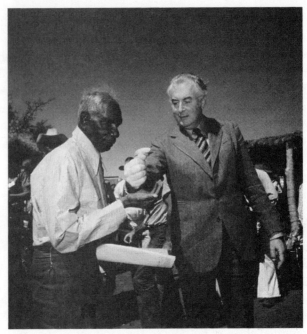

As he poured sand into Vincent Lingiari's hand, Gough Whitlam declared that the former Vesty lands now belonged to the Gurindji people.

ignore this, we're going to go back to the attitudes that prevailed in earlier times".' It should be noted, however, that there were many areas in which Fraser was only too prepared to erase the Whitlam imprint.

The new Act was an historic step. In the Northern Territory, for which it was responsible, the Commonwealth Parliament gave Aborigines a right to land by virtue of their aboriginality. It was a recognition of prior injustice and of the customs and spirituality of Aboriginal society in the age before the white man. The 1980s saw the push for land rights coupled with two other demands: a call for a treaty, and the bid for Aboriginal self-determination. It fell to the Hawke Government to grapple with these issues.

Bob Hawke's record in Aboriginal affairs was a compromise designed to conceal a political fracture. Hawke repudiated Labor's pledge for national land rights legislation; his government advanced the cause of Aboriginal self-determination; and when a treaty proved too hard Hawke initiated a reconciliation process best described as a transfer of the problem to the next generation.

The abandonment of the ALP's national land rights pledge was not a surprise, given Hawke's search for political consensus. The Woodward report to Whitlam envisaged not just legislation for the Northern Territory but offered a model that could be applied in the States. While Fraser had legislated for the Northern Territory, the Coalition was never prepared to contemplate a national approach. The ALP Government in Western Australia under Brian Burke launched a virulent campaign against any national bill and Burke lobbied Hawke directly. Hawke was never able to perceive how a viable political foundation could be established for national land rights legislation. It would represent a decisive assertion of Commonwealth power over the States; it would unite the entire Liberal and National parties against the initiative; the Labor Party itself was deeply divided over both the principle and the tactic; and there was evidence of a deep public backlash against the steady campaign for Aboriginal rights. The Hawke Government tried yet failed to develop a national land rights policy. But retreat left a guilty Hawke with the need for atonement.

The notion of Aboriginal self-determination had been adopted with varying degrees of commitment since the Whitlam Government's time. Hawke's retreat on land rights only intensified the pressure on his government to deliver greater Aboriginal self-empowerment. After the 1987 election the portfolio went to Gerry Hand who, in consultation with Hawke, devised the Aboriginal and Torres Strait Islander Commission (ATSIC), which replaced the government department. The philosophy was to invest Aborigines with the power to take decisions on policy, management and funding priorities. The theory behind ATSIC was to create an elected Aboriginal structure that could realise the aspiration of self-determination. It was an idealistic but flawed concept introduced amid a Bicentennial haze.

ATSIC was both an elected body representing Aborigines and a decision-making authority for financial assistance programs. There had never been a concept like this before. Hand told the Parliament: 'ATSIC is an acknowledgment by all of us that it is no longer acceptable for governments to dictate what is best for the Aboriginal and Torres Stait Islander people: they should decide for themselves what needs to be done.' Separate institutions of governance were being created for the Aboriginal people; it was both an advance and a risk. Hand stressed that the bill did not mean 'separate nationhood', but he was less exact in defining what it did mean.

The risk was always manifest: that the merit in greater responsibility would be offset by potential funding abuses, the excuse for the States to do less and, over time, the possibility that in some regions the health, education and living conditions of Aborigines might in fact decline, not improve. At ATSIC's core was the unresolved issue of how self-determination was to be realised and precisely what self-determination actually meant.

In June 1988 Hawke and Hand went to an Aboriginal festival at Barunga in the Northern Territory to which thousands of Aborigines had come and where they were welcomed by the Northern Land Council chair, Galarrwuy Yunupingu. Hawke threw spears and sat on the ground with the Aboriginal people while they outlined their hopes. There was a gift-giving ceremony and Hawke was presented with a series of demands in the Barunga Statement—a petition framed with paintings done by elders of the Western Desert and Arnhem Land people. At its core was a treaty, an idea which had gained momentum during the 1980s.

Hawke was remarkably forthcoming. He promised that 'there shall be a treaty negotiated between the Aboriginal people and the Government on behalf of all the people of Australia'. The timetable called for 'the conclusion of such a treaty before the end of the life of this parliament'. It was an exercise in self-delusion. Opposition leader John Howard responded quickly, saying it was 'an absurd proposition that a nation should make a treaty with some of its own citizens'. In reality, the Australian political system and the general community were deeply divided over the idea of a treaty. Neither the conceptual thinking nor moulding of public opinion had been done.

The idea had gained currency during 1978–83 when, at Nugget Coombs's instigation, an Aboriginal Treaty Committee was formed. It involved prominent indigenous and non-indigenous Australians including Judith Wright, who wrote a book, *We Call For A Treaty*. The committee asked for a compact covering five matters: protection of Aboriginal identity, language, law and culture; recognition of land rights; the conditions governing mining and exploitation of Aboriginal lands; the question of compensation; and the right of Aborigines to control their own affairs.

The issue was investigated by the Senate Standing Committee on Legal and Constitutional Affairs, which identified some of the constraints. Its 1983 report raised the chief problem, saying of the Aboriginal peoples that 'they are not a sovereign entity under our present law', which meant they could not enter into a treaty.

At the time of Hawke's pledge the unresolved problems over a treaty were immense: its legal or constitutional form; a credible negotiating authority on behalf of Aboriginal Australia; how the treaty was to be drafted; how the treaty was to be approved (by the Commonwealth Parliament or by the people); whether the treaty was to be symbolic or have legal force. The final problem was that the Australian people were scarcely ready for the idea, while the Coalition was opposed in principle. In this climate there was no means by which the idea of the treaty—giving closure to the past—could be realised.

The mistake of the Hawke government is that it raised expectations on which it could never deliver—national land rights and a treaty.

There was, however, a deeper philosophical issue: the conditions under which Aboriginal and non-Aboriginal Australians would relate to each other. During the treaty debate some Aboriginal leaders such as Michael Mansell said the aim should be a separate Aboriginal nation. He had very little support among other Aboriginal leaders let alone, one suspects, among Aboriginal people. But at the heart of this debate lay a profound confusion about what 'self-determination' meant. The Hawke Government was left in an invidious position—it needed an initiative to move the debate forward but it also needed to 'buy time' to allow some of these issues to be resolved. The result was the process of Aboriginal Reconciliation.

In January 1991 the Minister for Aboriginal Affairs, Robert Tickner, issued a discussion paper on reconciliation. It won the support of the Opposition and the support of the ATSIC chair, Lowitja O'Donoghue. It was also sanctioned by the Royal Commission into Aboriginal Deaths in Custody, which found that enduring change depended upon 'reconciliation of the Aboriginal and non-Aboriginal communities'. The Council for Aboriginal Reconciliation Bill was passed in 1991 and a council appointed, chaired by Patrick Dodson. The Act said that reconciliation was to be achieved by 1 January 2001, the symbolic centenary of Federation, a target which seems ambitious in retrospect. It raised the possibility of a document of reconciliation. The process offered nine years to try to advance the issue of rights and justice for indigenous Australians. A hallmark of the approach was its bipartisan nature across Labor and Coalition, a recognition that a shared commitment was critical to progress for Aboriginal Australians. But the following year the initiative was stolen back by the courts. The High Court made an epic judgment.

Eddie Mabo was a Torres Strait Islander who lived most of his life in Townsville but had come originally from the island of Mer in the Murray Islands group. In 1974 an official denied Mabo access to the Murray Islands when his father was dying, a move that stung Mabo. He and others went to the High Court seeking recognition of their rights over land in the Murray Islands.

Queensland premier Joh Bjelke-Petersen promptly passed a law abolishing any property rights held by Torres Strait Islanders at the time they became part of Queensland in 1879. Bjelke-Petersen was wiping the slate. He was using the Queensland Parliament to extinguish without compensation any such rights. Mabo's lawyers went to the High Court, which judged 4–3 that the Queensland Act was invalid because it conflicted with the Whitlam Government's 1975 Racial Discrimination Act. The substantive case then went to the High Court.

On 3 June 1992 the High Court decided 6–1 that Aborigines had common law rights to land that predated the 1788 British claim of sovereignty. It found that these rights had survived where the title had not already been extinguished by government action and where there was an ongoing Aboriginal link with the land. Prime Minister Paul Keating best conveyed the essence of the decision: 'It rejected a lie and acknowledged a truth. The lie was *terra nullius*—the convenient fiction that Australia had been a land of no one. The truth was native title—the fact that the land had once belonged to Aboriginal and Torres Strait Islander Australians and that in some places a legal right to it had survived the 200 years of European settlement.'

The Chief Justice at the time, Sir Anthony Mason, says: 'Our previous approach to the position of the indigenous inhabitants of this country was based on a fiction, namely that they did not own the land, that the land did not belong to them . . . In this day and age it was vitally important to ensure that these inaccuracies, these legends, these myths were dispelled . . . I have an overwhelming conviction that Mabo was right and that no self-respecting court could come to a conclusion other than the conclusion reached in Mabo.' The main judgment by Justice Brennan said the idea of *terra nullius* no longer commanded support in international law, that the common law 'should neither be nor be seen to be frozen in an age of racial discrimination', and that the Crown's acquisition of sovereignty meant that native title could be extinguished by the valid exercise of power.

Keating seized the judgment as an opportunity. He saw it as a chance for a new relationship between Aboriginal and non-Aboriginal Australians, a chance to admit and purge the past. In this frame of mind Keating went to Redfern in December 1992 and called for an act of recognition: 'The starting point might be to recognise that the problem starts with us, non-Aboriginal Australians. It begins, I think, with that act of recognition. Recognition that it was we who did the dispossessing. We took the traditional lands and smashed the traditional way of life. We brought the diseases, the alcohol. We committed the murders. We took the children from

Paul Keating saw the Mabo judgment as a chance for a new relationship between Aboriginal and non-Aboriginal people.

the mothers. We practised discrimination and exclusion. It was our ignorance and our prejudice. We failed to ask: how would I feel if this was done to me?'

Keating grasped the true dimension of the Mabo judgment—that it was not just about land but about confronting the moral vacuum at the heart of Australian nationhood.

Only the High Court could have repudiated the doctrine of *terra nullius*. No political party could have ventured safely into this ultra-divisive territory. It would have been too dangerous. In a nation deeply imbued with a faith in the rule of law, the High Court had not just the power but the standing to reverse the 1788 assumption of nobody's land. Only the High Court could tell this truth and have its new version of history and law accepted by the Australian people with such relative equanimity. The High Court was able to do what the politicians could not do. The very idea of a political and parliamentary debate on the doctrine of *terra nullius* was frightening to contemplate. The Court, in effect, was able to break the impasse in the political system about Aboriginal issues. With this constitutional fait accompli it was able to move the nation across the bridge to a reconciliation with its past and its indigenous people. It was a decisive moment on the path to reconciliation.

Once the law had been reversed, once the law accepted that Aborigines had land rights predating 1788 which could potentially endure to the present day, then the entire legal and moral basis of European settlement had been rewritten. This was the single most important step in recognising and seeking to redress the injustice of the past. It had the potential to redefine the relationship between Aboriginal and non-Aboriginal Australians.

The decision also broke the political deadlock over land rights. The land rights issue had been gridlocked because the Commonwealth Parliament was unable to legislate for national land rights due to the opposition of the States, disagreement between the major parties and substantial public resistance. The High Court took the issue from the parliament, rewrote the rules and then handed it back to the politicians. But the Court was able to do this only because Eddie Mabo and his lawyers fought for a judicial solution over a prolonged period.

The High Court decision changed the political power balance in an unprecedented way. Before Mabo the Aborigines had to ask for land rights and rely upon the generosity of the political Establishment. After Mabo the Aborigines had a negotiating weapon. They had a power called native title which gave them a negotiating leverage they had never previously enjoyed. These native title rights were buttressed by the Racial Discrimination Act of 1975 which prevented the States from making land grants, from that year onward, that discriminated on a racial basis in extinguishing native title. So, for the first time, the Aborigines had a hand to play.

In his Native Title Act, Keating, to use Frank Brennan's description, decided 'to turn necessity into a political virtue'. The Commonwealth had to deliver certainty to existing landholders, farmers and miners. That was a political imperative. But in the process Keating sought not a legislative slaughter of native title rights but a means of creating a workable system to allow Aborigines to claim native title. This was a courageous though realistic choice. It meant that Keating incurred an anti-Aboriginal backlash which later merged into Hansonism as scare campaigns mounted about people losing their backyards.

The Native Title Act was both a risk and an opportunity for the Aboriginal leaders. It was about what the Aborigines would receive in return for consent to the validation of existing title. The main uncertainty related to land grants made after the 1975 Racial Discrimination Act which might be in conflict with its provisions. The premiers insisted that all people who had received crown grants of land since 1975 must have these rights preserved. During its parliamentary passage Keating's bill was amended in favour of Aboriginal interests for two reasons. First, with the

Coalition taking a firm stand against the bill, Keating needed the support of the Democrats and Greens for its passage; and second, the Aboriginal leaders threatened to withhold their own endorsement. The politics of the Senate assisted the Aboriginal position. Frank Brennan says: 'Keating treated the Aboriginal negotiators as real political players. He eyeballed them, he bullied them and he caressed them. He made it very clear that once you step into this political ring we cut deals, you own the compromise and we do it together.' Keating convinced most of the Aboriginal negotiators that he had cut them the best result that was possible. It was the longest debate in the Senate's history. The bill was passed at midnight on 23 December 1993 amid tears, joy and applause.

The framework, if not all the detail, was impressive. The Act protected native title but such claims could not be made on current land holdings. It was assumed that pastoral leases extinguished native title but the Act did not make this explicit. Native title holders had a right to negotiate in relation to mining but no right of veto.

The Howard-led Coalition won the 1996 election accepting the Mabo judgment, but pledged to redraw the balance in the Act against native title. However, the High Court struck again. In the Wik case, by a tight 4–3 margin, the Court found that native title could co-exist with pastoral leases, which covered 40 per cent of the continent. It was a nasty shock for Howard and the National Party leader, Tim Fischer. The non-Labor side of politics sank into a bitter convulsion. The pastoralists were alarmed about sharing land and the miners were alarmed about their operations on pastoral leases. The government attacked the High Court and the farmers attacked the government. From the start there were only two issues: how severe would be the backlash, and how much would be translated into law?

Howard, under pressure from his own side, declined to extinguish native title on 40 per cent of the continent. As Frank Brennan said, the Senate would never pass the bill, the compensation would be too great and the High Court might find against any such law anyway. That didn't stop demands for such action. Howard opted for his so-called '10 point plan' compromise. The aim was to force back Aboriginal gains made in the Native Title Act and the Wik case. State governments would be allowed to override native title on pastoral leases. Howard, unlike Keating, did not bring the Aborigines into the compact and so they fought him.

During 1997–98 Howard's bill was deadlocked in the Senate with the prospect of a double dissolution election on native title. Labor, the Democrats and the Aboriginal negotiators refused to cut any deal with Howard. The bill was passed, finally, in a compromise between Howard and Tasmanian independent, Brian Harradine, only after the 1998

Queensland State election. Harradine was anxious to avoid any federal election on native title. Howard needed a settlement to take the wind from Pauline Hanson's One Nation and its ability to win Senate seats. The national interest was served by the bill's passage. But the struggle exposed the inadequacy of a Commonwealth Parliament without a single Aboriginal representative. After his election to the Senate, Aden Ridgeway said that native title 'is still sitting out there as a matter of unfinished business'. By late 2000 there had been twenty successful claims under the Native Title Act, with several hundred waiting to be processed.

The reconciliation process was fractured. Relations between the prime minister and Aboriginal leaders sank to a nadir not previously witnessed. The 1990s were a low and debilitating period in the dialogue. The core problem was the absence of trust—a failure to establish a personal bond between Howard and the Aboriginal leaders. It was an issue of the human spirit.

Howard came to the prime ministership suspicious of the pro-Labor Aboriginal leaders. This was reinforced by a conviction that, in Geoffrey Blainey's words, Australian history was now being shaped by 'a Black Armband view'. The loss of trust was not one-way. The Aboriginal leaders found it hard to accept the legitimacy of the new government and the authority of the 1996 election. They tended to see Howard as a throwback and an aberration. They overlooked the extent of public support for his positions. Their response was understandably emotional but unhelpful politically.

There were three overlapping issues which drove relations to this point—the Wik debate, the 'Bringing Them Home' Report, and Howard's refusal to apologise on behalf of the nation for past injustices.

In August 1995 the Human Rights and Equal Opportunity Commission was asked by the Keating Government to inquire into the separation of Aboriginal children from their homes. The terms of reference were deliberately selective: the aim was not a comprehensive review of the Commonwealth's policy of removal of Aboriginal and part-Aboriginal children, but rather a report on removal 'by compulsion, duress or undue influence'. In time this may loom as a serious mistake. The report was to be concerned only with removals without consent. It made little serious effort to examine the policy or its administration and was, in effect, a powerful and compelling oral history of tragedy and injustice. The April 1997 recommendations were for both compensation and an apology.

At this point the idea of the 'stolen children generation' passed into political discourse. The Howard Government's formal response, that 'there never was a generation of stolen children', was self-defeating. It was pedantic, ungenerous and futile. The idea had already taken hold based on a reality. The magnitude of the government's denial meant that it was hardly in a position to explain the legality, selectivity and welfare basis of the policy. In truth, the government's preoccupation with denial destroyed its credibility as a mediator between past and present.

This was a tragedy because there were vital issues at stake. The removal was based upon a racial outlook and a system of values that typified the previous age and is unacceptable today; it was a policy that in its own time was mainly seen not as evil but as beneficial; it was backed by law, administration and a social philosophy. Yet it left a legacy of emotional destruction.

The parliaments of New South Wales, Victoria, Tasmania and Western Australia passed resolutions of regret and apology. The South Australian Parliament passed a resolution of regret and apology in relation to the 'forced separation'. The Queensland Parliament used a similar formula. The Northern Territory Parliament declined to express regret or give an apology. The Commonwealth Parliament, finally, passed a motion of sincere regret in August 1999 but did not offer an apology.

John Howard says: 'My position in relation to the apology is very simply the fact that I don't believe in apologising for something for which I was not responsible. It's as simple as that. And I was brought up as a child by my parents to say "sorry" when I *was* to blame.'

The former chairman of the Council for Aboriginal Reconciliation, Patrick Dodson, says: 'One can think of reconciliation as a transformation in your own psychological and spiritual make-up. It's not just a re-arrangement of your prejudices. There really is a conversion experience that takes place and that concept, I think, was something the prime minister found difficult to grasp.'

The issue of compensation remains unresolved but is being pursued. In the Federal Court case brought by two Aboriginal victims, Lorna Cubillo and Peter Gunner, Justice O'Loughlin, after surveying the evidence, found against the interpretation of 'a policy of indiscriminate removal irrespective of the personal circumstances of the child'. He reported that the number of institutions able to receive children was small and that the number of patrol officers was small. And he was influenced by the patrol officers who gave evidence, some of whom had had a long and sympathetic association with Aborigines.

O'Loughlin found that it was the removal and detention, as distinct from the manner in which they were carried out, that were the causes of the injury. That is, the damage flowed from a lawfully conducted policy; and negligence in the application of the policy had not been demonstrated in the cases in question. The issue overall is far from being resolved and the Aboriginal people are determined to continue to press the case in the courts and in the parliaments, seeking a reversal on compensation.

The decade-long reconciliation process was only a partial success. Its symbolic culmination came at Sydney Harbour over 27–28 May 2000, six months short of the nation's centenary.

An estimated 150 000–250 000 people walked across the Harbour Bridge in hope. It was the largest crowd since the 1988 Bicentennial, a coming together on a great bridge for a reconciled future. For the first time reconciliation became a people's movement. This was an encouraging sign but it could not substitute for a divided polity. The hope came from the people and not their prime minister, who declined to march. Howard had become part of the problem, not the solution.

On the previous day, inside the Opera House, there was an inspired yet flawed ceremony to mark the reconciliation climax. The document of reconciliation was delivered to all Australia's political leaders on stage. 'We, the peoples of Australia,' it began, 'of many origins as we are, make a commitment to go on together in a spirit of reconciliation . . . One part of the nation apologises and expresses its sorrow and its sincere regret for the injustices of the past, so the other part accepts the apology and forgives.'

Howard took the document but declined to endorse its words. Howard was far from being alone. He was a symbol of how half the nation felt— the half that opposed an apology. Howard's tragedy is that he could not reach out to Aboriginal people. Such a gesture by a conservative prime minister would have constituted real bridge-building. That inability was Howard's tragedy and Australia's loss. The gulf was so small yet so large.

There was a feeling at the Opera House and the Bridge that the nation was waiting for a release from Howard. Yet Howard is not the real problem—that is the shadow across the hearts of many Australians. The next prime minister and government are likely to apologise. But the dispute over the apology has seriously exaggerated its meaning.

The apology is important but it cannot substitute for a reappraisal among Aborigines themselves. The focus, ultimately, must return to Aboriginal self-esteem, community and leadership. As the century closed Aboriginal leaders such as Noel Pearson and newly elected Democrat Senator Aden Ridgway began to talk a new language—of responsibility and self-help.

In his 2000 Chifley Lecture, Pearson said: 'I have come to the view

*Ordinary Australians turned
out in their thousands in
support of reconciliation during
the symbolic walk across
Sydney Harbour Bridge on
28 May 2000.*

that we suffered a particular social deterioration once we became dependent on passive welfare. The irony of our newly won citizenship in 1967
was that after we became citizens with equal rights and the theoretical
right to equal pay, we lost the meagre foothold that we had in the real
economy and we became almost comprehensively dependent upon passive
welfare for our livelihood. We find 30 years later that life in the safety net
for three decades and two generations has produced a social disaster.'

The profile of Aboriginal Australia is frightening. Life expectancy for a
man is 57 years compared with the national average of 75; for a woman
it is 62 years compared with 81. The unemployment rate is four times the
national rate; imprisonment is twelve times the national rate; Year 12
education is only 40 per cent of the national completion rate. Aboriginal
Australians are the poorest in a rich society; the most unhealthy in a
healthy society; the least educated in an educated society.

In the Northern Territory in the 24 years since the passage of the land
rights law more than 40 per cent of the territory has passed to Aboriginal

ownership. The Act has been a triumph in helping to rejuvenate Aboriginal culture, law and custom. But much of the land is non-economic and has not offered a basis for improvements in living standards. The 1998 Reeves Report on the impact of the Act reports that only 6.5 per cent of Northern Territory jobs are in primary production and that over the past three decades the proportion of Aborigines living in urban areas has risen from 17 to 40 per cent. Reeves concludes that the economic future for most Aborigines will not lie with land but with 'the possession of productively useful skills, technology and capital of the kinds in demand in the mainstream Australian economy'. It is an issue too often overlooked in the highly charged debate about past injustices.

A vital aspect of reconciliation ignored by the media was the emphasis on Aboriginal economic self-sufficiency. By the year 2001 it was obvious that neither land rights nor welfare, although essential, offered a satisfactory basis for the future. The comprehensive assessment by John Reeves QC of Australia's first land rights law concluded that any notion that land development was the key to economic progress was 'misplaced'.

In his first term in the parliament, Aden Ridgway says: 'We've got to break this welfare dependence and that cycle of being on the treadmill that leads us back to welfare. I think, if anything, the 1967 referendum was good for what it sought to do, but it was a double-edged sword. It not only cemented firmly this idea in the indigenous mind that there was an entitlement to welfare benefits, but we ended up becoming victims of a welfare economy. What we've now got to put back in place is the glue that binds the family together. And self-esteem in the context of culture is vitally important.'

The best speech on Reconciliation Day at the Opera House came from the Governor-General, Sir William Deane, who tried to put the pieces together. He said that 'reconciliation' was at a crossroads: that injustice in Australia must no longer be perceived as belonging to 'another country'; that the progress actually made should be recognised; that advocates of the Aboriginal cause should speak with moderation; that reconciliation was a help but no panacea; and that the real task was about living together or, as Gurindji leader Vincent Lingiari said in 1975 when the traditional land was returned, 'We are all mates, now.'

Lingiari's words should be immortalised. Their simplicity reveals the truth—it is about living together. That sounds easy but it's no easy task given the history: dispossession, destruction, denial of rights, assimilation, equality and the overthrow of *terra nullius*.

Anger and resentment have been natural reactions and they have fired much of the progress. In the months before his death that Aboriginal political warrior Charles Perkins said: 'I think we were, Aboriginal people, too passive. I think we just went along with a lot of initiatives by governments, by politicians, by well-meaning people—and we should've been a bit more aggressive, perhaps violent, perhaps more militaristic, perhaps more confrontationalist. Who knows?'

Another veteran of the fight for justice, Faith Bandler, says: 'Forgiveness is important. It's important in everyday life. I went through the Depression and the war, and after the war, for many many years, I felt I could never forgive the Germans or the Japanese. I think we've got to forgive. But it's hard. It's very hard.'

This phase of political action, from the 1967 referendum onwards, has not yet ended. It is about bringing a closure to the past and that means it must end soon. Closure is the 'unfinished business' and the essential requirement. Australia can't keep debating the past, since the entire purpose is to reach a settlement between peoples and then turn to the future.

There are three important conditions for closure. First, the issue of Aboriginal reconciliation must cease to be a source of major conflict between Labor and the Coalition since this guarantees a bitter polarisation of views. Second, the Commonwealth Parliament must cease to be a parliament of non-Aboriginals and become a parliament of some indigenous along with non-indigenous Australians so that it represents all peoples; and third the nation must progress towards a genuine spirit of reconciliation. This involves a reappraisal by non-Aboriginal Australians as well as Aboriginal people who must abandon, eventually, their victim mentality.

Frank Brennan says of this process: 'The time must come for any nation state to be able to say, enough of the past, we will now draw the line and once that line is drawn, it is to be said this is finished business. And basically we get on with the business of living. At the moment we're not ready for it. I don't think the trust is sufficient.'

The point of closure is reached when one side accepts its responsibility for past crimes and apologises, and when the other side, aware that there can never be full restitution, decides to forgive. This is the act of closure. It is not an end. It is rather the end of the beginning of how to live together.

INTERVIEW WITH
GOUGH WHITLAM

Gough Whitlam is now a unique link to our past—a leader who fought the battles of the 1950s and 1960s on the White Australia policy, state aid, Aboriginal land rights, independence for Papua New Guinea, the Vietnam War and developing diplomatic relations with China. His views are as enduring as they are undiminished.

There have been some extraordinary figures in the history of the Labor Party. Archbishop Mannix of Melbourne, for instance, and Billy Hughes. What's your impression of those two?

They were both immigrants. Billy Hughes, by sheer capacity and dialectic skills, became leader of the Labor Party [in 1915]. Mannix, of course, came out from Ireland for a very different reason. The British, under George the Third, were dissatisfied with the education of the Catholic priesthood in Ireland so they set up the Royal College of St Patrick, and by the beginning of the twentieth century Mannix was the head of the College— Maynooth, it's called. He was respected as an intellectual and as a person who got on well with other authorities. So he came out here as Coadjutor to Archbishop Carr, who was a very considerable figure. When Mannix became Archbishop [in 1917]—it was just three years before the Dublin Rebellions—he said, perfectly reasonably: 'How are we Irish-descended Catholics in Australia to be expected to have conscription to defend Britain, when Britain is assaulting the Irish in the same way as Britain said the Germans were assaulting the Belgians?' He was absolutely correct. Of course, it was very divisive and for a very long time after that the Labor Party lost a great number of supporters who were British and Protestant, like Hughes. It was really only when I became leader that you would get the Labor Party civilly receiving representatives from all parties. I'm not a Catholic. I'm no longer an Anglican. I'm not a believer. But I do respect people that have religious views, albeit Jewish or Christian or Muslim or Buddhist or Hindu. In this country anybody in a leadership position must have some knowledge of the culture, and that includes the religious background of all the people that make up this country and who inhabit neighbouring countries, the largest or the smallest.

John Curtin, the prime minister during most of World War II, was another remarkable figure. What was the essence of Curtin's greatness, if he was great?

He *was* great. He had been through all the industrial and religious and political agonies of the First World War, conscription and the lot. When at last he became leader of the party—only I have been leader of the party longer than Curtin—he had to devote himself with immense discipline to getting the respect of the public and of his opponents. He did have the respect of Menzies and Fadden. He did. He was treated very shabbily by some members of the Federal Caucus, but he stood his ground and he survived. Accordingly, we did have conscription in areas concerning our safety. For instance, he said: 'How is it possible for me to be regarded as a good Labor man if we send conscripts to Rabaul, but not a good Labor man if I send conscripts to Timor?' He was the first person to mention Timor in the party council.

Did Curtin resolve in World War II, in relation to conscription, the problem that Hughes couldn't resolve in World War I?

Yes, he did. Hughes *could* have done it, but he realised that 'wave the flag, beat the British drum' was effective then. When Hughes was prime minister the vast majority of the Australian population had been born in Australia and had been born of people from the British Isles. In the Second World War that was still the situation, but Curtin, of Irish and Catholic background, solved the problem and kept the party together. What I admire about Curtin is that he, with the assistance of Chifley, who was not only Treasurer but Minister for Post-War Reconstruction, wholeheartedly supported the new world which was being created by the United Nations—the reconstruction of the International Labour Organisation and all the new international bodies which were being created, the World Bank, all of them. Australia wholeheartedly supported every organisation flowing from the San Francisco Conference of 1945 and the Bretton Woods Conference of that time. Curtin and Chifley were great internationalists. They knew that Australia's future depended on being part of a well-ordered world, politically and financially.

I never met Curtin but I did get to know his wife, who continued to be a very strong force in the Western Australian branch of the Labor Party. When I became leader in 1967 I got a message of support from her that added: 'You were married on the twentieth anniversary of our marriage.' How did she bloody well know that? But she was a very strong woman and a great support for me.

There was a great dispute between Curtin and Churchill when Curtin was bringing our troops back to Australia across the Indian Ocean and Churchill wanted to divert them to Burma. How important was this as a moment for Australia?

It was essential to our survival in a physical sense as an independent nation. It was also essential to demonstrate to the UK and the US that Australia should not be taken for granted, because Roosevelt also wanted our troops to be diverted to Burma. If they had been, they would have been captured—as they were at Changi. But they got back here and they were

195

the troops who first defeated the Japanese in New Guinea. No doubt about it, the stand that Curtin took was essential to the postwar respect, such as it's been, that we've had from Britain and America.

You were raised in the age of the White Australia policy. It was the policy when you joined the Labor Party, when you entered Federal Parliament. How did you feel about the policy as a parliamentarian?

I was profoundly embarrassed by it and I did all I could to change it—and you remember, it was changed within five years of my becoming deputy leader of the party. There were other people in the caucus at the same time of the same mind and also in the States, in particular Don Dunstan, the premier of South Australia and the leader of the parliamentary party in South Australia. He and I were at one in this.

How hard was it in the mid-1960s to change Labor policy on White Australia?

Very difficult indeed, because the [Labor] leader, Arthur Calwell, was devoted to that policy, as was the Prime Minister, R G Menzies. During the time of Menzies and Calwell it would have been impossible for either of our parties to change the policy. Dr Evatt, of course, who was the leader, before Calwell, he never touched it, because he thought it was too prickly. But of course, it was impossible for a democratic socialist party like ours to enshrine a racial test. Yet Australia was promoting migration as long as people were white!

It all came up in the context of our attitude to neighbouring countries including our colony of Papua and our trust territory of New Guinea, because you had the absurd situation that people who were in our colony and trust territory couldn't come to Australia unless they entered a bond to leave when required. That is, we had people who were Australian-protected citizens in New Guinea and Australian subjects in Papua who couldn't come and live in Australia. There was the other question of migration. We were pushing migration from European countries and most Mediterranean countries such as Lebanon but we were restricting or forbidding migration from other countries where there was no question that they were as educated and productive as Australians—Japan being a very clear case.

Looking back on the White Australia policy, was this a stain on our history?

It is still held against us in many countries including our immediate neighbours, because when we talk about what we regard as unacceptable practices in neighbouring countries we give the impression that we think we're superior because we're English-speaking. We're allied with the UK or the US, but of course what we have to emphasise now is that we are primarily more important than being a former dependency of the UK or a deputy of the US. We are citizens of the world. We are a member of the United Nations. We ought to stress all those issues—social, humanitarian, political, defence—which are involved with the United Nations, with which all our neighbours are associated as closely as we are.

When you first went into Federal Parliament in the early 1950s, what was the attitude of most of the Parliament towards the policy?

They wouldn't touch it, they wouldn't touch it. It was always very embarrassing. At the Citizenship Conventions which were held over the Australia Day weekend in Canberra throughout the 1950s, I usually went along, and on one occasion I represented Doc Evatt and I ventured to mention it. But of course, the whole thing was, nobody was supposed to mention it. It was always very taboo, we were always discouraged from ever raising it. It was raised in discussions, but never in public.

How determined were you to get the Labor policy changed?

I was determined. I had been ever since I became deputy leader, and the first row I ever had with Arthur Calwell was when it came up in our caucus. He turned to me for support for his attitude and I said: 'Well, I always support you whenever possible, but on this issue I can't.'
    I think the policy change was quite basic. But I want to put it in context. The big blue in the party in the early 1960s, and this was a blue between Arthur Calwell and me, was not immigration but the attitude on Papua New Guinea. Dunstan knew it had to have self-determination and independence and I knew it too. Now, Evatt never visited Papua New Guinea. Menzies didn't until the 1960s. But I did, and I'd seen a bit of it during the war.

After the war the Labor Government introduced the immigration program. How important was this policy to Australia's future development and evolution?

Much more important than we realised at the time. At the time it was to push up our population so that in case of another war in the Pacific we'd have more people to defend ourselves; and the policy was limited to getting people from western Europe. It was gradually extended but very much to Menzies' distress, as you would have read in Alexander Downer's memoirs, edited by his son, about all these Greeks and Italians coming in. I used to live in areas where they were coming because the first Mediterranean migrants—Italians, Maltese and in due course Balkans—came to my electorate. What was not realised at that time was that the people that contributed to our social development were from the Mediterranean as much as from Britain. Germany and Scandinavia. I mean, where would we be culturally, for instance in music or in drama, if we had not brought immigrants from the Mediterranean as well as from Britain and the Netherlands and Scandinavia? Could you think of a British or Dutch or Scandinavian composer? I can think of a few but I could count them on one hand—but look at the ones from Italy and even France.

In the mid-1960s the Holt Cabinet began to modify the White Australia policy, with Hubert Opperman as Immigration Minister and Peter Haydon as his departmental head. How significant was the policy change made by the Holt Cabinet?

You remember, the proposals came from Opperman and Heydon—Peter Heydon, not Bill—in Menzies' time, but they were rejected. Now one shouldn't exaggerate the impact of these.

All that was done was to say that people who were coming to Australia shouldn't have to wait for naturalisation for various periods of time. For instance, diplomats from Asia: they had to wait fifteen years, until their wives could no longer bear children. Britons, of course, and Irish automatically became citizens. People from Europe only had to wait three years. People from other areas waited longer. But administratively, right up to our election in 1972 there had to be, from any country outside Europe, an application for entry referred to Canberra and there had to be a confidential report on their appearance. The photograph wasn't enough, because by a strong light or powdering you could reduce the colour of your exposed parts. It was said that the test was, in extreme cases, 'Drop your daks', because you can't change the colour of your bum. We changed all that.

Holt removed the objectionable different 'time zones' for naturalisation. But in practice they [the government] still made it very difficult for people who were not white-skinned to come to Australia. Furthermore, they continued this doctrinal vetting where officials were told to inquire into the politics of the people, to get reports on their politics, particularly in southern Italy and in the Balkans. There were absurd anomalies.

How determined were you, when you became prime minister, to eradicate the racist overtones surrounding our immigration program?

I thought very clearly that with our history of settlement here and our location in this region we could never have any policy based on race or religion.

For instance, take the Philippines. There was no question that because of the American occupation of the Philippines for 40 years (following 400 years of occupation by the Spaniards) there were many people whom the Americans had trained to be very good nurses and motor mechanics. It was absurd to say they couldn't make a living in Australia. There was some appalling cases where Philippine soldiers in the American Army marrying here were expelled or were told that we'd pay for them to go to California where America would accept them. Then, you remember, there was that absurd instance in Fiji, a British colony: a child couldn't come here for education because then she might bring the rest of her Fijian or Indian relatives. I mean, it was giving rise to all forms of illogical and odious prejudices. This was under the policy changes made by the Holt Government and continued by the Gorton and McMahon Governments.

About this time there was a change of policy in relation to the Aboriginal people. How did you regard the situation in the 1950s and early 1960s before this change?

I'll give you a very clear example. In the middle 1950s onwards, Paul Hasluck, who was Minister for Territories, arranged delegations from both sides of the parliament to New Guinea and also to the Northern Territory. That the cattle industry depended on Aboriginal stockmen and they were not paid properly, they were not housed properly. They were living in a state of servitude, as Governor-General Deane has described it. And that is a fact. We saw it.

When our Constitution was drawn up in the 1890s there were two references to Aborigines. One was that, in taking the census, Aborigines were not to be included. The other was that the Federal Parliament could make special laws for people who needed special laws—other than people of the Aboriginal race—in any State. Now, Menzies learnt in 1965 that Western Australia would lose a seat in the House of Representatives if Aborigines were not counted in the census. So he said, we will remove that section of the Constitution. On the 11th of November 1965, Menzies introduced a bill for a referendum to take out that ban on counting Aborigines. It went through the parliament in November 1965 and then Menzies was succeeded by Harold Holt. But before the parliament met in 1966 Holt announced that this referendum would not proceed, it would be dealt with after the elections which would take place at the end of 1966.

In 1967 Holt put both [the census question and the question of special laws] and they were carried overwhelmingly.

It was a complete turning point in this issue. But the real change in conditions for Aborigines arose when, in 1975, my government enacted the 1965 United Nations Convention on the elimination of all forms of racial discrimination.

The 1967 referendum gave Federal Parliament the power to legislate for the Aboriginal people, but what was the actual response of the following Gorton and McMahon Governments?

They still left the policy to the States to administer. There were suggestions that the Federal Government should act but, quite frankly, the Country Party resisted and they gave in to that resistance. When we were in government we ended the alienation of Aboriginal reserves in the Northern Territory and in 1975 we arranged with the Vesteys that they should give up some of their land at Wattie Creek and that that should be given to the Gurindji. You remember Vincent Lingiari, their spokesman. In October 1975 we put through the House of Representatives a land rights law for the Northern Territory. It couldn't be challenged by the States because they couldn't challenge what we did in the Northern Territory. It went through the House of Representatives and was on the Notice Paper for the Senate on the 11th of November 1975—so it was a couple of years before it finally went through.

Nugget Coombs wrote in his book *Kulinma* for me, the greatest compliment I have ever had ... To Gough Whitlam, the first and so far the only Prime Minister who was listening to Aborigines.

What we're talking about here is a change of values. Do you think that's right?

Yes, I do. You just can't categorise or grade other human beings. They all have to have the best possible opportunities and that comes through education. And I would think land is basic. It's vital because Aborigines knew how to live—they understood the soil and the vegetation. I mean, Aborigines lived quite well until we introduced, from 1788, some diseases. They knew what shrubs they could eat, what animals or lizards or fish they could eat.

199

And, furthermore, in the time of the Aborigines our land and rivers were in very much better condition than they are now.

How do you evaluate the progress we've made over the last 25 years?

Well, there are now some terrific spokesmen for the Aborigines. I don't overflow with admiration for the education that missionaries gave Aborigines. I've got to assert though that the Dodsons, who went to Catholic Missions, were given a very good university education and Noel Pearson, from a Lutheran Mission, was given a very good university education. They are also practical, and there is no doubt that those who vilify Aborigines could never win a debate with such people. Aborigines use the English language with extraordinary clarity and force.

Were you surprised after you lost office and the Fraser Government came to power that Malcolm Fraser proceeded with a version of your land rights legislation?

Yes, but not terribly because Malcolm soon showed, certainly by the middle of 1976—when he had to deal with South Africa—that he was against racial discrimination. There is no doubt that that had been Malcolm's attitude for well over twenty years.

Turning to foreign policy, was China the real bogie, the real enemy, in the Vietnam War?

Yes. And it was also thought at that time, although it was no longer the case, that China was in cahoots with Russia. It was no longer the case, and the poor bloody Australians didn't realise it.

The Coalition, including R G Menzies himself, had done very well out of the communist menace, inside Australia and around Australia. I believed in the same attitude as Attlee [the former British PM] and Chifley in 1949 that if, or more likely when, Mao Zedong and the communists took over the capital, Beijing, then we should recognise that government. Now, Attlee did, but because elections were imminent in Australia we didn't. And then in 1950 there was the Korean War and after the Korean War and the intervention of China there you always had the attitude that they would be a menace to all their neighbouring countries.

Australia later went to Vietnam. Was it in large part to keep the United States involved in the region?

That was the complete reason. The result was a complete disaster which flowed from ignorance and sycophancy and I don't think there is anybody now who would support what we did—the Menzies, Gorton and McMahon Governments—in Vietnam. You won't find any of the journalists, any of the academics, any of the politicians prepared to support what we did at that time. And as you can see from the books written by Americans who were involved in it, they didn't realise how strongly the Vietnamese wanted to rule their own country. I pointed out that the war in Vietnam was a civil war and was driven more by nationalism than by communism. The Vietnamese wanted to rule their own country. Dick Casey [former Minister for External Affairs] took me to task but I was right.

You took the decision to go to China when you were Opposition leader. What drove that decision and how important was it?

It was an essential change. It would have been difficult for us to do it if we had won as we should have in 1969, but we used the gap before we won the 1972 election [to look at] independence for Papua New Guinea and recognition of the People's Republic of China and we promptly set about both after 1972. It became politically possible for us to do it. If Canada next door to the United States could safely go to China and establish diplomatic relations, why couldn't Australia?

You were initially doing this while in Opposition?

Exactly. It was a very hazardous thing. Santamaria said I would be the Manchurian candidate for the prime ministership of Australia and our own prime minister, Billy McMahon, said Zhou Enlai was playing me like a trout. In fact, of course, it came off pretty well.

The meeting with Zhou Enlai was the most hazardous but possibly the most fruitful meeting I'd ever had. There I was, with a few very doubtful journalists from Australia, with Tom Burns and Mick Young, the Federal President and Secretary of the party, in this great hall at midnight with all the Chinese hierarchy and I was being questioned on the impact on our relations under SEATO and ANZUS. I said that SEATO was now an irrelevance but ANZUS was still important to us and the ANZUS pact had been made to reassure us when America made a soft treaty with Japan. That is, ANZUS was not directed against China. Zhou was a bit staggered by that. At the next meeting we had, over a dinner of course, he asked me again and I reassured him and he took the point.

Zhou would converse in Chinese, which gave him the opportunity to hear my questions and then think over his answer while they were translated. He got the impression I knew a bit more because when what I said was being translated back to him I inserted or corrected a few things, because at least I knew the Chinese words for the various countries involved. It was only when we were leaving that he spoke English to me. He could speak English very well. He said: 'You're very young to be the leader of your party? And I responded: 'I'm the same age as you were at Geneva in 1954'—when the Americans and the British and Chinese and Russians were all meeting at Geneva. His response was: 'You know, Dulles would not shake my hand.' It was a very good illustration to me of the impact that some crass Americans can have. Zhou Enlai understood what I said. As we were going out we had a very crucial conversation. I then went to Shanghai and stayed at the Peace Hotel and he sent a birthday cake for me there. I got on very well with him.

I was going on to Japan and I got a message from our ambassador there that the prime minister of Japan would be very pleased to meet me when I arrived the following day. I asked the PM: 'Did you know that President Nixon was going to visit China?' He didn't wait for it to be translated. He said immediately: 'We read about it in the paper.' In that period in 1971 I met the people in China, I met the prime minister of Japan, and I knew the impact that this change of American policy had had. Our diplomats didn't realise it, nor our prime minister.

America's change of policy could only have been done by a Republican president. Nixon had made his reputation on being an anti-communist, destroying American diplomats who had ventured to discuss matters with the Chinese, so nobody could say that he was weak on this.

From the moment you won the 1972 election you moved very quickly to establish diplomatic relations with China.

We asked our ambassador in Paris, where there was also high level Chinese representation, to raise the subject of having diplomatic relations, on the same conditions roughly as Canada had achieved the year before. So it didn't take long at all. I forget the exact dates but I think it was within about ten days. You can't ignore one of the largest countries in the world in area and the largest in population. But not only that, it is the nation which has had a national identity for longer than any other country on earth.

It is significant that one of the first things that any subsequent prime minister has done has been to visit China. I think at last we are being more realistic in regard to all the stuff that comes from ideologues in the United States who are adverse to China. You know, there are still people in America who advocate restoring diplomatic relations between America and Taiwan. We shouldn't take too seriously the things which are said in the United States against China and in favour of Taiwan.

Are you an optimist about the future of Australia/China relations?

Yes. There are some things in China, of course, which turn me off pretty strongly, like the fact that there is so much capital punishment. But person for person, the Americans are more bloodthirsty than the Chinese. One of the unfortunate things is that nearly all the countries to our north, northwest, northeast, still continue the death penalty but the United States is the only country in the Americas which maintains the death penalty. I condemn it in America and I condemn it in China.

Another of your foreign policy objectives was to deepen the Australia/Indonesia relationship and to develop a close personal relationship with President Suharto.

Or whoever was in charge in Indonesia. It is deplorable that Menzies—our first prime minister after Indonesia became independent—didn't make a visit for ten years, and the next prime minister to make a visit was Gorton, nine years later.

I thought it was appalling that Australian prime ministers had so belatedly visited Indonesia and that no Indonesian leader had visited Australia. Menzies, incidentally, urged Evatt and Calwell, the then leader and deputy leader of the Labor Party, to choose somebody to go with him, but they wouldn't commit themselves. So he asked me directly and I told him that

I didn't think I would at that time. It's appalling that there were those gaps. Evatt and Calwell never visited Indonesia and our foreign ministers Spender and Casey never visited Indonesia. There had been this neglect for so long. I visited there for the first time in 1967.

In 1975 President Suharto decided to resolve the East Timor issue by incorporation. Could Australia have stopped the Indonesian invasion by either diplomatic or military means?

Not a chance. Incidentally, the Indonesian paratroops and marines landed in Dili when Malcolm Fraser was prime minister. It was three weeks after I had ceased to be prime minister. I had discussed these matters with President Suharto in February 1973 in Jakarta, in Central Java in September 1974 and in Townsville in April 1975, and all those documents are open to the public. They have been declassified, anybody can get them. There were also letters that I sent to President Suharto. In particular, there was one which I asked Dick Woolcott, who was going there to present his credentials as ambassador, to give to the president.

I say that if people are wanting to ask whose hands were bloodied over this, it was the Portuguese. The simple fact is that for four centuries the Portuguese state and the Catholic church were culpably negligent in the way they treated that colony. It was the least developed, the least literate colony in the world. The Portuguese were great explorers, the first Europeans to get to Timor or Ambon, but they were the most inexpert exploiters.

Some people are suggesting we should have gone to war there. Now, the night before the Indonesian marines and paratroops landed in Dili, President Ford and Secretary Kissinger were farewelled in Jakarta and they were told that the landings would take place the next day. A few years ago, in the early 1990s, Kissinger was over here on one of his lecture tours and gave a luncheon speech, and he was asked, What about it? And he said: 'Yes, we were told. We thought it was like Goa.' It was another development in the dissolution of the Portuguese empire and they didn't object. There was already trouble in Angola with the Cubans there and they didn't want to get into another blue over a Portuguese colony.

People who comment on these things ought to look at what the American attitude has been all along on this. You remember there was a great move in Australia to keep [Dutch-held] West New Guinea away from Indonesia. It was the only former European possession which was not given independence, and Bobby Kennedy came out on behalf of John Kennedy to tell the Menzies Government: 'We will not strike a blow in defence of the Dutch.' And accordingly, Barwick advised Menzies and Menzies accepted that that was the end, that the Dutch would have to leave. And the Indonesians took over.

You really reinvented democratic socialism for the Labor Party after its long obsession with nationalisation. How much damage did the idea of nationalisation, in particular bank nationalisation, do to the party?

It did us a great deal of harm, there is no doubt. I can explain why it took place. The States had objected to some of the new banking legislation which involved the Commonwealth

Bank being the Reserve Bank, and the States challenged it. So Chifley, with Evatt's advice, said well, just nationalise the banks. The public weren't prepared for that. Then Evatt made the mistake of saying, well, the High Court's against us, let's go to the Privy Council— which was completely against our principles of ending appeals at the Privy Council. So it dragged on almost to the 1949 elections. If it had been dropped when the High Court ruled it out there would have been no trouble.

My whole objective was to use the Constitution as it stood, rather than trying to get an amendment to permit nationalisation. The High Court had said that, under Section 92, trade, commerce and intercourse between the States had to be entirely free, absolutely free. The High Court had developed this doctrine that the government can't take over any business. What I said was, there are ways you can achieve the Labor Party's objectives under the Constitution as it stands and in particular you can make grants to the States for purposes which you define. That's how we got federal aid for education and how we took over the whole cost of higher secondary and technical and tertiary education.

How important was the 25 per cent tariff cut in terms of economic change?

As we can now see, it was absolutely essential. It is not possible to quarantine an economy. No country is an island unto itself. Even a continent can't live unto itself. We can't live unless we sell our products, we can't sell our products unless we buy other products. We've got to face the fact that some things are developed on an international basis. You can't run airlines or even shipping lines or telephonic services or other forms of communication unless you have some international arrangement. Now, it takes a long time to get international arrangements regulating investment and taxation. But the fact is that we wouldn't have a fraction of the skills we now have in Australia if we were not using international networks.

You remember that Jim Cairns and I put this proposal to the caucus and it was carried 2:1. Frank Crean supported it too. All of the economically literate people in the caucus supported it, and they were right. I had to be strong about it, sure. But you remember how the tariff system was completely abused. John McEwen was a very effective and strong leader of the Country Party, a chap for whom I had very great admiration and who had some admiration for me—I first met him at my father's house in 1934. But in trying to get support for secondary industry, I must say, he debauched the system.

You also had great respect for Menzies?

He was a superb parliamentary performer and electoral performer. No better one on the other side. He'd taken two elections to get back from his catastrophic defeat in 1943. Well, he did get back. Similarly, I got back after our catastrophic defeat in the 1966 election. I went more than halfway in 1969, I went the whole way in 1972.

Despite the 1999 defeat of the Republican Referendum, do you think an Australian republic is inevitable?

Unquestionably. Within ten years.

How important is it for Australia and for Australians that we become a republic?

I believe, from the point of view of other countries, it's essential. There's no doubt that one of the difficulties we have in our region is that we preserve this farce that our Head of State has to live in England and, let's put it bluntly, belong to the Church of England.

Do you find it incredible when you look back that for 70 years Australia maintained the judicial supremacy of the Privy Council?

Yes, I do. The Constitution was drafted by people living in Australia and approved at referendums in five of the States and by a parliamentary resolution in Western Australia. But the British insisted on retaining the right of appeal to the Privy Council. That was the only alteration that the British made in the Constitution drafted by us in the 1890s and passed by the British Parliament in July 1900. The only alteration they made.

My government strongly believed, and I think most people agree, that the laws which Australians have to obey or administer should be Australia's. That is, the High Court should finally determine any questions of disputes between Australians or between Australian governments. There's no doubt that most of the High Court judges in the last twenty years have been very pleased that there are now no appeals to the Privy Council, because they didn't respect some of the decisions of the Privy Council. I needn't go into the details but the Privy Council was not as good as our High Court even in our High Court's most prejudiced days.

When you became prime minister you wanted to modernise our links with Britain and with the monarchy. What did you do?

I went to London on Good Friday 1973 and discussed these issues with the Queen. Her title, for instance. Up till then the Queen's title—in Australia, that is—was: Of the United Kingdom, Australia and her other realms, Queen, Defender of the Faith, Head of the Commonwealth. Then in 1973 she agreed that it should be Queen of Australia and her other realms and territories, Head of the Commonwealth and, oh, Defender of the Faith. But Britain was no longer mentioned in her title after 1973. We were the first country to do that. Nearly all the other Dominions followed.

You wanted the Queen to feel closer to Australians?

Oh yes. There's no doubt, and you remember there were many visits here by her and sometimes by Prince Philip and by Prince Charles—not so many by the cousins. There was no question that we wanted to build up the idea that we respected our heritage but that in our own region we should be shown to be independent.

The new title was in an Act to which the Queen herself assented at Government House, and then afterwards she came to lunch at the Prime Minister's Lodge. We had a senior trade union representative, Jack Egerton, the vice-president of the ACTU, and we had Reg Ansett representing the benign face of capitalism. Of course, I had to introduce all the people to the Queen and so I introduced Jack Egerton. And he said: 'I believe you've been naturalised, love.' The Queen *was* amused. She'd become Queen of Australia.

5

Farewell Great
and Powerful Friends

Australia was born when its troops were fighting for the Empire. On the eve of Federation, 250 000 people lined the shores of Sydney Harbour to farewell the NSW contingent leaving for the Second Boer War. It was not the struggle itself that counted for the Australian colonies—they acted from kinship and strategic needs. Security had been one of the Federation motives and the issue was self-evident: how could less than four million Australians defend their claim to the island continent? The principal answer to this question lay in the resort to great and powerful friends; and it remained the answer for much of our history.

Australia's great luck was that the British people colonised its lands. This meant that at Federation Australia belonged to the world's greatest Empire and its strongest navy. Australia did not speak to the world in its own right; it spoke as part of a mighty Empire—a considerable advantage. In 1901 Britain was not just a friend; it was family.

Federation united the colonies but the Imperial links remained. Australia did not pretend to conduct its own foreign policy or to manage its own place in the world. The Empire was not just a protector: it was a lens through which Australia viewed the world and, in turn, through which the world perceived Australia. It helped Australia to define its own role in a globe dominated by colonialism.

The Constitution gave Australia an 'external affairs' power. But there was no legal or strategic suggestion that its potentiality would be realised in the foreseeable future. This power meant that the Commonwealth would deal with Britain's Colonial Office, which brokered Australia's place in the world. Australia had no navy or diplomatic service. The practice of diplomacy, the power of treaty making and any decision to resort to war would rest with London, not Australia. This was the idea of a united Empire.

The Boer War established the 'great and powerful friend' tradition. A total of 16 000 Australians along with the same number of horses were despatched, and Australia lost around 500 dead in battle or by disease.

Departure of troops from Port Melbourne Pier on their way to the Boer War.

Queen Victoria sent a message of heartfelt gratitude. The war was popular and little understood. There were a few critics, Henry Lawson among them. But the 'great and powerful friend' tradition would endure for much of the century. Our military forces would be raised at home, despatched abroad, fight overseas and confront a strange enemy on foreign terrain— all in the name of Empire or friend or democracy.

There was one flaw in this wondrous arrangement: Britain's interests did not necessarily coincide with Australia's. (Nor did those of America, the second great and powerful friend.) This was a problem of varying but institutionalised intensity. Each Australian prime minister confronted this challenge of how to harness the Empire for Australia's own needs. It became a continuous process of give and take, manipulation and the search for common ground.

Australians had a keen grasp of where the threat lay. It was Japan. In the first 50 years of Australia's existence the shadow of Japan dominated defence and foreign policy. Japan was the pervasive factor in influencing Australia's Empire relations and then its ties with the United States. In 1902 Britain concluded, without reference to Australia, a treaty with Japan. Japan became the key Empire ally in the East and, by definition, Australia's own ally. This was not Australia's choice. Fears about the rise of Japan were accentuated with its 1905 war victory over Russia at the

Battle of Tsushima. This inaugurated a fluctuating 40 year period of distrust between Australia and Japan that would end in a brutal war. Japan, deeply hostile to the White Australia policy, now became the dominant naval power in the Pacific. At this point Australia's politicians cast aside the pro-Japanese British view and offered their own interpretation of Japan's dramatic rise. A future Defence Minister, George Pearce, asked: 'Is there any other country that offers such a temptation to Japan as does Australia?' The historian of this period, Neville Meaney, quotes a former deputy prime minister, Allen McLean: 'The stupendous struggle in the East must awaken the people of Australia to the fact that we have been living in a fool's paradise when we have assumed that our great distance from the military nations gave us immunity from foreign invasion. Japan has astonished the world. We now find one of the great naval and military powers within a very short distance of our shores.'

Australia's dilemma was defined by historian David Horner: 'Everybody in Australia recognised that to defend Australia by just relying on our own resources would not be possible. We had to look to the defence of Australia as part of the British Empire. Yet it was clear to many that the Japanese could sail south from Japan and reach Australia much faster than the Royal Navy could get to this area from Britain.'

Prime Minister Alfred Deakin responded with two initiatives: an approach to the United States, and a campaign to increase Australia's own defence forces. These two impulses would become part of a recurring Australian pattern. On Christmas Day 1907 Deakin called upon the US Consul in Melbourne. His purpose was to make a personal appeal to the American president, Teddy Roosevelt. The president was sending a great American fleet around the world and Deakin wanted it to visit Australia. Norman Harper recounted the story in his history of the US alliance. Deakin wrote to the American ambassador in London: 'The appearance in the Pacific of such an armada is an event in the history not only of the United States but of that ocean ... no other federation in the world possesses as many features of likeness to the United States as the Commonwealth of Australia and I doubt whether any two peoples are to be found who are in nearer touch with each other.'

Such flattery saw the American Government accept Deakin's invitation. The British were appalled at such Australian impertinence. Winston Churchill, parliamentary undersecretary at the Colonial Office, wrote: 'It ought certainly to be discouraged from every point of view.' The Admiralty would be embarrassed by the size of the US fleet. Roosevelt's vision was of America as a Pacific power.

On 20 August 1908 the most impressive fleet yet seen in Australia entered

To celebrate the visit of the Great White Fleet in 1908, a replica of the Statue of Liberty was placed in front of the Daily Telegraph offices.

Sydney Heads. The sixteen battleships were painted white, a symbol of peace. By dawn's early light both of the main roads to Watsons Bay were thronged as rarely before. The Governor-General, Lord Northcote, reported: 'Hundreds of thousands of people lined the shores of Port Jackson, while every available vessel in the harbour was crowded with sightseers. I am credibly informed that the number of people who took part in the welcome constituted the largest gathering at any time in the history of New South Wales.' *The Sydney Morning Herald* said in an editorial: 'It is likely enough that America may become the first line of defence against Asia.' There was a romantic touch to the reception. Harper quotes from *The Age* editorial: 'We Australians would love to think of ourselves and the great American republic as travelling through the centuries with ever increasing cordiality and love for one another.' An American journalist, Franklin Matthews, declared: 'Fleetitis is raging all over the Antipodes.'

Deakin wrote that the reason for such popularity was 'not so much because of our blood affection for the Americans but because of the distrust of the yellow race in the North Pacific'. Deakin saw America as an extra source of support, not as a substitute for Imperial ties. His US initiative was a one-off; its significance was as an omen, not as a strategic reality in its own time.

Public and political sentiment in Australia moved decisively towards a stronger defence effort. In 1907 Deakin pledged to establish an Australian navy, with backing from the Labor Party. Beneath the surface was a lack of confidence in British defence guarantees and a suspicion of the Anglo-Japanese alliance. Australian naval plans had to be co-ordinated with London since Australia ultimately depended upon the British Fleet. But an assertive and intelligent Australian nationalism was emerging across both sides of federal politics. The young Commonwealth began to take the initiative.

After a frustrating series of negotiations with Britain, involving both Deakin and Andrew Fisher's ALP Government, vessels were commissioned for construction in British shipyards. The Australian Navy was designed for operation with the British Navy. It was agreed at the 1911 Imperial Conference that the RAN would operate under British command in times of war. On 4 October 1913 its vanguard, the flagship and two cruisers, sailed into Sydney Harbour. Further vessels were under construction. Australia was the only Dominion to commission its own navy before World War I.

Deakin had also proposed in 1907 a system of universal compulsory military training for young men. This policy was bipartisan and had strong backing from Labor, which had helped to create the climate for the initiative. Labor's Billy Hughes argued for universal service, in effect, to honour the principles of egalitarianism and socialism. The system was finally established under the 'Fusion' government when Joseph Cook was Defence Minister. The scheme applied to men from 14 to 20 years of age and involved sixteen days' training a year. In what Neville Meaney described as a 'classical exposition of the Australian crisis', Cook called Australia 'the most distant, the richest and the most vulnerable part of the British Empire', where there were 'not far from our shores two or three million of the best trained troops in the world'. Japan lay at the heart of Australia's defence initiatives.

Military historian Jeffrey Grey says that in 1911 a total of 92 000 youths were in training; over three years the size of the militia increased by 50 per cent; and in World War I about 15 per cent of the AIF (Australian Imperial Force) consisted of former 'boy soldiers'. The Royal Military College, Duntroon, was established in 1911. Meaney estimates that in the few years before the Great War Australia increased its defence budget by more than 200 per cent.

On the eve of war Australia's worry about Britain's reliability deepened further. Britain, alarmed about the rise of German naval power, gave priority to reinforcing the heart of the Empire. In the Pacific it would rely upon the Anglo-Japanese alliance. Meaney recounts Joseph Cook's re-action: 'The Pacific was being made safe and secure not by the might and majesty of the British Fleet but by the Japanese treaty. That raised for Australia very serious questions ... They were under treaty obligations with a nation whose people they might not admit to their shores. They had their White Australia policy and they must at all costs defend it.'

The features of these pre-1914 efforts were the high degree of bipartisanship across the Liberal and Labor Parties, the embrace of universal conscription, the conviction that Australia needed a dual strategy of Empire and self-help, and the recognition that there was a threat and it was Japan. Australia was the first English-speaking nation to introduce compulsory military service in peacetime. But there was a paradoxical legacy—Australia was better positioned to rely upon a volunteer army during World War I itself. Military historian David Horner remarks: 'We saw, in that period before the First World War, two strands of Australian defence policy that have existed throughout the whole century. That is, the strand of being part of the Empire, the Imperialist strand if you like, and at the same time, one that was in those days called the Australianist view: that is, we should defend Australia from within Australia.'

As the Labor Party leader Kim Beazley says, independence is not obtained by repudiating great and powerful friends. It is an advantage for a small or middle-size power such as Australia to have such friends. The traditional challenge for Australian policy has been to exploit such alliances in Australia's own interests. And the growth of a sense of Australian national interest, of relating to the world as Australians rather than as extensions of Empire or great partners, has been an integral part of this process.

Australia's leaders in the years preceding World War I displayed remarkable enterprise. The conclusion is irresistible—their skill and vigour rate far higher than the 1930s leadership in the prelude to World War II.

The Great War (1914–18) posed the greatest threat to Britain and the Empire for more than a hundred years. It was a European war but the European powers ran their own empires. What happened in Europe would determine what happened in Africa and Asia and the Pacific. Australia had a direct and high stake in the outcome of World War I. Its vital interests were engaged. Australia's leaders knew this in both an instinctive and a strategic fashion.

In August 1914 the Empire responded as one. Prime Minister Cook said: 'So far as our defences go, I want to make it quite clear that all our resources

On the duckboards, Western Front.

in Australia are in the Empire and for the Empire and for the preservation and security of the Empire.' This was not a controversial statement; it was expected by the public. Australians initially accepted that their forces would be under British command. Cook told Britain: 'In the event of war the Government is prepared to place the vessels of the Australian Navy under the control of the British Admiralty when desired. It is further prepared to despatch an expeditionary force of 20 000 men of any suggested composition to any destination desired by the Home Government, the force to be at the complete disposal of the Home Government.'

Australia's response to the war was virtually unanimous. The Liberal and Labor Parties both saw Australia as an integral part of the Empire. And there was a palpable sense that the war would be the making of the nation. Geoffrey Blainey points out that, at the time, national greatness tended to be measured by war deeds. The peaceful progress of the nineteenth century had been no preparation for the horrors of a full-scale twentieth century war.

Australia's first action was in the Pacific, and Japan was a war ally. In September 1914 Australian forces took Rabaul, the capital of German New Guinea. This occurred under the British policy that Australia and New Zealand deal with German possessions south of the equator and that Japan take German territories north of the line. When Australian troops sailed to the Middle East en route to Gallipoli they had a Japanese escort.

William Morris Hughes, 'the little Digger', became prime minister in 1915. Australia's role was tied indissolubly to his plans, passions and prejudices. The Governor-General, Sir Ronald Munro-Ferguson, wrote of him: 'In some respects he is not unlike his countryman Lloyd George. His judgment is better; his insight clear; his capacity for affairs great. He is highly strung and at times violent. He stands out above his whole party in intellect, courage and skill.'

Hughes was a globalist. He had a crude strategic vision which he pursued with relentless drive devoid of any capacity for self-doubt. More than any other senior politician of the early Federation, Hughes was convinced that Australia was a target of malevolent design. His purpose was to maximise Australian influence in the seat of Empire in order to secure the Empire's support when Australia's day of reckoning came. Hughes knew the future enemy; it was the current wartime ally.

He said: 'All our fears or conjectures that Japan was and is most keenly interested in Australia are amply borne out ... It is to me quite clear that in the event of even a temporary reverse to the allies, the Japanese Government might not be able—even if they so desired—to keep Japan behind Britain.'

David Horner summarises the Hughes strategy: 'He saw that we needed to play our part in the Empire but also had his eye on the fact that the quid pro quo for that was that the Empire would be expected to defend us in our area of the world.'

Gallipoli was merely the start of the war. It would be fought in the trenches of Europe; and Britain would have no greater ally than Australia. Wave after wave of Australians paid the final price. The battlefields of the Western Front would be the site of Australia's ultimate sacrifice for its great and powerful friend, for its family bond. Australia, along with other Empire nations, saw much of its next generation slaughtered on the Somme, at Pozieres, Passchendaele and Bullecourt.

On 1 November 1917 a long sought aspiration was realised—the formation of the Australian Corps. It united all the Australian divisions in a single force and was finally put under the command of Australia's John Monash. In 1918 the Australians were involved in the decisive battles of the war leading to the armistice. David Horner says: 'What a lot of people

Billy Hughes touring the battlefields of the Western Front in 1918.

perhaps don't realise is that Australia played a very major part in 1918, one of the few occasions in which the large Australian army has taken on perhaps one of the best armies in the world, the German army, the main enemy in the main theatre, and defeated it. Perhaps, as has been suggested, [it was] the most important military contribution that we've made in any war—part of the British overall effort admittedly, but the Australian Corps, along with the Canadian Corps, made the main thrust in 1918.'

Hughes went to Britain during the war to try to maximise Australia's influence. In 1916 he was an electrifying campaigner for the war effort and he returned to London in 1918. During these visits Hughes discovered by dint of experience that Britain's interests did not always coincide with Australia's.

On both trips Hughes visited the Australian troops and in 1918 his visit preceded the battle at Hamel, one of Australia's finest efforts. Hughes's biographer, L F Fitzhardinge, quotes from an account given by Joseph Cook, who was also travelling with the prime minister: 'Hughes, often as not, lay full length on the ground, looking into the faces of the soldiers and chewing a stalk of grass. He seemed wrapped up in the men and was gazing into their faces all the time.' Hughes later recalled his experience to the Governor-General: 'I saw a great thing last week in France. I talked to the boys who were going into the Hamel stunt. I can't tell you how splendid they were: words are poor things to describe them. I thought that with a million such men one could conquer the world.'

The Great War symbolised Australia's early destiny—a blood sacrifice for family, friend or Empire followed by a campaign to convert the sacrifice into political capital. Hughes understood the process. Indeed, he was its prime originator and arch-practitioner.

Hughes went to the 1919 Paris Peace Conference to exploit Australia's blood sacrifice and to persuade the great and powerful on behalf of the nation's security needs. He was accompanied by his personal secretary, Percy Deane, who had the rare ability to avoid being fired by his autocratic boss. Deane commented: 'What the Digger stood for in war, Mr Hughes stood for in the negotiations which led to the peace.'

There had never been a peace conference to match it. Leaders and diplomats from around the globe came to strike a new order, unaware that they were doomed to fail. The most ambitious was the academic patrician from Virginia, US president Woodrow Wilson, with his dream of a League of Nations. But Wilson confronted a bunch of professional hardheads: Britain's David Lloyd George, French president Georges Clemenceau and, down the line, the talkative Hughes. Hughes had insisted on separate Australian representation at the peace conference and separate membership of any newly formed League of Nations—significant steps towards Australian autonomy and representation. Australia had a marginal role but Hughes gave it a high though not necessarily statesmanlike profile.

He stayed at the Hotel Majestic, just off the Champs Elysees, where he fumed about Wilson. As a realist Hughes had only contempt for the international idealism of the US president. The antagonism was strong and mutual. For those Australians who later bemoaned the Australian deference to America, Hughes offers a stunning therapy. 'He is great on great principles,' he said of Wilson. 'As to their application: he is so much like Alice in Wonderland . . . Give him a League of Nations and he will give us all the rest. Good. He shall have his toy! What shape is it to assume, you ask. None know. He least of all.'

The conflict between Wilson and Hughes came to a head over Australia's determination to have direct control over German New Guinea. It was a clash between the idea of colonial security and the US anti-imperialist tradition. Hughes was driven by power factors and, for him, fear of Japan was paramount.

He began his presentation on 24 January 1919 in the Quai d'Orsay, armed with a large wall map. He lectured world leaders on the strategic significance to Australia of the Pacific islands, notably New Guinea, declaring that: 'New Guinea was the biggest island in the whole world save Australia. If there were at the very door of Australia a potential or actual enemy, Australia could not feel safe. The island was as necessary to Australia as water to a city. No state would suffer if Australia were safe. Australia alone would suffer if she were not. Australia had suffered 90 000 casualties in this war and lost 60 000 killed. Her troops everywhere had fought well.'

Hughes wanted Australian annexation of German New Guinea, while Wilson wanted the territory controlled under a League of Nations mandate. For Wilson the 'League of Nations would be a laughing stock if it were not invested with this quality of trusteeship'.

Wilson later lectured Hughes on world opinion and said that Australia couldn't hold up the conference. Lloyd George described the scene: 'Mr Hughes, who listened intently with his hand cupped around his neck so as not to miss a word, indicated at the end that he was still of the same opinion. Whereupon the president asked him slowly and solemnly, "Mr Hughes, am I to understand that if the whole civilised world asks Australia to agree to a mandate in respect of these islands, Australia is prepared still to defy the appeal of the whole civilised world?" Mr Hughes answered, "That's about the size of it, President Wilson".'

But the two men were playing to their respective galleries. Behind the scenes Lloyd George had brokered a compromise. There would be a mandate system under which New Guinea would be administered under Australian law. Hughes had won a wide degree of Australian control. As for Wilson, his own Congress rejected US participation in the League of Nations.

On the issue of war reparations, Hughes was a loud and offensive Australian. He wanted Germany punished to the hilt, with full compensation of war costs to nations such as Australia. He suffered a humiliating defeat in his capacity as Chairman of the Reparations Committee and his campaign for a vindictive peace, much worse even than the Conference endorsed, revealed a politician limited by his passion for vengeance. Hughes would be better remembered for his fights than for his achievements.

His performance in Paris would be the most assertive in Australian diplomacy for nearly half a century. He proved to the world that Australia and the Dominions were more than British lapdogs. Hughes defined the purpose of Australian policy—trying to influence the great and powerful. Every subsequent prime minister would struggle with this mission.

After the war the world was a more dangerous place for Australia. The British Empire was weaker and Japan, as Hughes foresaw, would eventually become an enemy. The domestic divisions of the war were enduring and Australia lacked the vigour of the prewar period. Between the wars

Australia would be trapped, too weak to defend itself but hostage to a declining Empire too weak to control the Pacific.

Singapore became the grand illusion of Australian defence policy for the next twenty years. Australia knew its vulnerability but deluded itself by invoking the Imperial sentiment. It had no separate intelligence or diplomatic resources with which to pursue a vigorous foreign policy. Its leaders were not taken seriously by Britain in the discussion of defence policy and their failure to devise a consistent position meant that they didn't warrant being taken seriously. Australia was caught unprepared by World War II. Official war historian Bob O'Neill says: 'Australia did indulge in a great deal of self-delusion over the whole Singapore issue. If you go back into British official records in the 1930s on Singapore you can see there are various marginal notes: "Do not pass this information on to the Australians". The British themselves had a fair idea that the policy was not going to work if it came under real pressure from the Japanese.'

There was a sense of Australian fatalism. Australia's Director of Military Intelligence and Japan expert, E L Piesse, had slammed Hughes for his anti-Japanese tactics at Paris which only played into the hands of Japan's imperialists and militarists. But Japan was on the march anyway. The Anglo–Japanese alliance expired in the early 1920s to be replaced by a four power Pacific Pact, an optimistic development initially, but in Tokyo the expansionists gained sway. In 1931 Japan invaded Manchuria, the precursor to its expansion. In 1935 Piesse warned: 'The possibility of war with Japan must be faced. If war does occur no British naval forces could leave European waters that would be of any use in defending Australia.'

The Australian Army chiefs knew that Singapore was a phoney fortress and warned to this effect. Their self-interested analysis, in retrospect, seems obvious—that Japan would not attack until Britain was preoccupied in Europe and, since the Royal Navy would be absent, Australia would need a far stronger army for its self-defence. Australia's problem, in essence, was its national weakness. Whether measured by its economy, its small population or its infrastructure, Australia was extremely exposed. It had one great asset. Its geography made Australia a hard place to invade.

Surveying the interwar years, historian Jeffrey Grey says: 'It is clear that little or nothing was done to increase the government's ability to carry out its military responsibilities. Australian governments of both persuasions chose to believe that another major war would not occur, or that if it did, somebody else would fight it on our behalf.'

In September 1939 World War II came, again as a conflict in Europe. The similarities with the Great War were apparent but false. Prime Minister Robert Gordon Menzies invoked the ties of loyalty and security with Britain. Crowds sang 'Land of Hope and Glory' but, unlike the first war, there was no spontaneous rush to join up. Hostilities were distant and summer was coming.

Menzies was cautious and saw the gravity of the challenge. His biographer, Allan Martin, documents Menzies' concern about Japan: 'This is not 1914 when there was no real problem of Australia's security from attack and when land forces in Europe were the determining factor. In this war Australia's own security must be attended to.' Indeed, Japan was preparing to strike.

Australia, faithful to the Empire strategy, raised forces to serve in Europe, Africa and the Middle East over three years. At the time, Labor opposed the despatch of the troops. But the evidence is that Menzies made a measured judgment about the departure of the Second AIF from Australia to the Middle East. Reviewing his decision Jeffrey Grey says: 'In 1939 the Japanese had not attacked in the Pacific and the threat posed by Hitler was real. It was unthinkable in any case that a homogeneous society like Australia would stand by and allow Britain to face the German onslaught alone. Nor should it be thought that a British defeat did not pose serious economic and strategic dangers for the Dominions.'

Australian troops fought the Germans, Vichy French and Italians. In World War II, as in the Great War, these forces were engaged in a decisive phase of the conflict, notably at Alamein where General Montgomery gave the Australians responsibility for the key thrust against Rommel's Africa Corps. It was a victory that Churchill hailed as a turning point of the war.

In the War Cabinet there was deep concern about Singapore. The appreciations put before ministers were stark: in any Pacific war Britain could only make a limited contribution; America would be unlikely to declare war if Japan attacked only Dutch or British possessions; and America and Britain would give priority to the Atlantic and Europe. The Deputy prime minister, Arthur Fadden, wrote: 'If Australia were to be abandoned by these two great powers until the war in Europe was decided, we and our countrymen might well be pulling rickshaws before long.'

In early 1941 Menzies, worried about the reliability of Singapore, went to London. Welcomed by the British prime minister, Winston Churchill, Menzies was impressed yet repelled: 'The cabinet is deplorable—dumb men, most of whom disagree with Winston but none dare to say so. The chiefs of staff are without exception "yes" men. Winston is a dictator; he cannot be overruled.'

Menzies was feted; he rallied the home front and was deeply impressed by the fortitude of the British people enduring a pounding from Hitler. But Menzies, even more than Hughes before him, faced the reality not just of diverging Australian–British interests but of conflicting interests.

David Horner summarises the Menzies visit: 'When Menzies arrived in London he got a nasty surprise in respect of what he expected to get from Churchill. He was hoping to get support forces to be sent to the Far East and what he found was that Churchill wasn't interested in the Far East. Churchill was interested in fighting the war in the Middle East. He didn't really have his mind focused on the Far East.'

Churchill was ebullient, manipulative and friendly. He told Menzies: 'I think Australia will have to be mauled a little.' Menzies, as Horner says, better grasped where Australia stood and realised that he had little leverage with Churchill. Australia's ties with the Empire had been insurance against a crisis, yet when the crisis came the insurance policy could not be redeemed. Menzies returned emptyhanded and undermined. He complained at Rose Bay that he must now play domestic politics. Menzies had lost the support of his own party and, eventually, a new Labor Government was formed under John Curtin.

When Menzies resigned the prime ministership he wrote a private letter to Curtin: 'My dear John, I've ceased to be prime minister and we shall therefore no longer be opposite numbers at the table. I want to thank you for two years and four months in which my task, always difficult, has frequently been rendered easier and at times rendered more tolerable by your magnanimous and understanding attitude. Your political opposition has been honourable and your personal friendship a pearl of great price. Yours sincerely, Bob.'

Curtin took office after two independents switched their support in the House of Representatives. It was a supreme irony. Curtin, jailed for anti-conscriptionist activity in the first war, now found himself as the only politician equipped to leader the nation effectively in the second war. He came to power in October 1941, when the war was about to engulf Australia. The two landmark events were the Japanese attack at Pearl Harbor on 7 December 1941 and the fall of Singapore on 15 February 1942. It was a period of permanent crisis, tragedy, alarm and reassessment. Australia came close to the edge.

The Japanese attack on Pearl Harbor brought America into the war. The event that Australians had feared for half a century had occurred— Japan on the attack through the Pacific. Australia felt more vulnerable than at any point in its existence. But Japan's war entry resolved the strategic dilemma facing the Empire. Australia now had two great and powerful friends as allies. Curtin addressed the nation on 8 December 1941, declaring war on Japan: 'Men and women of Australia. We are at war with Japan. This is the gravest hour of our history. We Australians have imperishable traditions. We shall maintain them. We shall vindicate them. We shall hold this country and keep it as a citadel for the British-speaking race and as a place where civilisation will persist.'

It was a war on two fronts. Churchill and Roosevelt had agreed before Pearl Harbor on the strategy: it was 'beat Hitler first'. Australia had been neither consulted nor initially told about this epic decision. The war with Japan would be secondary. Australia had the most to lose from this strategy and it became the principal obstacle for Curtin in his desperate appeals for reinforcements at Singapore.

On 10 December HMS *Prince of Wales* and HMS *Repulse* were sunk by Japanese bombers off the Malayan coast. It was an omen of doom. All prospect of British naval forces defying Japan—on which Australia had been depending since Federation—was dashed. Churchill confronted the grim reality: 'I put the telephone down. I was thankful to be alone. In all the war I never received a more direct shock. The full horror sank in on me. There were no British or American capital ships in the Indian Ocean or the Pacific except the American survivors of Pearl Harbor . . . over all this expanse of waters, Japan was supreme and we everywhere were weak and naked.'

Curtin's initial hope that American entry into the war would see US reinforcements was dashed too. Richard Casey, Australia's Minister in Washington, reported: 'While lip service is paid to the importance of Singapore, its importance is clearly subordinated to the Philippines in American minds.' On 23 December Curtin cabled Roosevelt and Churchill: 'The fall of Singapore would mean the isolation of the Philippines, the fall of the Netherlands East Indies and attempts to smother all other bases. It is in your power to meet the situation . . . we would gladly accept United States commander in Pacific area. Please consider this as matter of greatest urgency.' The same day Australia's representative in Singapore, V G Bowden, cabled: 'I must emphasise that the deterioration of the air position in the Malayan defence is assuming landslide proportions. As things stand at present, the fall of Singapore is to my mind only a matter of weeks. If Singapore and the AIF in Malaya are to be saved, there must be very radical and effective action immediately.' Hong Kong fell three days later.

Curtin's direct appeals to Churchill and Roosevelt both failed. The truth is that it was too late for Singapore to be reinforced. The risk was that any reinforcement would only have increased the size of the forces that would be lost to the Japanese.

In trying to rally the Australian people Curtin now issued one of the most famous declarations in the nation's history. Penned by his press secretary Don Rogers and based on Curtin's brief, it was splashed across the Melbourne *Herald*: 'Without any inhibitions of any kind I make it quite clear that Australia looks to America free of any pangs as to our traditional links or kinship with the United Kingdom. We know the problems the United Kingdom faces. But we know too that Australia can go, and Britain still hold on. We are therefore determined that Australia shall not go and we shall exert all our energies towards the shaping of a plan, with the United States as its keystone, which will give to our country some confidence to be able to hold out until the tide of battle swings.'

This reflected a truth—only America could save Australia now. Australia was being driven by the survival instinct. The assumption of British protection upon which Australia had relied since 1788 was dying.

But the reaction was most unfavourable. Menzies condemned the appeal as a 'great blunder'. Churchill was unimpressed and bemoaned Australia's 'mood of panic'. He offered to broadcast to the Australian public. Roosevelt told Casey the statement would not 'ingratiate Australia with the United States' and that it tasted of 'panic and disloyalty'.

The article carrying Curtin's declaration is significant not for its impact upon the US but for its insight into Australian thinking. Curtin had no wish to repudiate Britain or Empire. He was making an appeal to the home front. He was trying to rally a despondent nation, anxious to instil a more resolute hope and purpose in a somewhat fatalistic community. Kim Beazley says of the article: 'It was addressed primarily to the Australian people. What he was saying was: we need new friends, we need to think anew strategically; and don't think you're actually going to be able to have anything by simply relying on someone else. You've got to get off your backsides and do the job yourselves.' Curtin was worried about the morale of the people, the lack of urgency, the oscillation between panic and 'she'll be right', a trait that concerned him throughout the war.

Foreign professionals were not impressed with Australia's response to the external threat. In his book on the alliance Norman Harper quotes two views. The first came from the American Minister in Canberra, Nelson Johnson: 'These people are with difficulty waking up to the fact that they are going to have to fight for their right to live freely in Australia . . . I find it difficult to understand what they are doing or thinking. They are in a state of funk and yelling for help, now, from the United States while they cast blame on the British for failures in the past, some of which they should share responsibility for.' The second view came from the British High Commissioner: 'The reaction of the Australian people to this emergency has in some respects fallen short of that which one would have expected of a people remarkable for their sanity and courage.'

Official war historian, Paul Hasluck, said that Canberra 'was more badly scared than any other part of the continent and that it was widely expected that Canberra would be bombed and perhaps occupied'. But the very senior ministers kept their nerve—including Curtin.

Australian troops were in action in Malaya during January 1942 as the Japanese thrust south. On 23 January Australia's representative, Bowden, cabled that the Singapore situation was 'desperate and possibly irretrievable'. David Horner has reconstructed the unfolding story. Australia's High Commissioner in London, Earle Page, reported on a meeting he had attended of the British Defence Committee about Singapore which had discussed whether 'evacuation should not now be considered'. Page vigorously opposed evacuation at the meeting. He sent an alarming cable to Canberra on 23 January. Acting on this cable and in the absence of Curtin, the Foreign Minister, Dr Evatt, amended a message to Churchill to include: 'After all the assurances we have been given, the evacuation of Singapore would be regarded here and elsewhere as an inexcusable betrayal.' The minutes of Australia's War Advisory Council, which included both Government and Opposition leaders, show endorsement of this message.

Churchill was provoked. He replied in full measure: 'I really cannot pass without comment such language to me as "inexcusable betrayal". I make all allowances for your anxiety and will not allow such discourtesy to cloud my judgment or lessen my efforts on your behalf . . . You have made it clear in public that you place your confidence in the United States. I have some recent and I believe true knowledge of the view they take and I doubt very much whether they would share your opinion.' Page reported that, in the British War Cabinet on 26 January, Churchill 'went off the deep end about Australians generally'.

Churchill and Curtin subsequently settled their differences. It was as natural for Curtin to seek reinforcement at Singapore as it was for Churchill to be cautious about strengthening a lost cause.

Singapore fell on 15 February 1942. Churchill described it as Britain's greatest military defeat. It was Australia's worst military disaster. The 8th Division was taken into captivity and one-third, more than 8000 men, would not survive. There was an enduring legacy of bitterness. It was the decisive failure of the 'great and powerful friend' strategy and a psychological turning point.

The truth, however, is that Australia has had difficulty in coming to grips with the Singapore tragedy. Evatt's 'betrayal' cable echoed down the decades and has been taken up even by a subsequent prime minister, Paul Keating.

The Curtin Government had to bear the responsibility for the unfortunate failures of earlier governments. And British governments had deceived Australia over Singapore for far too long. But when the crisis threatened it was extremely negligent for military authorities not to make evacuation plans in advance. The flaw in Australia's position was that it demanded that Singapore be reinforced while it was close to assuming that the cause was already lost. If, as the evidence suggests, Britain betrayed Australia, it also suggests that Australia's self-delusion for so long made it a party to its own betrayal. David Horner says: 'We went along with the Singapore strategy, and if we are to blame Britain we equally must blame ourselves for going along with that strategy. So I wouldn't use the term "betrayal" to describe what happened to Singapore.' Bob O'Neill says that Australian leaders deluded themselves over Singapore and 'what was behind the wishful thinking was the terrible thought of having to find the economic resources to build the defence force that was going to be necessary if Singapore was seen to be a broken reed'. The point, of course, is that any such task was not remotely within range of the weak Australian governments of the 1930s.

The betrayal claim has been exploited as a political device. It helps to excuse Australian weakness. It is a convenient anti-British weapon. But there is an enduring message: that relying upon the great and powerful has its limits. The task is to understand those limits in terms of military capability and political will. The lesson of the Singapore story is that Australia must develop defence self-reliance within its overarching alliance strategies. Singapore was the ultimate warning in Australia's first century— yet it remains a wake-up call for each generation to interpret and reinterpret.

Four days after the fall of Singapore, Japan bombed Darwin: 243 dead, 350 wounded, six ships lost. There was looting and people streamed from the city. Hardly a good omen for a nation likely to face further attack. The official statement was a lie, a cover-up of the real damage and number of deaths. But the bombing of Darwin settled the minds of senior ministers—defence of continental Australia was the absolute priority.

Curtin now confronted what would prove to be his most difficult decision of the war. In February 1942 he cabled Churchill saying, 'if possible, all Australian forces now under orders to transfer to the Far East from the Middle East should be diverted to Australia'. Curtin was laying claim to his own troops. He was acting on a firm appreciation of the military situation from the Australian Chiefs of Staff, in particular the insistence of the Chief of the General Staff, Vernon Sturdee. But the British command had taken another decision—with Singapore fallen they wanted to divert an Australian division for the defence of Burma. Churchill prosecuted this line. He deflected Curtin's request and made his own. When Curtin declined to accept the British position Churchill decided to apply the pressure.

At 9 pm on 20 February Churchill ordered the Admiralty to instruct the convoy carrying the Australian troops across the Indian Ocean to change course and steam north to Burma. Churchill then cabled another appeal to Curtin, forceful and intimidating. 'A vital war emergency cannot be ignored,' he said. 'This one [division] is needed now and is the only one that can possibly save the situation. I am quite sure that if you refuse to allow your troops to stop this gap ... a very grave effect will be produced upon the President and the Washington circle upon whom you are so largely reliant. We must have an answer immediately.' Churchill did not inform Curtin that he had already diverted the convoy.

President Roosevelt reinforced Churchill's request. 'I realise that your men have been fighting all over the world,' he began. 'I nevertheless want to ask you in the interests of our whole war effort ... if you will reconsider your decision.'

The great and powerful had spoken. Their appeal was based upon the need for a co-operative and united war effort. The Opposition members of the War Advisory Council, including Menzies, Billy Hughes, Fadden, McEwen and Percy Spender, urged Curtin to bow to the request. But Curtin was reinforced by General Sturdee, who said he would resign unless the troops came home for the defence of Australia.

Curtin again told Churchill the troops must return. Yet Churchill in a 22 February cable was defiant: ' We could not contemplate that you would refuse our request and that of the President of the United States for the diversion of the leading division to save the situation in Burma ... We therefore decided the convoy should be temporarily diverted to the northward.'

Only now did Curtin discover Churchill's unilateral action. He was appalled and shaken. It typified the way Churchill ran the war. Curtin went for a long walk around Mount Ainslie before replying: 'We feel a primary obligation to save Australia not only for itself but to preserve it as a base for the development of the war against Japan. In the circumstances it is quite impossible to reverse a decision which we made.'

Curtin prevailed.

Kim Beazley says: 'The pressure from Churchill on Curtin at the time . . . was the most intense that any Australian prime minister has ever been subjected to by an ally in any circumstances in the nation's history.'

David Horner closes the debate: 'Curtin was right on this issue. I don't think there's any question about it. Had those troops been diverted to Burma . . . almost certainly they would have gone into prisoner of war camps in Burma and they would not have been available for the defence of New Guinea later that year.'

This would have been a catastrophe for Australia. Historian Geoffrey Serle depicted the event as a triumph for the 'young green tree' over the 'old dead tree'. Gough Whitlam says that 'it was essential to demonstrate to the UK and the US that Australia should not be taken for granted'. The crisis revealed the gulf between Australian interests and Imperial strategy. The stakes were very high and Curtin's nationalism delivered the right decision. It was a landmark event—Australia at this point told the great and powerful that there were limits to their strategic plans, and occasions when such plans had to accommodate the legitimacy of smaller partners. It was a literal and symbolic point on the road to maturity.

America's General Douglas MacArthur arrived in Melbourne on 21 March 1942, ordered from the Philippines to Australia by President Roosevelt. MacArthur gave Curtin what he had long sought—a new commitment from the United States. Australia, after it was secured, would be the base for a counter-offensive.

MacArthur had a profound impact upon local morale. Four days earlier, after landing on Australian soil, he had declared: 'I came through and I shall return.' His actor's skills were precisely what Australians needed. MacArthur was hailed as the country's saviour. From his arrival at Melbourne's Spencer Street railway station he lifted the spirit and confidence of Australia's political leaders. But MacArthur was disappointed at the small number of forces available in Australia and somewhat sceptical about what he found. After watching a House of Representatives debate for 90 minutes he remarked: 'If Australians fight as well as they can argue, we are certain of victory.'

Curtin and MacArthur formed a unique partnership based upon mutual self-interest. MacArthur was a warrior, a conservative, a self-styled man of

General Douglas MacArthur and John Curtin formed an alliance for survival.

destiny dealing with Curtin, a Labor man and lapsed pacificist. When they met in Canberra MacArthur played the perfect script. He put his hand on Curtin's shoulder and said: 'Mr Prime Minister, we two, you and I, will see this thing through together . . . you take care of the rear and I'll take care of the front.' It bordered on farce, but it worked.

Curtin and MacArthur both fought the 'beat Hitler first' strategy—Curtin for Australia, MacArthur for himself. Curtin trusted MacArthur and MacArthur called Curtin the 'heart and soul' of Australia. Toasted at a private dinner in the parliamentary dining room, MacArthur said: 'My faith in ultimate victory is invincible . . . We shall win or we shall die, and to this end I pledge you all the resources of all the mighty power of my country.' He had no authority to make such a claim. But MacArthur was taking command, psychologically and literally.

At midnight on 18 April 1942, under a directive agreed by Curtin and Roosevelt, a foreign general, MacArthur, took control of all combat units of the Australian armed forces. A significant degree of Australian sovereignty was conceded in the cause of survival. Curtin wrote to Macarthur: 'You have come to Australia to lead a crusade the result of which means everything to the future of the world and mankind. At the request of a sovereign nation you are being placed in Supreme Command of its Navy,

Army and Air Force.' MacArthur said he would deal directly with Curtin and only with Curtin. As David Horner says, the Australian Chiefs of Staff were now replaced by a foreign general as Curtin's main adviser. The prime minister, of course, still took advice from Australia's senior military officer, General Blamey, in his capacity as Commander-in-Chief. But the critical decisions in Australia's survival crisis came from the Curtin–MacArthur duo. This was the high tide of US influence on Australia and a dramatic symbol of the war's role in recasting Australia's outlook.

Japan chose a strategy of isolation of Australia rather than invasion. Australia's immediate position was secured in the two great naval battles of Coral Sea and Midway. As American and Japanese carriers chased each other in the warm waters of the Coral Sea, Curtin delivered what Geoffrey Serle describes as possibly his finest parliamentary speech: 'Men are fighting for Australia today. Those who are not fighting have no excuse for not working.'

Defeat at sea forced Japan into trying to take Port Moresby by land. This produced a series of debilitating battles in which the Australians were forced initially to retreat along the Kokoda Track before staging a recovery and pushing back the overextended Japanese until they were defeated. These New Guinea land battles saw furious tensions between MacArthur and Blamey along with Curtin's weakness as a war leader in dealing with MacArthur. Nearly 2200 Australians were killed in the campaigns, which assume a special place in the Australian story. 'I see the battles fought by the Australians in 1942 as the most important ever fought by Australians in relationship to the direct security of Australia,' Horner says. 'If we had not fought those battles successfully, Australia would have been under threat, certainly of attack and perhaps of invasion.'

The overall picture of World War II is very different from the Great War. Australia lost 34 000 killed, far fewer than in the first war and off a larger population. Many nations were laid waste yet Australia was almost untouched. In economic and social terms Australia emerged much stronger from the war. This is the key contrast with the first war, which left a legacy of division and demoralisation. The political and psychological change was important—Australia became a more confident and assertive nation as a result of the 1939–45 war. The World War II generation proceeded to lead the country for another generation. The war crisis had imposed a greater sense of responsibility upon Australia. It began to operate more confidently, to pursue its own interests more resolutely and to devise its own solutions to domestic and external problems.

At the same time, Australia was not deluded into any revolutionary rethink. As the war advanced Curtin turned back to Britain, more aware of the difficulty of dealing with the United States. His biographer, David Day, stresses that in 1944 Curtin and his military advisers believed that Australia would look to Imperial defence in the postwar period. Curtin praised the Empire and its blood ties. He wrapped himself in the Union Jack, and not just as political protection against Menzies.

Curtin and his colleagues were realistic about their ties with America. They no more thought they were creating a special relationship with the US than they believed they were severing ties with Britain. The notion that World War II substituted America for Britain as Australia's main partner is myth. Bob O'Neill says: 'I don't think a great deal of what they [the US] did was because they sought to save Australia. They recognised that Australia was a very useful base to have on the flank of their advance and they did what they had to do to secure that base. If there had not been these other interests, I don't think the Americans would have been terribly interested in Australia's future.'

The war gave Australia great experience in dealing with the United States. It seeded a new tradition. But it did not create an alliance—it created something else, the idea that a US alliance would be highly desirable since Britain was in decline and America was on the rise. Between the idea and the reality fell the US postwar retreat. In the immediate postwar period the US demobilised quickly. Australia looked to Britain and strong ongoing Commonwealth co-operation. But the most significant change was that Australia started to operate in the world in its own right; it became actively involved in the United Nations and other international organisations; and it began to develop a new role and policy in Asia.

The strange legacy of World War II was peace and a new, different war, the Cold War. Communism was on the march. This was the defining event for Australia and for most of the postwar world. The Cold War would last for about 45 years and its influence would be pervasive in terms of strategy, values and national perceptions. It was a global contest between political systems and ideas—communism against democracy, as well as a contest for national advantage between the United States and the Soviet Union along with numerous other players.

It was the Cold War that created the conditions for the Australian–American alliance. Without this war there would have been no such alliance. The Cold War had a more enduring impact on US thinking than did World War II, because it internationalised US foreign policy on a permanent basis as the Soviet Union became a permanent global rival.

But before Australia negotiated over the Cold War with the US, it had to deal with Britain. Britain was not yet extinguished as a global power. The first major Cold War decision by the Menzies Government involved a strange mixture of elements: it would send Australian forces to the Middle East to fight the Russians in any new world war. It was the decision of a nation in transition during a world in transition. The Chief of the Imperial General Staff, Sir William Slim, had visited Canberra in mid-1950 and, in an extraordinary meeting, persuaded the Menzies Cabinet to commit forces to the Middle East in any new conflict. This was Menzies, in the first twelve months of his prime ministership, bound to a foreign policy vision of the past. He was utterly shaped by the war experience and by the British linkage. Menzies was still claiming vindication of his wartime decision to commit Australian forces to the Middle East against Labor's opposition.

However, the principal impact of the Cold War was the formulation of a new American strategy. The US was looking for global allies. This did not make the Australia–US alliance inevitable but it gave Australia a terrain on which to work. In relations between great and medium-size powers the initiative often lies with the smaller party because it has more at stake and invests a greater diplomatic effort. This has often been true of Australian–American ties. It is the chief ingredient in explaining how the alliance was formed. It was at Australia's initiative; it was an Australian triumph; and it was largely the work of the Liberal Foreign Minister, Percy Spender.

The backdrop was one of the most frightening phases of a frightening Cold War. By the late 1940s the Russians controlled Eastern Europe; in 1949 the Chinese Revolution was completed with Mao Tse-tung victorious; the Soviet Union had just acquired the bomb; and North Korea was about to attack South Korea. In the West there were fears of a new world war. In Australia the Menzies Government was in power, fiercely anti-communist at home, pro-British abroad, worried and looking for friends.

Spender had a vision and the self-confidence to realise it. His departmental head Sir Alan Watt said he was 'no starry-eyed idealist but a realist who liked to see himself as a man of the world'. A self-made Sydney lawyer, Spender came to promote a relatively old Australian idea: a military alliance across the Pacific. It had been floated by Alfred Deakin, pursued by Joe Lyons and pushed by Dr Evatt before Labor's 1949 defeat.

In his first major statement to parliament on 9 March 1950, Spender outlined his proposed Pacific Pact: 'What I envisage is a defensive military arrangement between countries that have a vital interest in the security of Asia and the Pacific.' Spender nominated Australia, Britain, other Commonwealth countries and 'particularly the United States whose participation would give such a pact a substance that it would otherwise lack'.

Spender's statement concealed his real intention—he wanted to reorientate Australia from Britain towards America on a permanent basis. His son, John Spender, says: 'He saw that a power shift had taken place as a result of the Second World War and that Britain would never again be the same and that, for all of the past and the history and the tradition, our future lay in alliance terms with the United States.'

In June 1950 Spender got his golden opportunity. North Korea launched its frontal assault on South Korea. The US under President Truman led the defence and secured a UN Security Council resolution authorising action. The Menzies Government condemned the 'communist expansion' and made ships and planes available. The firm initial response of both Australia and Britain was against sending troops. But Spender had other ideas. In an adroit display of influence he engineered Australia's military commitment to South Korea and compelled Menzies to follow him.

In the process Spender would initiate the brand of 'great and powerful friend' diplomacy that would shape Australian polity throughout the Cold War and beyond. It was a decisive break from the tradition of the world wars. Australia would be strong on diplomatic rhetoric but extremely cautious in military commitment. It would be the era of political wars— Australia would fight in Korea and in Vietnam not primarily for the Koreans or Vietnamese but for its own political goals and its alliances. It was Korea that delivered the US alliance and Vietnam was the price paid for that alliance. In the process only a small number of Australians were killed in action in the second half of the century compared with the first half. It would be an era in which Australia both appeased and manipulated the great and powerful. It relied more on diplomatic politics than on military action to secure its aims. By most measures it was a highly successful strategy.

In July 1950 Menzies, in London again, was lobbied hard in a cable from Spender: 'My appreciation of the military position in Korea is that the US, though not prepared to admit it, is in a very difficult if not desperate position. From Australia's long-term point of view any additional aid we can give to the US now, small though that may be, will repay us in the future one hundred fold. My personal view is that we must scrape the bucket to see what we can give.'

Spender was chasing a US alliance. For Menzies it was merely an illusion. But Spender read the Korean situation correctly. Menzies had hardly boarded the *Queen Mary*, bound for New York, when the British Government began to change its mind. On the morning of 20 July, Spender was recovering from a duodenal ulcer at 'Summerleas', the Moss Vale home of Sir Charles Lloyd Jones. He was rung by Alan Watt with the news that Britain was about to commit ground forces to Korea. An announcement would be coming from the British Parliament, probably the next day. Spender saw the sequence: Britain would commit troops and the 'Dominions' like Australia would be forced to follow in a re-run of the old Empire pattern. He was horrified.

Watt and a young officer, Arthur Tange, drove straight to Moss Vale. After they arrived Spender told Watt that Australia had to commit forces and commit immediately. The priority was to show the Americans that Australia took its own decisions without waiting for a British lead. The days of following Britain into war were over. With Menzies on the Atlantic, Spender rang the acting prime minister, Country Party leader Arthur Fadden, in Queensland.

Fadden was most displeased. In Spender's own account of the conversation he says that Fadden interjected more than once to say, '"You know the views of the Big Fellow"—meaning Menzies. His view was that we could do nothing without Bob's approval.' Spender told Fadden that 'when the prime minister was absent, he, Fadden, stood in the position of prime minister'. It was for him to decide. It was impossible to have such a crucial decision-making discussion with Menzies by radiophone to the ship. But Fadden refused to decide. Why couldn't they wait till Menzies got to New York? Why the urgency? Why couldn't the cabinet be called together? Spender proceeded to reject each delaying proposition. The struggle continued. Eventually Fadden said: 'I will have to leave it to you.'

That was enough for Spender. He and Watt drafted the statement. Watt rang the ABC. It was carried on the 7 pm news bulletin. Australia was going to war in Korea.

Sir Arthur Tange says: 'Australia contributed forces to Korea for its own diplomatic reasons, not through any sense that it was our duty to protect the people of Korea. I think that should be said candidly.'

The official historian for the Korean War, Bob O'Neill, summarises Spender's calculations: 'Spender thought that if the United States saw Australia simply following in Britain's wake, Australia would get no credit at all. If Australia could get ahead of Britain and appear to be the most supportive member of the Commonwealth that would really register in the State Department, the Pentagon and the White House.'

The hardest part was breaking the news to Menzies. Spender rang him on the ship. 'He was obviously put out. He said little. But even over the distance of some 12 000 miles I was aware of the sourness in his voice.' Menzies, of course, stepped ashore in New York and claimed the decision as his own. He went to Washington, addressed the Congress and was hailed a hero.

Spender himself went to Washington to continue his campaign for the treaty. On 13 September 1950 he entered the Oval Office for a supposedly brief formal call on Truman. O'Neill's judgment is that this meeting 'was the real turning point which led to the ANZUS Treaty'.

Truman was in good humour and Spender went for the human angle. He referred to the unfavourable newspaper reviews of Truman's daughter Margaret in her recent singing performance. O'Neill continues the story: 'That engaged the President and he responded with a tirade against critics and the press and went on for quite some time. He looked at his watch and said, "Good heavens, I've used up nearly all of the time allocated to your visit. Did you have some serious purpose in coming to see me?" And he (Spender) said, "Well, there is this matter of a security commitment to Australia. We've been trying to achieve this for some time".'

Truman had a favourable impression of Australia from his own life— he expressed admiration for the Australian soldiers with whom he had fought on the Western Front in World War I. He praised Australia's Korean commitment. Spender left the Oval Office confident that he had Truman's in-principle support for the treaty. But the battle would not be easy: Secretary of State Dean Acheson was opposed and the US military chiefs didn't like the idea.

The deal would be done between Spender and Truman's foreign affairs adviser, John Foster Dulles, and the pivotal issue would be Japan. The US objective was a Japan Peace Treaty to lay the basis for Japan's redevelopment and a degree of rearmament as part of the anti-communist coalition. Spender said that Australia, given its history, could not accept a rearmed Japan and would require additional protection.

The key negotiation was conducted in Canberra in February 1951 when Dulles toured the region to secure support for the US proposal, in effect, to make Japan a Cold War ally. Spender told Dulles that Australia's price would be 'a satisfactory security arrangement in the Pacific'. Australia's war sufferings at Japan's hands were too close. After four days the draft was completed. Spender went to the Lodge, showed it to a surprised Menzies, and got a brandy for his effort. The ANZUS Treaty was signed at San Francisco on 1 September 1951. It was Australia's half-century year.

The British were not happy. Spender had seized a window of opportunity and America was formalised as a new great and powerful friend. There was also another friend—Japan. The Cold War was being harvested in a productive way.

Menzies had never believed the treaty to be possible but, once it was delivered, he exploited the US connection as his own. The ANZUS Treaty was weaker than NATO, which provided an automatic guarantee of US support in the event of conflict. ANZUS specified that each party in the case of an armed attack in the Pacific area, or on any of the parties, would act to meet the common danger 'in accordance with its constitutional processes'. The treaty's real significance was to give Australia access to US defence thinking, planning and military strategy. For the first time, Australia was involved in a major military pact that excluded Britain.

America was a different kind of friend and partner from Britain. There was no Imperial, historical or family tie. This was a partnership of powers, large and medium. It was based upon mutual self-interest in the Cold War environment. It was about utility, performance and results. The advantage to Australia was that the US was the leading superpower. Over the Cold War era Australia would invest much in this alliance in the form of money, machines and men. There would be vast defence installations constructed as part of the US nuclear strategy—facilities that most Australians would never see and never think about. The non-defence civilians who did see them would leave in awe, with a deep impression of the scale and magnitude of the US alliance. The relationship would touch every aspect of Australian defence and foreign policy. But it developed in tandem with another powerful force—the rise of an authentic Australian outlook and vision, notably in Asia.

World War II produced three startling legacies in Asia: the revolt against colonial empires, the rise to power of Asia nationalism, and a series of security crises involving communism. Australia sought to integrate its alliances with the great and powerful with its new goal of effective relations in Asia.

In the late 1940s the Chifley ALP Government offered firm and constructive support for Indonesian independence against the Dutch. At times Australia was in disagreement with both Britain and America on this issue. It was a turning point for Australia—a transition from having sought Empire guarantees against Asia to backing Indonesian nationalism against its own colonial master. It was a declaration of Australian optimism and a commitment to collaboration with a new Asia, a vision only partially realised.

Australia sought and achieved a settlement in its 50 year struggle with Japan. The old enemy was converted into a new friend. Australia's initial instinct was for a punitive peace but this surrendered to the new geopolitics: fear of China, the lure of Japan's markets, and the communist scare as a replacement for World War II hatreds. The symbol was the 1957 Australia–Japan Commerce Treaty negotiated by Sir John McEwen. Within the parliament it was the war veterans and former POWs who sanctioned the shift in public opinion required to underpin the Japan treaty.

McEwen undertook this initiative in a solo capacity, saying later that 'if I were to fall on this the government would not have to fall with me'. McEwen, in fact, saw that the great and powerful friends did not constitute Australia's economic future. Britain was moving towards Europe; the US would not be a replacement market. Australia had to look to Asia and Japan. It was a judgment reached not only by McEwen but by influential advisers such as Sir John Crawford and a handful of visionary businessmen who established the Australia–Japan trade relationship which locked Australia into Japan's industrial boom. By the late 1960s, only a generation after the war, Japan had become Australia's major trading partner.

As the threat from communism intensified, Australian diplomacy became more frenetic. It was the US alliance that would take Australia in 1965 into its third biggest war. There are many ways of interpreting the Vietnam War. Vietnam was the price Australia paid for the US alliance; it was the logical culmination of Australia's Cold War strategy of relying upon the 'great and powerful' in combating communism; it represented an Australian judgment that ANZUS was not enough and that the US must become entrenched in a regional military commitment; and finally, it symbolised the tactical skill but strategic failure of Australia in managing its great partner.

There were three major stepping stones. First, Australia's commitment under Menzies to the forward defence concept. This policy became entrenched in the minds of senior cabinet ministers. It was founded on military co-operation with Britain and America in Asia to bolster the se-curity climate and keep the great and powerful friends in the region. The Menzies Government helped Britain during the 1950s Malayan Emer-gency when there was a communist-inspired insurgency. In the 1960s Australian troops were involved with British forces in defending the new

Federation of Malaysia against Indonesia's confrontation. The United States, unlike Britain, was not worried about Indonesia's radical national leader, President Sukarno. America's fear was closer to China—it was Vietnamese communism. In 1962 Australia sent some advisers to Vietnam, being anxious to support the US position there. A White Paper subsequently prepared for the Whitlam Government described forward defence as 'a policy developed in Australia independently of any outside pressure. The cornerstone of this policy was seen as a compelling necessity to commit the power of the United States to the Asian area'. By the early 1960s it was clear that the chance of winning a greater US military role in Asia lay only in Vietnam.

Second, Australia saw a linkage between Indonesia and Vietnam. Indonesia was Australia's main worry. The official historian for the Vietnam War, Peter Edwards, says: 'For Australia, up until late 1964, even early 1965, by far the biggest problem in the region was not Vietnam, it was Indonesia's confrontation of Malaysia.' During this period Australian forces were involved in action against Indonesian troops. The cabinet, acting on the view that Australia's security situation was deteriorating, announced in late 1964 a selective conscription scheme. Australia was preparing for a range of options—but Menzies' statement revealed that the main worry was Indonesia rather than Vietnam. The logic within the Menzies Cabinet was manifest: the Indonesian problem meant a US regional presence was essential but the focus of that commitment was going to be Vietnam.

Third, Vietnam slotted into the Australian diplomatic mindset—that notion of keeping the great power in the region by making a politically significant but militarily modest war commitment. This sort of thinking had become ingrained in Australia's mind. It was our technique of exploiting the 'great and powerful friend' connection. And it is how we entered the Vietnam War.

The Counsellor in the Australian Embassy in Washington, Alan Renouf, wrote in his famous May 1964 cable: 'The problem of Vietnam is one, it seems, where we could without a disproportionate expenditure pick up a lot of credit with the United States, for this problem is one to which the United States is deeply committed.'

Peter Edwards has shown convincingly that the Menzies Cabinet agreed to commit an Australian battalion before any formal US request was made. Australia was running ahead of America. In the critical cabinet committee meeting of 7 April 1965 Menzies, McEwen and Holt led the charge. There were two motives: to deny South Vietnam to communism and to bolster the US military presence in the region. The latter was the dominant instinct. Menzies said the psychological effect on the US of an Australian commitment would be 'phenomenally valuable'. Holt said that 'whatever the final outcome of the US intervention', Australia had to help. McEwen agreed that Australia had to back the Americans to encourage them to stay. Foreign Minister Paul Hasluck, generally a Vietnam hawk, and Labour and National Service Minister William McMahon urged a delay but were overruled.

In a misleading speech, Menzies announced the commitment of an Australian battalion to a half empty House of Representatives on 29 April 1965: 'The takeover of South Vietnam would be a direct military threat to Australia and all the countries of South East Asia. It must be seen as part of a thrust by Communist China between the Indian and Pacific Oceans.' This interpretation was an insult to Vietnamese nationalism and misjudged China's role in the war.

For the first time Australia was fighting a war without Britain. The Labor Party opposed the commitment. It warned that Australia was misleading, not helping, its great and powerful friend.

The thinking that shaped Australia's entry was the source of the problem. In Vietnam, as in Korea, Australia's main concern was the United States relationship and alliance, not the Vietnamese or the Koreans. For this reason Australia failed to make a sufficiently careful appreciation of the nature of the Vietnam conflict. The nexus between Vietnam and conscription was also a fatal blunder. Much of the anti-war movement would be driven by anti-conscription sentiment. The final irony was the Indonesian upheaval of September–October 1965 that became a pivotal point in the transition from Sukarno to Suharto. This 'solved' Australia's Indonesian security problem for the next 30 years—an outcome within the shadow of the Vietnam commitment.

Harold Holt replaced Menzies as prime minister nine months later. In July 1966, in his televised speech at the White House, standing next to President Lyndon Baines Johnson, Holt said: 'And so, sir, in the lonelier and perhaps, even more, disheartening moments which come to any national leader, I hope there will be a corner of your mind and heart which takes cheer from the fact that you have an admiring friend, a staunch friend, that will be all the way with LBJ.'

It was, of course, nonsense as well as craven. The entire 'political war' tactic of Vietnam, Malaysia and Korea was a repudiation of being 'all the way' with anybody. Peter Edwards says: 'Harold Holt was never really "all the way" with LBJ. Australia was really operating within a framework that it had operated in for at least a decade and a half—giving very strong political support but only supplying relatively small forces.'

Malcolm Fraser was Minister for the Army and then Minister for Defence during the period of Australia's involvement in the Vietnam War.

This is to deny neither the sacrifice nor the pain of the Australians involved. A total of 50 000 Australians served in Vietnam and 501 were killed. Western intervention failed and the war was lost. The US was politically and psychologically scarred. It retreated from the Asian mainland for a long and undefined time. Australia's objective of entrenching a US regional presence was defeated. Yet the deeper aspiration for a stable Asia was advanced; indeed, a new economically successful Asia would emerge. Retreat and defeat in Vietnam forced a landmark reassessment within sections of Australian politics. The Nixon Administration redefined the US role in Asia in terms of the Guam Doctrine. Kim Beazley says: 'The Vietnam failure did lead to a greater maturity in Australian foreign policy. We were instructed to develop that maturity, I might say, by the United States. A seminal influence upon the getting of maturity for Australians was President Nixon's Guam Doctrine which was that the United States, like the Lord, helps those who help themselves.'

The policy of forward defence with the great and powerful had delivered Australia a number of foreign policy successes. But the biggest commitment, Vietnam, came in the wrong place at the wrong time and that terminated an era which had a limited shelf-life anyway. In the 1970s

Britain had joined Europe, and the United States, after the Vietnam War, had abandoned the idea of major military commitments. It was the end of an era. The days of Australia's 'great and powerful friends' diplomacy for the anti-communist cause in Asia were over. The dawn of true national responsibility was at hand.

The key to the future now lay in the policy towards China. The symbol of Australia's strategic decision to deal on its own terms with the world came with the opening to China and the establishment of diplomatic relations with Beijing as soon as Gough Whitlam came to power. The growth of stronger ties between Australia and Asian nations was linked with a more mature relationship between Australia and its great and powerful friends. These trends went hand in hand.

Whitlam decided to confront the Asian security issue at its source. The China bogy and the 'domino' theory had shaped the failed policy on Vietnam. For Whitlam the key to changing the politics of the region and denying the Coalition its 20-year-old anti-communist electoral weapon at home lay in normalisation of relations with China.

In 1971 he travelled as Opposition leader to Beijing—the first step in a reorientation of Australia's Asia policy. Whitlam had the satisfaction of being followed by the US envoy, Dr Henry Kissinger, and later President Nixon, who astonished the world with their new policy of detente with China. It reinforced the new Australian policy and ensured that it would be more fruitful. The fear, isolation and suspicion that had dominated Australia–China relations was dissolved with remarkable speed.

The Whitlam policy would soon be a bipartisan one. Every prime minister after Whitlam had a deep commitment to the China relationship and a belief that it would be fundamental in Australia's future. Malcolm Fraser was a champion of the relationship. Bob Hawke accorded China a priority and spoke of 'enmeshment' with Asia. Hawke's successor, Paul Keating, pledged himself to 'engagement' with Asia. When a shadow fell over our China relations in 1996, John Howard restored the equilibrium in an early 1997 visit.

But Australia did not substitute Asia for the great and powerful friends. Any such notion of a 'zero sum game' at work was a false one. The idea of 'great and powerful friends', so central to our identity and history, died with Menzies or, more precisely, with the demise of the Menzian age which was certainly terminated in 1972. Of course, this was not the end of relations with Britain or of the alliance with America. But it signalled a transition in Australian self-esteem, identity and strategic vision. It was an evolutionary process with many turning points and twists, not all of which are mentioned let alone comprehended in this essay.

The dividing line between Menzies and Whitlam was colonialism. Menzies' mind was cast forever in the colonial mould: supporting Britain at Suez, the United States in Vietnam, a white South Africa, Australian rule in Papua New Guinea; with a lack of affinity for any sense of Asian engagement. Whitlam, by contrast, projected an independent Australian vision.

Under Fraser and Hawke, Australia had to integrate its Cold War alliance with its Asian relationships. Hawke comments: 'I said the future of Australia is going to depend upon us becoming more and more enmeshed with Asia. Remember, in 1983 we were still very much in the depths of the Cold War. Within that context the relationship with the United States remained profoundly important. I did everything I could to strengthen that, [but] we had to make decisions in terms of Australia's interests.'

Keating faced a different situation: the zenith of Asian economic progress. 'I believed that at the end of the Cold War, when I became prime minister, all of Australia's vital interests coalesced in Asia—trade, security, cultural. If we put the question in the negative, do we have vital interests in Africa? The answer is no. Do we have vital interests in South America? No. Do we have vital interests in North America? Some. Where do we have our vital interests? Where we live, in Asia.'

In its past Australia was rarely the lapdog of the powerful that its internal critics depicted. Australia tried to manipulate the great and powerful as much as they manipulated Australia. The results varied because our clout was limited and our allies were strong. The point, though, is that Australia was fortunate to have Britain and America as allies and it was sensible to cultivate such allies in an unpredictable world. Such alliances made Australia a more outward-looking nation than it would have been otherwise, and they also involved Australia in ambitious, far-flung and costly military engagements. It was a serious business whose ultimate testament is 100 000 Australians killed abroad in the cause of this view of nationhood in partnership with the great and powerful.

These relations were reinforced by race, culture, language and convenience or, in short, by a common heritage. This was tied, in turn, to Australia's own identity as a white Anglo-Celtic nation shipwrecked between Asia and Antarctica. From Harold Holt onwards—when the

White Australia policy was slated for demolition—Australian leaders began to draw a nexus between a changing identity at home and successful relations in Asia. Keating took this idea to its ultimate with his 'engagement' concept: that Australia had to change itself to truly succeed in Asia.

Australia's transition into an independent, multicultural nation which negotiated its own way with Indonesia, Japan, China and other Asian countries was the major step in its new maturity. This was a choice about national destiny and a response to the changing priorities of Britain and America as they retreated from global entanglements.

Australia seems now to have reached a stage of national maturity defined as accepting responsibility for its own fate and place in the world. How successful Australia will be in this new stage of its history is a very open and rarely discussed question. Its dealings with Asia are still conducted in the shadow of the past—witness for example, Hansonism in the late 1990s. Its links with Asia won't always be smooth and may become very troubled or worse—as the deteriorating relationship with Indonesia after the East Timor independence vote shows.

Australia's aim is to integrate its old relations with its new relations—to ensure that it never has to choose between past and future, between the European connection and Asian engagement, between America and China. In short, it seeks to have the best of all options in a shrinking globe. This was the motive driving the Asia-Pacific diplomacy of Hawke and Keating. They wanted to create an Asia-Pacific community, a community that incorporated Asia and North America, because this is the Australian requirement. The idea has yet to be realised.

John Howard argues that Australia has a unique vantage point—its European tradition, its strong links to America and its new engagements with Asia. Malcolm Fraser, a pessimist, says that Australia will be forced eventually to choose between Asia and America and that its answer must be Asia. Bob Hawke and Paul Keating are optimists; they believe that Australia can be enduringly international—engaged in Asia but deeply linked with Europe and North America.

Australia's strategic dilemma is that it doesn't fit naturally into any group shaped by identity or geography. Australia is not part of Europe by geography; it is not part of North America by geography; it is within Asia but not an Asian nation. It falls within no natural regional group. It is no longer an outpost of Britain in the Antipodes, nor any longer a compliant ally of

America. Such liberation is now rightly celebrated. But that liberation constitutes a risk as well as an opportunity.

The challenge facing an Australia without great and powerful friends will prove to be more daunting than most people believe. The debate about this challenge at the end of the 1990s was complacent and superficial. Much will depend upon Australia's intelligence, insight and cultural adaptation. The risk is that Australia might fail to develop effective partnerships in Asia and find itself a victim of growing isolationism.

The more likely result, however, is that Australia will be smart enough to take the best the world has to offer. This has been our tradition—borrow from abroad and translate to home. The key lies in a deepening of Australia's engagement with the world and engagement must be driven by a sense of intelligent curiosity and national self-interest.

INTERVIEW WITH
JOHN HOWARD

Australia's prime minister, John Howard, stresses both the egalitarian and aspirational themes in our political culture. For Howard, Australians have a rare skill in knowing when to keep the past and when to move forward. He sees Australia possessing a 'distinctive independent culture'. He says a republic will come only when no significant section of the population opposes the change.

In recent times Australia's been going through a period of great economic change. How do you describe this?

The change we've had over the last twenty years has been the greatest, probably, since the great Depression. It has been modernisation, it's been the inevitability of Australia being part of globalisation. It was essential, unavoidable and I believe overwhelmingly beneficial.

I think the first decisive event was the floating of the dollar. That set in train a number of very significant changes which aided the globalisation of the Australian economy, followed by tariff reform. Industrial relations reform was delayed until the advent of the Coalition Government in 1996, as was taxation reform. We've had an erratic record on fiscal policy: there was tightening in the 1980s by the Hawke Government and then it was allowed to lapse in the early 90s by the Keating Government and it was brought back to centre stage by the coalition. But if you look at the last twenty years, you've really got five pillars, I think—financial reform, tariff reform, industrial relations reform, fiscal consolidation and, finally and importantly, taxation reform. Now, all of those things were necessary. Without them, this country wouldn't have survived the Asian economic downturn, and they all played a part.

How personally committed are you to these changes?

If you look back at my 25 years in politics, particularly my time from the early 1980s onwards, you'll see a consistent pattern of support for each of these. I was the Treasurer who established the Campbell Committee and started to implement some of its changes, but to its credit the Hawke Government followed on and reversed Labor hostility to financial reform. I've been very strongly committed to those reforms because I've seen them as essential to the shaping of the modern Australia, essential to giving Australia a show in the modern world.

This really amounts to a fundamental change in economic culture. How do you see this change affecting people?

My view is that change was going to be imposed on Australia whether we liked it or not. The lesson of the early 1970s—the failure of the Whitlam Government as an economic manager in the early 1970s—was its failure to accept that we had no option but to adjust to change. It was being imposed on us by the rest of the world. The quadrupling of oil prices, the end of the system of fixed exchange rates—those two things alone transformed the world environment in which we lived and we had to come to terms with that. I mean, you don't, as a country of our size, have an option. Not even a nation of Japan's size has an option. And governments either have to adjust and take their people with them, or suffer even greater consequences. It's a mistake to believe that you can produce a more people-friendly outcome by resisting economic change. You can facilitate change in a way that produces a people-friendly outcome, but you really don't have an option of staying as you are, because if you try and do that, you'll burn more people in the process.

When you were Treasurer in the Fraser Government, you began to push some of these economic changes but you didn't get all that far. Was that a frustrating period, when you look back on it?

In a number of areas it was, particularly in financial reform and also in tax reform. I had wanted a broad-based indirect tax in the early 1980s and it's only in the last year that we have seen it finally come into effect. It's a big change that's been needed for a long time. Reform can be frustrating and very slow.

Both Malcolm Fraser and Doug Anthony were people who, I guess, acquired their political and economic experience at a time when the old paradigm worked and understandably they didn't think change was necessary. The Menzies period was a period of immense stability and growth. But it was at a time when the Australian economy was protected, globalisation hadn't come, we lived in a world-wide fixed exchange rate era, and therefore it was understandable, if you grew up in that culture that you thought it would always work, no matter what the circumstances.

It is therefore correct to say that the Howard Government is the first coalition government that's really been committed to these economic changes?

That is certainly true. The Howard Government is the first. But to be fair to our predecessors, it's the first government that's lived in an environment where, unambiguously, that's what you had to do. The Fraser Government really came into power, as did the Whitlam Government, at a time when we were sort of on the cusp, where people still thought there were options. When the Hawke Government came to power, and particularly during the later years of the Fraser Government, it was clearly apparent that unless we changed in order to accommodate the changed world circumstances, we weren't going to make it.

Now, in the process, as a result of all these changes, is Australia in danger of losing its egalitarian tradition?

If that egalitarian tradition is under pressure, it's not because of the changes. It's because of the changed world environment in which we live. You've got to remember that no society can as easily erect its separate and distinctive social paradigm or mindset as used to be the case. It's under pressure and one of the things that I've tried to do with things like the 'social coalition', and balancing economic liberalism with modern conservatism in social policy, is to try and hang on to that egalitarianism.

But are you personally concerned that, given that this is a new world of globalisation, we're likely to see changes in the Australian tradition such that the 'fair go' idea is likely to be lost?

I feel a need virtually every week of my prime ministership to recommit myself to ways of maintaining it. I think you can have globalisation and economic modernisation, I'm sure you can, in a way that protects the 'fair go'. Remember that part of the erosion of the 'fair go' is really a consequence of social rather than economic change. The thing that has produced poverty in Australia, more than perhaps anything else, has been the greater degree of marriage failure. Look at the profile of single-parent families—they are overwhelmingly not the product of teenage pregnancy but of relationship and marriage breakdown. They are social changes that were set in train separately from economic change. I mean, they're a product in part of the social revolution of the 1960s rather than the economic globalisation of the 1980s. I think, although the two rub against each other and influence each other, you've got to keep that in perspective.

Is there a danger that the bush, which has been so important in the makeup of the Australian identity, is being left behind as a result of economic change?

It is understandable when the whole country is doing well that, if you're not doing as well relatively, you feel that you're missing out. And the bush has had to cope with some world forces, like low commodity prices, that no national government can influence. The bush has always been part of what we feel ourselves to be as Australians. The Australia I grew up to love as a kid included the bush, and one of the fascinating things about our self-identity is that even those of us who've lived all our lives in the cities feel an empathy with the bush and feel that in many ways the bush is more Australian than any other part of the country. Now, that's not true but it's a natural sentiment, and it's a very warm sentiment.

I've been a supporter of economic reform and in Government and in Opposition I've campaigned very hard for necessary economic change. But I've always been a pragmatic politician, I've always understood the need to take Australians with me. I think Australians will always back reform if you can satisfy them on two counts. The first is you've got to convince them that it's good for Australia. We did that with tax reform in 1998. We won that election because we persuaded people that, although individually they might have questions and misgivings, overall it was good for the country, it would make our fuel cheaper in the bush, it would make our exports cheaper, our business costs lower and cut our personal tax. And the other thing you've always got to do in Australia is to persuade people that it's fair. If they think something is unfairly penalising one sector of the community, they won't accept it because they do have an innate sense of fairness.

Markets are more important in terms of influencing outcomes, so doesn't that mean at the end of the day that Australia must become a more unequal society in terms of disparity of income?

Providing those at the bottom are protected and looked after, disparities between, I guess, the middle, upper middle and higher still groupings don't matter quite so much. The important thing is to make sure you have a strong social security safety net, and it's also important to Australia that we maintain an aspirational element in our society. One of the things people perhaps have misunderstood about our history is that we have been very egalitarian but we've also been very aspirational, and it's always been part of the Australian psyche to start with nothing and to work your guts out and leave more to your kids than you inherited. That's been the driver behind a lot of the small business ethic. It's a very important part of the contribution that postwar immigrants made to Australia.

Australia began its life as part of the British Empire. How important is the British heritage to you?

It's immensely important, the language, the literature, the culture, the sense of humour, the civil conduct of political affairs—for all the rumbustiousness of the Australian parliament, the civil conduct of political affairs in an open media. And I think, very importantly, a sceptical political culture. I guess it's more a Celtic deposit than an English deposit but one of the great things about the Australian political culture is that it is sceptical. It's one of the things that marks us out very much from the Americans.

Over time, of course, we've moved away from Britain, and we became an independent nation. Is it possible to identify when that actually happened, when Australia became independent?

I think emotionally Australia became independent in World War I. We fought as an Australian army. We fought in an Australian military tradition. I still have a memory of seeing an old diary of my father's from World War I with an entry written in September 1918 and the line simply read, 'Relieved by a Pommy Division'. I mean, this was a private in the Australian army unit in France in 1918. That's what he wrote. Now, that was somebody who saw himself as part of the Australian army, not as part of the British army—whatever the command structure.

Menzies was the founder of the Liberal Party. Looking at the positives of Menzies, why do you think he was such a successful politician?

Menzies was highly intelligent. He'd learnt the hard way, he'd had a lot of reverses and that taught him through experience a lot of skill. He understood the essentially middle class mood of the Australian community, he understood the mainstream of the Australian community very well, he was a lot more Australian, Menzies, than he was ever given credit for by many of his critics. He was British but he was overwhelmingly Australian. He had a great under-standing of political opportunity and he was a lot more generous on issues than he was given credit for. I think one of the great things Menzies did was State aid for Catholic schools. People saw that as political opportunity and it was a political advantage to the Liberal Party but it really did more than anything else in Australia to end sectarianism. The Second Vatican Council had gone down the path of the more ecumenical approach, but I think that [state aid] was an act that signalled to 25 per cent of the Australian population that a hundred years of discrimination in the education of their children was coming to an end. I think that was a very important thing.

What is the message we should draw from the 1999 Republican Referendum? What does the outcome tell us about ourselves?

It tells us first and foremost that Australians do not feel other than that we are a distinctive independent culture in a society, owing much to our British inheritance but recognising that we've moulded and shaped it. The genius of Australia has been to keep the good bits of our inheritance and to throw out the bad bits. I mean, we kept the civil culture, we kept the language, the literature, the law, the scepticism, but we threw out the class consciousness and class division. We're also not as eccentric, not as eccentric as some of our British fore-bears, so I think we've been very clever in doing that. The 1999 Republican Referendum showed that people didn't feel self-conscious about our identity. To some degree the whole Republican campaign was based on people feeling embarrassed about our current political or national state. Now Australians don't feel embarrassed about it. Some may argue that it's anachronistic but they don't feel that we're other than an independent country. I guess the other thing that the 1999 Republican debate told us was that, to bring about that kind of change, you've almost got to allow a state of affairs to develop where there is no significant section of the population left who opposes change. A change of that order is not like an election, where 50.1 per cent is enough and people accept it. It's not like that.

Are you pleased you put the issue to the people?

I can honestly say I did exactly what I said I would do. I kept faith with my own personal view. The Australian public was never in any doubt as to where I personally stood. I didn't kid them before I became prime minister that I had a different view, and I always said that I would accept the outcome. I'm pleased we had the debate, I don't think we've been anything other than enhanced by the debate, and the issue can continue to be debated and discussed and nobody knows what the future will bring.

The process was totally fair. Just remember that the 'yes' case had on its side the whole of the Labor Party, most of the Australian Democrats, 30–40 per cent of the Liberal Party, every State premier with the exception of Richard Court, and you know, putting it mildly, 95 per cent of the Canberra Press Gallery, and the editorial support of all newspapers except the *West Australian* and the weekend *Financial Review*. I don't think anybody could say the 'yes' case didn't get a good airing. The question faithfully reflected what people were asked to do. I said at the Constitutional Convention I would put what emerged, and I did, and I allowed a free vote in the Liberal Party, and the Liberal Party came out of that stronger. I don't think it mattered that I was taking a different position from Peter Costello and others. I think people are smart enough, mature enough, to understand that two people belonging to the same political party can have a different view of something like that.

Why are you a monarchist?

Because I think the present system works. It's a reflection of my Burkean conservatism when it comes to institutions. I mean, I will change an institution and campaign with passion and vigour to change it, as I did with Australia's industrial relations system, if I think it is holding the country back. But I'm not going to throw out something that's given us—helped to give us—immense stability, particularly when we've moulded and adapted it to the Australian climate in a very effective way, so that for all practical purposes the Governor-General, now always an Australian, is the Head of State.

I subscribe to that old doctrine of Benjamin Franklin that death and tax are the two inevitabilities in life. I don't think anything is inevitable other than those two things.

I'm very happy with our current constitutional arrangement. Very happy.

Moving on to foreign policy, what's the most important decision you've had to take as prime minister concerning Australia's place in the world?

Undoubtedly, our commitment to East Timor. The whole East Timor issue was the most important foreign policy challenge that I've had as prime minister, and it was a very important moment in our relations with the region. It was difficult—it did require us, at a critical juncture, to really press the case with the government of Indonesia and to play a very active role on a broader world stage in getting the UN coalition together. East Timor did place a strain on our relationship with Indonesia but there was a very clear path for us to go down, and I have no regrets about any aspects of it.

Throughout most of our history Australia has had great and powerful friends, notably Britain and the United States. But given your own experiences as prime minister, how important at this time do you think our great and powerful friends are?

From a purely defensive and military point of view, the relationship Australia has with the United States remains tremendously important. The United States is the only world power left, since the end of the Cold War and the collapse of Soviet Communism. Our relationship with Britain is a different, more intricate, cultural emotional sort of relationship. Britain has a role but a very limited role militarily in our part of the world now. She played a part, pretty quickly I might say, in East Timor. But America remains the strategic and defence bedrock. It is not a relationship that prevents us on occasions having a very different view of the world in our own region. There have been significant differences in nuance and emphasis in our relationship with China for example in the time I've been prime minister, as opposed to the Americans', and I hope we may have played some part in contributing to a slightly different American view towards her relationship with China as a result.

No country, even the United States, is ever utterly master of its own destiny—I don't think you can ever say that. But Australia is as much the master of its own destiny as any prosperous twenty-first century nation of only twenty million people in our part of the world can hope to be.

I think we do make independent Australian judgments, but we've been doing that for quite a long time. We made some independent Australian judgments in World War II, we made some independent Australian judgments in the 1930s, we made them in the 1950s and 1960s. We're not indifferent to the blandishments of others, but we do make independent judgments.

In East Timor we are playing a leadership role. When you look at it in historical perspective, why is the East Timor commitment so important?

The East Timor commitment was important both symbolically and as a reflection of national will. Foreign policy should never so detach itself from the national will and the national feeling as to be sort of unidentifiable. I think it's very important that the people should feel ownership of their nation's foreign policy, not feel that it is being conducted for them or separately from them. Australians felt quite deeply about East Timor. I was impressed by the passion and feeling that was coming through to me on talkback radio and everywhere from the Australian people, and it was right across the political spectrum. There were left-wing socialists writing their letters, saying through gritted teeth, 'I agree with you', as well as people whose affection for East Timor had been conditioned in World War II because they'd been helped by the East Timorese people against the Japanese. It had particular historical Australian characteristics.

If Australia had not played a leadership role in East Timor, it's arguable that there wouldn't have been a United Nations force. The reality of international affairs is that somebody has to act as the catalyst for getting the force together. It's not that Australia sought a leadership role just for the sake of saying, 'we're the leader'. It wasn't an exercise in national ego. It was the reality that we were there. We were seen by the rest of the world as having a particular affinity; I was able to talk on a very direct basis with the Indonesian president right up until the decision was taken to allow in the peace enforcement operation. It would have been a denial of our international responsibilities for Australia not to have assumed a leadership role. We would have been letting others down, particularly the East Timorese people.

At the end of the day, is Australia going to have to choose between its past and its future?

No. I have always rejected the theory that Australian foreign policy involves a choice between our history and our geography. I have sought in the time I have been prime minister to assert what I call the 'intersection' theory of Australian foreign policy—that we occupy a unique cultural, historical and geographical intersection. We are a nation whose roots are Western, British and other European, we have strong links with North America, both historically and based on our common values and commitments; but here we are in

Asia geographically, with hundreds of thousands of Australian citizens of Asian descent. I see all of those influences as an asset, not a liability. The choice theory implies that our past associations are a liability instead of an asset. We can do things in the region that the Americans and the Europeans can't, because although we have the assets of our associations with them, we don't have the liabilities. We're not a world power, we're not a former colonial master, except in a very limited way in Papua New Guinea, so all of those things come together to give us assets in the region that others don't have. So I don't see a choice at all.

I think one of the mistakes we made for a while in our relationship with Asia was to fret too much about where we stood. Whether we were Asian, or part of Asia, enmeshed with Asia, or in Asia—forget that. We should really be as we are, and that is Australia, not denying for a moment our past associations or seeking to adjust them in order to please. What's important is the authenticity of our dealings with people on particular issues, as we've demonstrated. Way back in 1957 we were able to forge a trade agreement with Japan and it's still in my view one of the really pivotal events in postwar Australian history. It was only twelve years after World War II; it was an act of great political courage as well as economic foresight.

The 1957 commerce agreement with Japan laid the foundation of the modern economic relationship between Australia and Japan, whereby Japan is clearly our best customer. It sent a signal to the community only twelve years after the war that we were prepared to work with our former enemy.

We're not an Asian nation. We are a modern Australian nation, in many ways a projection of Western civilisation in our part of the world but with a real difference. We are at a special intersection of history, geography and culture and that gives us enormous assets, and we should stop fretting about how we precisely define ourselves. We shouldn't waste time with the sort of endless national navel gazing about which definition best fits us. I think it's a pretty unproductive exercise.

The American alliance has been enormously important to us now for many decades. At the end of the day, do you think we can rely on the Americans?

If this country was under direct, unambiguous assault, yes. I do believe that, yes. But I don't think that is likely to happen. I don't see anybody who is going to be in that sort of situation in the foreseeable future.

When Australians look back, how should they see the legacy of White Australia, which was a policy that we had for more than half our history as a nation?

I think truthfully they should see it, with the perspective of time, as a mistake, but something that I guess was inevitable given the history of this country and the attitudes that people had in those days towards people of different races. I don't think we should see our ancestors, our forebears, in many cases our parents or grandparents, as being any more racist than we are, just different. On an individual basis we are a nation that given the opportunity is fairly generous. We changed and we're better as a consequence, and we are seen as a more open, tolerant society.

I think on the issue of ethnic and social diversity, we're about right. I think we've come back from being too obsessed with diversity to a point where we are very proud and conscious of those ongoing distinctive, defining characteristics of being an Australian which we tend to identify with what I might call the old Australia. But we're also very appreciative of that chunk of our contemporary identity which is owed to postwar migration, and I think we've reached a sort of happy accommodation. I remember going some eighteen months ago to the reunion of the people who worked on the Snowy River Scheme, and I had the sense that here in the space of my own lifetime was the working through of the two [elements] into an integrated whole. I think we've got the right balance. We went through a period of obsession with assimilation where people had to forget their past and I think that then the reaction went too far in the other direction, where we thought we could build a federation of cultures. I don't think you can. I think you have to have certain mainstream identifiable characteristics that everybody can own, but you should allow everybody to treasure and protect their own individual heritage. I think we've got the balance right. I've used the expression, 'we have an Australian multiculturalism'. I think that it does capture that sense I was just describing.

Unity and diversity are both important. You can slave too much over particular words. I think this is a besetting Australian malady on occasion. We get hung up over one or two words. I want Australia to be distinctive, to have distinctive Australian characteristics that are different from English or Irish or French or Italian or Chinese—quite different. But I also want all Australians, whatever their heritage, to feel comfortable and free in a way that contributes to the national unity. I think we have got what I loosely call Australian multiculturalism in that sense.

If we look at the phenomenon of Hansonism in the 1990s, to what extent was Hansonism a cry, if you like, from the Anglo-Celtic heartland?

I think at heart Hansonism was a cry from people who felt that they were missing out economically. Along the way, Hansonism acquired these sorts of anti-Asian, anti-migrant overtones as more a device rather than a reality. Most of the people who were attracted to Hanson were no more racist than you or I. Most of the people who were attracted to Hansonism were no more racist than the average Australian. If you look at the areas where Hansonism flourished—I was struck not so long ago when I saw that the Wide Bay region of Queensland had the highest level of unemployment of any region in the country, or one of the highest, and that was the area where Hansonism did best in the 1997 Queensland election.

I was heavily criticised for not more savagely attacking Hanson at the very beginning. My answer to my critics is that the course of history has demonstrated that I was right. I mean, people now see Hansonism more as an expression of people in the bush feeling a bit left out than as an expression of racism. Now, I saw it in the 'being left out' terms rather than racist terms and that is why I handled it as I did. I thought some of the demonstrations against Hanson were so organised that they were being used as a political wedge against me by some of my more traditional political opponents.

Your government, as you say, has accepted the phrase 'Australian multiculturalism'. Why do you think this is the best form of words?

I think multiculturalism used on its own has meant different things to different people, and that's always been the problem. It's not a word I've used a lot and it's not a word I use a lot now. I don't mind saying that. To some people it means giving everybody the right to enjoy their own heritage. If that's what it means to everybody, well, that's great. To other people it means preserving differences to the point of their becoming divisions, and to a lot of people that's not right, including an enormous number who migrated to this country after World War II. So I don't use the expression a lot, but when I do I tend to call it Australian multiculturalism. I think it reminds everybody that we are Australians together, before anything else, but we do respect the fact that people have their own heritage. I think emphasising national unity is very important although fragmentary tendencies are not a big problem in this country, not of the type we've seen in Europe and elsewhere which are really regionally based. We've got a very good ethnic spread in this country, and we don't even have the sort of divide that Canada has had between its francophone and other derived populations.

What is required in this country to make Aboriginal reconciliation a reality?

You need time, infinite patience, and an understanding that if you set unreal goals and benchmarks you are doomed to fail. You just have to be very patient and you have to keep trying. You have to preserve good will. Now, that's speaking as an Australian who doesn't have Aboriginal descent. To Aboriginal leaders. I mean, there's good will all around the Australian community. No matter what's happened, people want to make it work, but it just takes time. If I look back, it was probably, it's always been, a mistake to say, we've got to achieve something by a particular date. You just have to keep working at it. I mean, what is important about Aboriginal reconciliation is how people feel about it at any given time. Not whether they've reached a certain point by a particular time.

Is it essentially an issue for the heart?

No, it's an issue—the heart part of it's been arrived at. I think people want to make it work, trying to find a way of doing it. I mean, some people think, you know, you achieve it all by symbolic acts and using particular words. Other people don't think those things matter at all, and all that matters are services and opportunities and economic advancement. Now it's a mixture of the two. Symbolism is important, but also achievement is important.

Trust is important.

Well, trust is important in any society. But that also implies—I mean, trust in political life also means not setting unreal expectations and not pretending that you can achieve something by uttering a word or saying a particular thing just for the sake of being able to say, well, I've said that.

How important have the Mabo and Wik cases been in terms of establishing a better basis for Aboriginal reconciliation, for people to be able to live together?

Having read the Mabo decision, it seemed to make a lot of sense. I didn't necessarily share some of the historical judgments made by some of their Honours. But that was not material to the judgment. High Court judges declare the law, they don't declare the history or the politics of a country. Now, I thought that was a very good judgment. It made a lot of sense. I thought, in retrospect, the *Wik* judgment fell into a different category. I felt Wik, I felt we had a line and then Wik came along and seemed to blur that. I think it was very unfortunate that we had to go through all the problem over the status of pastoral leases. I think that caused quite a negative reaction in rural Australia and understandably, because everybody had operated, including my predecessor Paul Keating, on the basis that a grant of a pastoral lease extinguished native title. That seemed to be the clear line coming out of Mabo.

Do you think we've reached a settlement now that we've had the Wik decision and the government's legislation following the Wik decision?

I think the status quo in relation to native title has been broadly reached. I think there could be some changes at the edges and it might vary a bit from State to State. There's certainly a feeling of exhaustion in the community about further debate on this issue.

My reading of the mood of the Australian people is that it's very mixed, it depends on where you are. There's a much more ready acceptance of it, in theory anyway, in the cities than there is in many rural areas and that's understandable. You don't have pastoral leaseholds in Kooyong or Killara. But you do have them in wide areas of Queensland and Western Australia and you have to accept it and we have to, as an overwhelmingly urban community, understand the feeling of people in the bush. Their sense some months ago of insecurity was not contrived, or not based on any hostility, but [there was] a certain bewilderment that a world they thought was settled had suddenly been changed. You have to try and accommodate both points of view on this.

I think you have had in all this some legitimate but competing interests. I mean, there's a general feeling that the concept of native title is proper—that is a general feeling—but the working out of it in detail has disturbed and unsettled a lot of people for quite legitimate reasons.

Has the cause of the Aboriginal people been too politicised, so that basic living conditions have taken second place to political issues—particularly land rights?

I think at a number of points in the last few years the Aboriginal cause has been hurt by excessive politicisation. The reality is that a government is elected by all of the Australian people and if any particular section of the community becomes too identified with one or other side of the political debate, to the extent that their capacity to talk to the incumbent government is weakened, well, you know, that's a negative. I think many of the bread and butter issues, if I can put it that way, of Aboriginal affairs have suffered in the process of the politicisation. It always disappoints me that real progress that is frequently made as a basis of good will between communities, governments and Aboriginals is forgotten and overlooked and played down.

I think there was a point where some of the Aboriginal leadership felt that the Howard Government was just a passing phase for a year or two. I think that changed and I welcome the constructive attempts that a lot of people in the Aboriginal community are making. I don't expect them to agree with me—how they vote's their business—but I do think that everybody's got to remember that they have obligations to the people they represent.

How would you explain your position on the question of the apology?

My position in relation to the apology is very simply that I don't believe in apologising for something for which I was not personally responsible. It's as simple as that. And I was brought up as a child by my parents to say sorry when I was to blame. Now, I think it's just too simplistic to say to the whole community, well, because these things were done—and there's a lot of debate about the degree and the intensity and the level of responsibility and there remain arguments about the processes involved in relation to the Human Rights Commission inquiry—to say, well, let's get it over with and say 'sorry', and then it's all fixed. That always seemed to me to be, apart from anything else, completely lacking in sincerity.

Do you think that one of the problems with the 'stolen children generation' report was that it tended to apply the values of today to a situation that existed decades ago?

I have no doubt that in relation to the separated or stolen children it was a case of applying the values of today to the deeds of yesterday. Many of the people who involved themselves in the deeds of yesterday did so for the best of motives, and many of them or most of them are now dead, and those that are alive, some of them, feel as though their life's work has been destroyed and dishonoured. I mean, these are very difficult issues. I can feel for the people who suffered the trauma as separated children, of course I can. There remains an enormous debate in our community about the basis on which some of those children were removed. In earlier years children were removed from their parents whether they were Aboriginal or non-Aboriginal, though not in the same way. You have to be very careful about applying today's standards to yesterday's behaviour.

I think the way in which we treated our Aboriginal people in earlier years remains the greatest blemish in our history. I've said that on a number of occasions and it remains my view. I've no doubt about that. It's one of the things we did badly. Now, in dealing with it you have to be frank, you have to acknowledge past misdeeds, but you also have to be careful not to collectively apportion blame. I mean, one of the things Australians will cop is responsibility for things that they did. But part of the Australian character is to see through something that is a little artificial, and it's a bit artificial to pretend that the current generation can accept responsibility for what an earlier generation did. I found, as I went around the community, a feeling: 'Look, we're very sorry about what happened, but we didn't do it; if we'd have been there we'd have behaved differently; let's get on with life, let's help them now, let's move forward, let's give them support and good health services and jobs and housing and all sorts of opportunities.' There's a great amount of good will in the Australian community for Aborigines.

What you were hoping to achieve with the proposed Preamble to the Constitution, in reference to the Aboriginal people?

I hoped through the Preamble to give for the first time a positive, ennobling recognition in the Constitution of the place of the indigenous people. That was the driving force behind the Preamble. I'm very disappointed it went down.

   I think the Preamble was defeated because the overwhelming preoccupation was with the republic. It was impossible to get a focus on the Preamble. People understandably said, well look, I don't quite know about this, so I'll say no.

Looking back over your predecessors, who do you think was Australia's most important prime minister, and why?

I regard Menzies as the greatest prime minister Australia's had. The reason is that he really laid the foundations of the modern postwar Australian nation. I mean, you can't underestimate the importance of those years after World War II when we welcomed millions of people from around the world, and we had very strong economic prosperity, and that provided people with a sense of achievement, a sense of identity and of well-being and a self-belief. I also admire Menzies' political skills. They were consummate and I would put him a fair distance ahead of any others.

We've been a hundred years a nation. When you look back, what do you think has been our greatest success?

I look back on that hundred years and our greatest success I tend to see not so much in a single event but rather in a characteristic. I think one of the great characteristics that Australians have, perhaps uniquely, is that we have found the best synthesis between individual effort and achievement and self-reliance and the need to work as part of a team. I think it explains a lot of things about Australians. It explains for example our immense success on the sporting field. We are very strong as individuals and we get all the advantages of it, but we are sufficiently cognisant of the need to work as part of a team, to discipline ourselves. We see it in the capacity of our fighting men. The characteristic of the Australian army from World War I on was its great individualistic character. But remember, in World War II in the prisoner of war camps in Thailand the death rate of the Australians was lower than the death rate of any others, and one of the reasons was that we were more disciplined in our habits. If you look at the sweep of Australian history, that tells you something about us. I mean, we've been able to preserve the best of our individualistic, even larrikin, streak but we haven't kept it to the detriment of working together to achieve a national outcome, a team outcome, when that's been necessary. I think that explains a lot about us and to me it's one of our most endearing characteristics and also one of our huge strengths.

What would you consider to be the main area of disappointment or failure?

I don't think there's any doubt that our failures in relation to Aborigines and Torres Strait Islanders represent, in the sweep of Australian history, our greatest blemish. That's not to pretend that it was an easy challenge but I don't think we've handled it well. I don't think we've handled it well for a long time. We're doing a lot better now and we're all trying a lot harder, but I think it has undoubtedly been our greatest area of failure and disappointment; but more so in the past than now. I mean, we are making up ground very effectively.

Interview with
Kim Beazley

Kim Beazley's focus inevitably shifts to the great issues of national survival and sustainability. For Beazley economic growth, a nation-building immigration program, Word War II and current relations with Asia are part of a larger tapestry—the ability of Australia to survive and realise its historic mission.

Do you think that the shift to a republic can be a natural and unifying event for Australians?

It *is* a natural thing for Australians. It is where our heads are. Australians are now natural republicans. I think it's a matter of argument, that we've always been natural republicans. But there is no question now that there is a commitment on the part of the majority of Australians to the idea of an Australian Head of State.

There's no question in my mind that the Australian people have left the monarchy behind. The problem for those of us who argue for a republic is how to devise a mechanism that enables the Australian people to express their republicanism. It was Paul Keating's view, and it is mine too, that the only way you can do that is to start with a plebiscite in which the Australian people make their own declaration. Once you've done that, I think it is much easier to debate various models of a republic.

Is it possible to describe when we left the monarchy behind—to identify a turning point in this transition?

There have always been republican Australians. We were a very innovative democracy in the late nineteenth century, the view about ballots, the view about the independence of mind of the ordinary citizen, was accompanied by a republican veneer. But of course there was also an enormous counter-strand of Empire loyalism. I think the republican process began in a serious way in the 1940s when we began to untangle our foreign policy from automatic commitments to various Imperial relationships.

But in terms of a political consciousness for republicanism, widely spread in the Australian community, I think it is more recent. It's a phenomenon of the 1980s when we changed our definition of what sort of people we were. We were no longer white Anglo-Saxon Protestant. We were a multicultural society and we got comfortable with that notion. And as we started to address the rest of the world and saw ourselves effectively as a nation in itself, making its way in a difficult but opportune region, our political consciousness started to reflect the actual reality of our political situation. Republicanism has been a natural part of a broad-based, as opposed to a specialist, agenda since then.

Looking at the development of our political consciousness, when do you think, in the hearts of the Australian people, they regarded themselves as being a genuinely independent people and country?

I think the 1970s and 1980s. Part of that was externally induced. There was a real shock in the Australian community, which we've forgotten now, when Britain entered the European Community. There was a real shock when we confronted a failure in our central alliance during the course of the Vietnam War. It dovetailed with a changing Australian character as we accepted multiculturalism and changed the racial definition of who is an Australian.

But at one stage in our history we did love the monarchy, didn't we?

I think there's still many Australians who have very good regard for the monarchy. But it's become more and more a distant thing, more and more somebody else's Head of State, but disconnected from our needs.

I think at the turn of the century, and for much of our history, we held the monarchy in high regard, basically because within the strand of Australian democracy and individualism there was, if you like, a counter-strand, or accompanying strand, a sense that we were creating a better Britain in the southern hemisphere. We were essentially British, and you can find plenty of comments from Australian prime ministers about our British character and plenty of comments of Australian cricketers going to Britain as 'going home' or going to 'the old country', but we were creating a better Britain, a classless Britain, a healthy Britain, here in Australia. And that was, if you like, our point of distinction.

Is the real problem now that we don't know how to write a republican Constitution? We have to agree on a republican Constitution and on a republican model. How difficult is this for us?

This has always been at the heart of the problem of arguing for a republic. Not many Australians understand but the monarchy actually sits at the heart of our constitutional arrangements. So when you are making adjustments around the monarchy, the knock-on effects will invariably be there. That is why I think the most appropriate way to approach the republic is to do it in stages. Firstly, give the Australian people ownership of the issue, a plebiscite on the republic. Secondly, give them ownership of the model. Present several alternatives to them, with the consequences of those alternatives. What adjustments do you make in relations between the Head of State and the prime minister. What adjustments do you make to the powers of sections of the parliament—like the Senate over the issue of Supply. If we have a second set of plebiscites in which all those issues are teased out I think we might then arrive at a settled view of what is potentially quite a complex issue.

Even at a period of time when the monarchy has been enormously popular in this country, there has been a contradiction in our hearts. We've never really felt like subjects. We've always felt like citizens, even though we are still, in constitutional terms, subjects.

The Republic is inevitable. It will come but it will only come when it's in the hands of those who love it. It used to be said that the republic will only come when it is put forward by the Liberal Party. I don't think that that is any longer true. You can see that there are large numbers of traditional conservative voters who strongly favour the republic. And they'd support it, irrespective of whether it was a Liberal or a Labor prime minister putting it forward.

From the time of Federation, we've always relied upon great and powerful friends. Did we have any other choice? Was this the strategic reality?

Great and powerful friends have always been important to Australia but we're not unique in that regard. Great and powerful friends are important to any middle-sized or small power. This is not something to be sneered at. It's something to be understood. You don't need to judge your sense of independence by the fact that you identify the need for great and powerful friends. In most circumstances independence is often reflected by the skill with which you manipulate the relationship with great and powerful friends in your interest. That's always been the challenge for Australian foreign policy and we've not always done very well with it.

What was John Curtin's great quality as a wartime leader?

I think Curtin's great quality was clear, strategic vision, in looking at the threats to Australia and, domestically, looking at the level of mobilisation necessary to ensure both that our strategic vision was properly supported and that the Australian people felt they owned part of the crisis.

Curtin was a very strong wartime leader. He had the weaknesses that all of us have had. But those weaknesses he set aside, for the war, until his death. He did not lose his fears but he was not governed by them.

How do you interpret his wartime Melbourne Herald *article in which he made his famous appeal to the United States?*

I think Curtin, based on his experience in dealing with Churchill and on a long-held understanding of the vulnerabilities of Australia to Japan, had uncoupled in his mind the 'eternal verities' which seemed to dominate our policy to that point. That article was about inducing in Australians a sense of realism. It was about allowing the United States, not then readily defined as an Australian ally, a comprehension of the Australian mind. It was also a statement to the Australian people that it's time you abandoned any of your illusions about our situation and about who will come to our aid, and started serious thinking about yourselves, the contribution you will make, and the requirements upon us as a nation to survive.

He was saying, don't think that the eternal verities defend you. You've got to get off your backsides and do the job yourselves.

What did the fall of Singapore mean for Australia?

The fall of Singapore meant the collapse of our illusions. It also meant a very serious threat. After almost two years of war, effectively, there was not in Australia a single combat-ready division. There were several overseas, but in Australia there was not one. The fall of Singapore not only collapsed illusions, it exposed a very real strategic problem for this country. We were saved from invasion, in the first instance, largely by a decision of the Japanese. Their opportunity was not seized and ultimately it was cut off. But, when you look at the defence we were mounting, it was a very close thing indeed. We were not prepared internally to deal with the consequences of the collapse of Singapore.

We had the great rift between Curtin and Churchill over the return of the 7th Division from the Middle East and Churchill's effort to divert that division to Burma. How important was this Curtin/ Churchill rift?

This is a critical moment in Australian history. If there's any single justification for John Curtin's rise to power, it is this act. This is its justification. Remember, Menzies, one of his predecessors, believed that he was wrong. And there is no doubt in my mind that even though Menzies would have accepted in the first instance the advice of his military chiefs, he would have broken under the sort of pressure that was applied to Curtin. Curtin did not break, even though the correspondence was intense and acts of a deceitful nature were committed in an attempt to force him to comply. Had Curtin not stood firm, those troops would have been lost and the effect on Australian morale and on our military capability would have been truly massive.

How intense was the pressure from Churchhill?

The pressure from Churchill on Curtin, at the time of the argument over the withdrawal of Australian troops from the Middle East, was the most intense that any Australian prime minister has ever been subjected to by an ally in any circumstances in the nation's history. When you contemplate it at the end of the first hundred years of our existence as a nation, it is all the more creditable to Curtin and all the more amazing that he was able to withstand a daily pressure by Churchill to force his hand.

Is it fanciful to see this event as fundamental to the birth and development of an Australian nationalism?

I think that the stand taken over the withdrawal of Australian troops was a critical moment in the ongoing development of a keen sense of Australian nationalism. It was a forcing of a strategic reality upon us—it was not a statement that great and powerful friends weren't important and that relationships with what was then regarded as the Mother Country weren't important.

You can't see in this act the genesis of Australian nationalism, because Australian nationalism really began in the nineteenth century. What you can see is a catalyst for something within us emerging as an active public policy.

You feel very emotional about Curtin. What is it about him that you admire so much?

I admire Curtin enormously. Some people might say of me, 'But then he would'. I'm a Labor leader and I'm very Western Australian. But what I admire in Curtin is his willingness to think originally about our strategic circumstances, to think logically about the requirements of Australian survival, and not to be distracted by prevailing opinion or old verities. I admire his consciousness of the requirements for Australian survival. I particularly admire it, given the context of his personal difficulties with his own life. He was a flawed man in many ways, and to be able to rise above those flaws and seize the hour for Australia is all the more creditable.

What was John Curtin's great flaw?

John Curtin had all the normal characteristics of an Australian male and one of those is a love of a bit of a drink from time to time and sometimes far too much. His struggle with alcohol verged on a problem with alcoholism. He controlled that and he was not blackmailed by it. He also had a very highly developed sense of danger, if you like. He had real fears, not quite Churchill's black dog, but a propensity to pessimism, to despair, and to combine that problem with alcohol is a pretty lethal combination. To rise above that is substantial.

John Curtin and Douglas MacArthur needed each other. What was the nature of this extraordinary relationship?

In some ways, John Curtin made Douglas MacArthur. We always look at it the other way around. But MacArthur had been defeated in the Philippines. He came back to Australia. He was being given little support in Washington and Curtin became for him a very important diplomatic arm. Until the middle of 1944 there were more Australian troops under MacArthur's command than Americans. Australian troops made MacArthur's reputation in New Guinea. Finally, I think Curtin gave MacArthur a view about how you organise society. The type of society that emerged in Japan bore no small resemblance to the sort of social democratic society that had been organised in Australia during the course of the early 1940s.

After MacArthur came, we handed over to MacArthur, a foreign general, responsibilities for our combat forces. What does this tell us about Australia's predicament?

The fact that we handed authority over Australia's forces to MacArthur suggests, of course, that we had a very keenly developed sense of our survival. A view that in the final analysis, Australia on its own could not resist the Japanese assault on its territory. That was a correct perception. Unless there was a firm advocate in Washington for the Australian point of view then the possibility of our point of view being neglected was more an absolute certainty. I think Curtin understood very early on that, in MacArthur, he had a potent player in the American political scene, a player who would always have to be taken note of in Washington.

What is the key to the American alliance? Does the key lie in World War II or in the Cold War?

The key to the American alliance does not lie in World War II. What World War II did was to show to the Australian people that a relationship with the United States could be critical to their survival and was more likely to be critical to it than the older relationship with the United Kingdom. It put the American arrangement at the forefront of Australian thinking.

But it was the decision by the United States in the aftermath of World War II, to play a permanent international role in containing the Soviet Union, the internationalisation of American foreign policy under the Cold War, that underpinned the development of the Australian/American alliance and its character for the bulk of this century.

What was the key factor leading to the negotiation of the ANZUS treaty?

For Australia the key factor was to place it within the framework of Japan. Nowadays it's hard to understand this. But really, our thinking on foreign policy matters, from the time of Federation up to the conclusion of World War II, was how to deal with the main threat. The main threat was Japan. And so the Americans could never get out of us the sort of relationship they wanted in the containment of Communist powers if they didn't settle our minds on Japan.

We had a very schizophrenic attitude about Japan at the time of Federation. On the one hand, we recognised it as the most likely threat to our security. On the other hand, in dealing with that threat, we swung between paranoia and defensiveness. We were constantly trying to get the British to acknowledge, in their relationship with Japan, the fact that the Japanese might go sour on us. Japan was always seen as the real security bogey for Australia. Take a look at the conscription debates during World War I. There is very little talk about pacifism in the classic religious sense. The talk is all about the wrong war in the wrong place, and if we use too much manpower in that war, what will be left when the real threat emerges. Japan featured very prominently in those conscription debates.

How much credit should one give Percy Spender for the ANZUS treaty, as opposed to Menzies?

I think you've got to give Spender almost the entire credit for the treaty. I think Menzies found the post–World War II adjustment difficult to make. He did not find the way in which the world was developing and the collapse of the British Empire an easy thing to cope with. And he reposed in the notion of Empire, and in the relationship with Britain, very great personal faith and ideological commitment.

Was Vietnam the price Australia paid for the United States alliance?

Vietnam was the price we paid for the way in which the United States alliance had developed in our consciousness and the way in which we'd come to interpret threats to Australia in the region. And finally, it was the price we paid for the way in which foreign policy was cynically manipulated for domestic political gain. The combination of those three elements thrust us into the Vietnam War.

Was Vietnam a mistake for Australia?

Yes, it was a mistake for Australia. A difficult mistake to avoid, there's no question about that. In the early phases of the war both the Labor Party and the Liberal Party were agreed on a small Australian commitment. But as the American buildup occurred it became pretty obvious to many Australians that the Americans were overplaying their hand and investing far too much militarily in that conflict. It took a while for that consciousness to grow. It grew faster in the Labor Party than it did in the Liberal Party.

I think that if it had grown a little faster in the Liberal Party and that an opportunity hadn't been seen for manipulation of the Australian political process by the Liberal Party, then the commitment would've been much smaller and the cost to Australia much less.

The real motive behind the Vietnam commitment was, firstly, to ensure that the United States maintained an interest in the region; secondly, to utilise the American alliance in Australian domestic political concerns; and thirdly, to insert great and powerful friends on a continuing basis in the region around us.

When did we move beyond this particular stage of the 'great and powerful friends' relationship? When did we mature?

The Vietnam failure did lead to a greater maturity in Australian foreign policy. There's no question about that. We were instructed to develop that maturity, I might say, by the United States. A seminal influence on the getting of maturity for Australians was President Nixon's Guam Doctrine, which was that the United States, like the Lord, helps those who help themselves.

As a result of the Vietnam War, and more particularly Nixon's Guam Doctrine, Australian foreign policy makers universally accepted that from that point on, whatever the character of Australia's relationship with 'great and powerful friends' and with the United States, Australia would, by and large, have to make its own way. That alliance with the United States was essentially a backstop, as opposed to an all-embracing concern.

How should we see the East Timor troop commitment, under UN auspices? How significant is this a landmark for our regional policy?

We're doing something in Timor on behalf of the international community. Let's make no mistake about that. This is not an Australian interest. It's an international interest but it's our area. It's an area in which Australia finds itself. The logic of the development of a policy of defence self-reliance is that in Australia's immediate approaches Australia has to be prepared to assume primary responsibility.

You talked about engaging with Asia, in a philosophical and historical sense. How much can Australia survive in this part of the world on its own terms?

If our view is that engagement is irrelevant in this region, we are going to find ourselves in a very difficult situation, very quickly. If we are not playing an active part in regional organisations, if we are not seen as constructive players in regional affairs, if we are not seen as having a view on what constitutes progress in this region, and being prepared to make a helpful contribution to it, we will slip from people's charts. Sooner or later, a crisis will grow in this region which will ultimately threaten substantial damage to our survival or our interests.

On social and economic issues, do you think Australia's in danger of losing its egalitarian tradition?

I do think that. Part of our egalitarian tradition was the view that you were responsible for your mates. It wasn't 'the survival of the fittest' view but a firm view that the rising tide raises all boats. I don't think that that sentiment is there as strongly in our national ideology, as it used to be in our parents' time or perhaps even just a few years ago.

I think several things have eroded it. Firstly, direct attacks on the right to collectively bargain and the value and importance of a union movement. I don't think people fully understand that the strength of Australian commitment to democracy, at least the commitment by ordinary Australians, throughout most of this century has been bound up in the sorts of organisations to which they've attached themselves. One of these has been the union movement.

The trade union movement is under threat from the government, from the character of industrial legislation that is being developed. The union movement is also under threat in so far as it is unsuccessful in making itself relevant to the new, burgeoning service areas. But it's not under threat in terms of public support. If you look at any set of opinion polls, even though only about 30 per cent of the Australian workforce is unionised, 60 to 70 per cent of Australians still regard the union movement as important.

How do you see the market-orientated reforms of the Hawke/Keating period? Was this the right way to go?

Australia had to develop its economy in a way that allowed it to be part of the globalisation of economic processes. We are a nation of only 19 million people. That is not enough for a domestic economy to survive on its own. We have to be a trading nation. The economic reforms were an essential underpinning of success in that regard.

How does Australia, then, meet the challenge of running an open and competitive economy on the one hand, yet maintain a sense of social justice and equity on the other?

We can maintain an open, competitive economy, and a sense of social justice, by understanding that social justice is a product of choice. We are drawn into a global economy by technology more than we are by choice but we are capable of negotiating the terms and conditions of our relationship with that economy to a considerable extent. The starting point is to sustain our skills. The second point is to sustain our families. We've got to regard those who rear children as making a special contribution to our society, and ensure that tax and social policy underpins that. Get those two things right, and there'll be comfort in this community. Get it wrong, and you'll have a permanently disaffected population.

Those who are empowered by the new economy are those who are skilled and who can make adjustments in their skills. Those who are disenfranchised by the new economy are those who, for reasons perhaps of a non-English-speaking background, or some form of disability, or some form of deprivation in economic terms, have their disadvantages constantly reinforced. It is the job of government to cross that divide.

The major problem in our relationship to the global economy is the way in which it divides us into global haves and have nots. That is now the critical fault line in Australia but it is not a single fault line. It is a jigsaw puzzle fault line. It divides regions from regions. It divides the bush from regional centres. It divides regional centres from outer suburbs. It divides outer suburbs from inner suburbs. It divides people who have skills from people who don't have skills. And the key to resolving those divides is not the market. The key is the democratic political process and the key for the individual is the individual's franchise—his or her vote cast in favour of a government that will negotiate their participation in the global economy more effectively.

We started the century with White Australia, we finish it with multicultural Australia. How great, how dramatic is this transformation?

The key transformation is in White Australia. In definitional terms, Australia has been multicultural since the nineteenth century, and deliberately multicultural since the 1940s. But we've only been multiracial in a process which started in the 1960s and was cemented in the 1980s. We changed our definition then of what it was to be an Australian. Up to that time the starting point of the definition of Australian had been the word 'white'. After that time a starting point of being an Australian was defined by a commitment to democrative values and a tolerant outlook.

The change from the definition of who is an Australian, the dropping of the term 'white', is absolutely critical because it allows us to survive. It means that we have the capacity to make the mental adjustments we need to make, to develop the sorts of relationships in the region around us where the earlier definition won't wash.

The change from White Australia is a landmark in Australian consciousness and in dealing with the issues of Australian survival.

You move around the country a lot. How tolerant a society are we? How tolerant a people are we?

There is a tolerance meter which swings about in different parts of the country and at different points of time. But the level of tolerance that Australians have for each other is probably greater than in just about any other nation on earth.

What's happened to our support for the idea of immigration. Is it eroding?

Yes, support for immigration is eroding and that's a problem. The Australian population and the characteristics of the population are not in the long term sustainable. In defence, in economic development terms, in industrial terms, we cannot sustain the level of aging that is foreshadowed for our population. We will not be a dynamic nation if we merely drift along in the way in which we are drifting now. But we have to change the character of our migration policy. Migration policies of the 1940s and 1950s simply will not suit. There'll be different policies, successful policies, but nevertheless, immigration policy, a good immigration policy, is essential for the long term survival of our nation.

The public has decoupled, in its mind, immigration from nation-building. The two have to be brought back together again. A good population policy is central to that. A good population policy is not just about immigration. It's about birthrate. It's about regionalism. It's about location. It's about skills. That's all part of a population policy, but having said that, immigration is essential to it.

Does this relate to the point we were discussing before, the terms and conditions of our survival as a country?

The character of the region in which Australia is situated is one of enormous change and fluidity. Australia is a small player in this region but a not unsubstantial economy and Australians as a people are clever adjusters to their environment. What we have to accept, is that the process of adjustment is never ending. We will never get it forever right. We will only get it right at different points.

The survival issues entailed in immigration are closely bound up in the dynamism of the economy and the capacity for it to support decent armed forces, decent defence capabilities and, of course, an inventive community.

Are Australians comfortable with the idea of a multicultural society?

Australians are comfortable with it, by and large. From time to time there's an annoyance with what some regard as political correctness. From time to time there is a concern or a fear, or anger, with somebody who's not entirely of the same cultural background. But by and large it doesn't last long. Most Australians know that, given the character of the region in which we live, given the character of the things we enjoy, tolerance and multiculturalism are related.

Tolerance and multiculturalism are in fact fundamental to our new identity, as is multiracialism.

Pauline Hanson casts a shadow over multiculturalism and multiracialism, because her movement demonstrates that if people do not feel a sense of comfort with where the nation stands they can get deeply defensive. But it is not a static thing. It is not a rigid view of the world. It is not one that is not capable of being subject to argument.

What is uniquely Australian is our capacity to draw on reserves of tolerance and 'live and let live' attitudes which are deep in the Australian psyche.

We've seen in this decade the Mabo and Wik judgments on native title. Do you think the Australian people support these judgments?

I think, ironically, Mabo and Wik reflect what Australian people think—individuals as opposed to official Australia. We've always accepted that the Aborigines were here first. We've always accepted that they had a relationship, an important relationship, to the land. We've accepted that view attitudinally, but not legally. It's been convenient for us not to accept it legally and it's provided opportunities for governments to engage in acts of great deprivation. But when the High Court ruled that there were people with an original title to this land, very few Australians thought of it as anything other than a statement of the bleeding obvious.

I do think that the consciousness of acts of deprivation done against the Aboriginal people, over the course of the last couple of centuries, is something which calls for atonement in our community. It's been a sad thing for me, over the last few years, that it has been so difficult for our national parliament to respond.

How important is an apology?

The apology is very important. I mean, it's got too much focus simply because it hasn't been done. If it had been done and we'd got on with it, I think all Australians would have found it acceptable and really quite easy. The more it has been allowed to rankle in the Australian political system, the more difficult it's appeared to be to get the correct format for some form of atonement to be made. But it is necessary to do that in order for us to be able to move on.

You had a very emotional response to the report on the stolen children generation. How shocked were you?

I did have a very emotional response and still do to the report because it indicated to me that responsibility was not at arm's length from myself. I'm one of those who find it quite easy to apologise for events that I know I'm not responsible for. I can quite readily apologise for events which occurred in the nineteenth century, though I wasn't there. But when you read the stolen generation report—the injustices and the sad acts occurred right into my lifetime in politics, in institutions the inhabitants of which I actually met as a child. I was taken aback by the enormity of the stolen generation report and that also contributed to emotionalism on my part.

Aboriginal reconciliation—is this essentially a question of the heart and a generosity of spirit?

Reconciliation, generosity of spirit—these are always in the first instance questions of the heart. Now, there may need to be restitution of a more physical nature. But what the Aboriginal community in this country is looking for in a reconciliation process is an act of the heart. And they're not really looking for it from the Australian people generally, because by and large, in most parts of Australia, they get on well with their fellow Australians. They're looking for the official statement—the official statement of the heart.

Is this our greatest failure as a nation? And how confident are you about the future?

Australian history is always a source of enormous pride to me. I take great joy in the achievements of Australians. I take inspiration in our struggles, our struggles for survival in a harsh environment, in an unkind world. If we have one blot, one blot in our history, it is the relationship with our indigenous people. That's not to say that relationships are static and that things haven't got better. But one thing that Paul Keating said to me once, which I always found terribly important, particularly as a Labor leader, was that each Australian prime minister is his own Aboriginal Affairs Minister—whether that Australian prime minister likes it or not. And to a considerable extent the reconciliation process, the ability to correct injustices, is dependent upon what is going on in the heart of the Australian prime minister of the day.

Illustration
Acknowledgements

The author and publishers would like to thank the following organisations for permission to reproduce material used in this book. Every effort has been made to contact copyright holders. Where an omission has occurred, the author and publishers will gladly include acknowledgement in any future edition.

Text illustrations:

Photographs are listed according to the page on which they appear.

(p. 2) Mitchell Library, State Library of NSW, ML:658.405/2; *(p. 5)* Mitchell Library, State Library of NSW, ML:F980.1/A; *(p. 6)* Royal Archives, Windsor Castle; *(p. 10)* Mitchell Library, State Library of NSW, wk@play 02074; *(p. 13)* National Library of Australia; *(p. 14)* Australian War Memorial AWM G579; *(p. 17)* Mitchell Library, State Library of NSW, ML:QA923.59/I73; *(p. 23) The Royal Tour of Australia and New Zealand, 1953–54,* Daily Telegraph and Sunday Telegraph, Sydney; *(p. 28)* News Limited; *(p. 29)* News Limited; *(p. 53)* National Library of Australia; *(p. 56)* Mitchell Library, State Library of NSW, ML Melb Punch; *(p. 58)* National Archives of Australia, NAA (Qld) J2483/1, 1906/314; *(p. 59)* John Oxley Library, NN63220; *(p. 68)* Mitchell Library, State Library of NSW, ML: GPO1 44806; *(p. 69)* Mitchell Library, State Library of NSW; *(p. 74)* Department of Immigration & Multicultural Affairs 68/4/26 (2525); *(p. 76)* Department of Immigration and Multicultural Affairs, photographer John Crowther 79/46A/1 (5019); *(p. 100)* Mitchell Library, State Library of NSW; *(p. 102)* Noel Butlin Archive of Business and Labour, 31/39/272, NN 6244; *(p. 106)* Museum of Victoria, MoV MD A5/15; *(p. 118)* State Library of Victoria, SLVic:H84.217/64; *(p. 158)* Mitchell Library, State Library of NSW, *Australasian Sketcher,* 25 December 1875, p. 150; *(p. 162)* Mitchell Library, State Library of NSW, ML:F980.1/A; *(p. 166)* National Archives of Australia, NAA A263/5, 6A; *(p. 167)* National Archives of Australia, NAA A263/5, 8A; *(p. 170)* National Archives of Australia; *(p. 172)* News Limited; *(p. 175)* News Limited; *(p. 180)* News Limited; *(p. 185)* News Limited; *(p. 191)* News Limited; *(p. 208)* Mitchell Library, State Library of NSW, ML Melb Punch; *(p. 210)* Mitchell Library, State Library of NSW, ML:GPO1 49231; *(p. 213)* Mitchell Library, State Library of NSW, ML:PXD19, no. 11; *(p. 215)* Melbourne University Archives; *(p. 227)* News Limited; *(p. 238)* News Limited.

Cover illustrations:

(Top) Mitchell Library, State Library of NSW, ML GPO1 44809. *(Bottom from left to right)* Australian War Memorial, negative no. H11574; National Archives of Australia A1200/19, L28536; Mitchell Library, State Library of NSW, *Wonder Book of Empire*; National Archives of Australia, NAA (Qld) J2483/1, 1906/314; Mitchell Library, State Library of NSW, ML Q393.41; Mitchell Library, State Library of NSW, ML GPO1 44806; Mitchell Library, State Library of NSW, *Sydney Mail*, 25 October 1916.

100Index years

Page numbers appearing in *italics* refer to illustrations.